SOMEBODY'S DAUGHTER

INSIDE THE TORONTO/HALIFAX PIMPING RING

PHONSE JESSOME

Look beyond the surface

'96

NIMBUS
PUBLISHING

D1067246

Nimbus Publishing Limited
P.O. Box 9301, Station A
Halifax, NS B3K 5N5
(902)455-4286

Design: Arthur B. Carter
Printed and bound in Canada

Canadian Cataloguing in Publication Data
Jessome, Phonse.
Somebody's daughter.
ISBN 1-55109-174-7
1. Prostitution—Nova Scotia—Halifax. 2. Pimps—Nova Scotia—Halifax.
3. Prostitutes—Nova Scotia—Halifax. 4. Halifax (N.S.). Police Dept.
Metro Prostitution Task Force. I. Title.
HQ148.J47 1996   363.4409716225   C96-950180-3

This book is dedicated to the memory of Joe Jabalee, a teacher who always found the time to foster the talents of his students and to help them develop a strong sense of self worth. You will live on in the accomplishments of those students, Joe. For those of us you have left behind, we miss you.

Contents

Preface

First, I want to offer a few words on purpose and approach. This book is not an academic assessment of the problem of juvenile prostitution in Canada, nor does it suggest solutions to that problem. My intention here is to provide a window on that violent underworld so you, the reader, can have a clearer understanding of who the girls in the tight skirts really are.

All the incidents described in this book are real, although some of the dates, times, places and names have been altered. The current and former prostitutes who agreed to share their stories asked that their names be changed, and that has been done. The jailed pimps who cooperated in the research for this book made the same request, and it has been honored. The names of other pimps who would not cooperate, but whose stories are contained in this book, have also been changed. This approach permitted me the luxury of combining certain stories to make this a more concise and readable book. There are those who will compare this book to the well-publicized cases it describes and draw conclusions as to the real identities of the pimps and prostitutes. That would be a mistake; some of the characters presented here have been created from the experiences of more than one person involved in those cases. My purpose was not to repeat the coverage given to those incidents in the media, but rather to take you inside the lives of the people caught up in them.

Many people have contributed their time and expertise in order to make this book possible and to them I say thank you. I will not individually list them because to do so would risk omitting someone and consequently offending a person to whom I owe a debt of gratitude. Many of the people you will meet in the pages of this book, many more are not identified but have added to the content in various ways. One person I wish to single out is Miles States, a former pimp who had no reservation in sharing his experiences and allowing his name to be used. He is a valuable and, unfortunately, under-utilized resource.

Book writing is very much a team effort. My name is on the cover, but there are others without whom it would never have been completed. I would like to thank my publisher Dorothy Blythe at Nimbus. Also a special thanks to Joanne Elliott who worked long and hard to chase these pages to the printer. Perhaps no one worked as hard on this book as my editor Liane Heller who took a mass of information and helped shape it into a digestible form.

I thank my employer, ATV, for allowing me to use the resources of its considerable video archive to supply most of the pictures in this book. Thanks to Kevin "fuzzy" Hilliard and Gary Steele for transforming the moving pictures of the video tape into the pictures contained here.

Finally, thanks to the task force officers who shared their experiences with me. To those officers whose names and stories I did not use, do not feel offended. Your efforts and experiences have been included in the stories of those officers I choose to represent the larger group in this book.

Part One:
Horror and Hope

It was late in January 1992 and nineteen-year-old Annie Mae Wilson was spending the final moments of her life watching television. Annie Mae was lounging on a couch in her sister's apartment in the north end of Dartmouth, Nova Scotia, enjoying some time with the new man in her life, her new pimp. Annie Mae ignored the irritating sound when the old brown phone in the kitchen began to ring. Unlike the newer phones with the electronic warble, Annie Mae's phone had a real bell inside activated by a tiny wire connected to a small lead weight that slammed repeatedly into the bell when someone called. It was appropriate enough that a bell sounded; the call represented the tolling of the bell for Annie Mae.

Annie Mae's sister took the call and shouted to the nineteen-year-old. When Annie Mae heard the familiar voice on the line, she knew she was in trouble. Bruno Cummings was in a rage. Bruno was calling from another Dartmouth apartment where he was playing cards with a group of friends. Like Bruno, they were also pimps. Bruno was upset because in his opinion he, not the young man on the couch in Annie Mae's sister's apartment, was her "man" on Hollis Street in Halifax and he knew she had not been working for him. Annie Mae's decision to switch pimps didn't really bother Bruno; it was how she was doing it. Pimps take their game seriously and don't like anyone breaking the rules. When a girl leaves one pimp and chooses another she is required under the code of The Game to pay her former pimp a leaving fee. Leaving fees are one of the methods, torture and terror being two others, used by pimps to keep young women from breaking free of the prostitution game. The fees run from a few hundred to a few thousand dollars, depending on a girl's age and appearance and the level of respect her pimp has earned in the street. Contrary to popular myth, there are very few street

1

pimps who share the profits with their young girls. Pimps take all the money and give their girls an allowance for clothing and food, ensuring that a young woman cannot save enough money to pay her own leaving fee. If a girl wants to break free of a pimp she usually approaches a new man and convinces him to pay the fee, but the girl is still in The Game.

Annie Mae had been a prostitute since she was fourteen and she knew the rules. By not paying the leaving fee Annie Mae was committing the ultimate act of defiance: she was showing complete disrespect to her man or, in the words of the card-playing pimps, "dissin' Bruno, big time."

Bruno knew he had to regain control of Annie Mae. If he let her walk away without paying a fee, his short career as a pimp was over. The message would spread in the street in minutes; Bruno's girls were open targets for any pimp who was shopping for someone new. No pimp would ever bother to pay Bruno a leaving fee again. Bruno did not like the idea of supporting himself with his part-time, legitimate job, bagging groceries. He had already lost more in the poker game that afternoon than he could make at the super market in a week.

Annie Mae knew she had gone too far when she slammed the phone down and now she paced her sister's apartment trying to decide what to do. Annie Mae had worked the streets of Halifax, Montreal and Toronto for more than five years. She knew an angry pimp was not to be trifled with and she knew she was once again getting herself into trouble. Annie Mae had developed a reputation that was not all that uncommon in prostitution. She was known as a "Choosy Suzy," a girl who liked to jump from one man to another. None of the pimps felt Annie Mae was a threat to The Game, they considered her a lifer who was just a little restless. Annie Mae thought she could get away without paying Bruno a fee because he was a minor player. At least that was what she had hoped. Bruno, she knew, was considered small time by most of the players. He had no ambition and never bothered running his girls in Montreal or Toronto. Bruno was content to make a few dollars from his girls in Halifax and then live the big life wasting it all at the poker table with the real players. But Annie Mae now realized she had misjudged Bruno; he would not stand for her leaving without paying the fee. She decided she better take the initiative. Bruno had not mentioned where he was calling from but Annie Mae knew how to reach him. She quickly dialed the number of Bruno's pager and left a message for him to call her. It was one of Bruno's card-playing buddies who was wearing his pager that afternoon and he returned the call.

Annie Mae was on the right track when she realized the mistake she had made. Her problem was in the approach she took when she tried to fix it.

"You tell him when he gets some man sense he can give me a call," she told his buddy. Annie Mae had instantly gone from being frightened to defiant and instead of easing the tension between herself and her former pimp, she had unwittingly pushed Bruno to the breaking point.

When the card player wearing Bruno's pager passed on her angry message, everyone at the table heard it. There were a few chuckles but one man was not laughing. Richard "Biker" Benson flashed a sinister smile when he heard what Annie Mae had to say. Biker was an older, well-respected player who had girls in Montreal and Toronto. He was also a violent man. He did not like Annie Mae and had slapped her around once—after she had left his brother, another pimp. Now Biker could force Bruno into dishing out some pimping persuasion to the errant girl while he watched the fun. He enjoyed beating his girls and seeing other pimps beat their girls almost as much as he enjoyed the hefty profits he earned in The Game.

"Bruno, you ain't no man at all. You think you got respect, and you let a 'ho dis' you like that. Man, you're nothin'." Biker pulled the right strings as he taunted Bruno while the younger pimp tried his best to ignore it. The other card players picked up the theme and Bruno began pacing the room as his anger grew. Bruno's closest friend and fellow pimp could see where Biker was pushing and he didn't want Bruno going in that direction. He told Bruno to cool off and let it go.

Bruno ignored the sound advice of his friend and hatched a plan that he felt would help him regain the respect he had lost and get Annie Mae out of his life at the same time. Biker offered to drive Bruno to Annie Mae's sister's apartment so the disrespected pimp could set her straight, and Bruno accepted. During the drive across Dartmouth Bruno sat quietly in Biker's car thinking about how to carry out his plan. He had decided the best course was a fast decisive one. Biker, unexpectedly, and with obvious excitement, pulled out a small black gun from beneath his jacket. Bruno knew Biker often carried a gun but he wasn't sure why he would be pulling it out now.

"Just in case my man, just in case." Biker smiled at the weapon and returned it to its place.

Annie Mae's sister's apartment was on the second floor of an older brick building just off Windmill Road in Dartmouth's North End. Bruno pushed his way through the plate glass door and ran up the stairs to the dimly lit hallway. Biker clambered up behind him and followed Bruno to the apartment door. Bruno Cummings stood just over six feet tall and weighted close to two hundred and thirty pounds. He was not muscular or athletic but he was an intimidating presence in that small hallway. The angry pimp pounded the wooden door and waited. Annie Mae's sister opened the door. She recognized Bruno and quickly raised her hand to her mouth as she turned to look into the apartment where Annie Mae was lying on the sofa with her head in the lap of her new man.

"She's dissn' you big time man." Biker was staring past Bruno at Annie Mae. "You gotta do somethin' now."

Annie Mae jumped up when she saw the two pimps in the doorway. She walked toward Bruno but before she was able to say a word Bruno lashed out with a fast powerful punch that landed square on Annie Mae's nose. The slim young prostitute reeled backward from the force of the blow. Instinctively she threw out her hand for balance and caught a fistfull of Bruno's long curly hair. The sudden tug on his hair fuelled Bruno's temper higher and he struck again, this time hitting Annie Mae on the left side of her face. The punch spun her head violently to the right, twisting her neck well beyond its normal range of movement. Biker and Bruno watched her collapse on the floor with a sickening gurgling sound. They saw blood coming from Annie Mae's mouth and nose, the result of the first punch to her face. They did not see what the violent twisting motion from the second blow had done. The vertebral artery had ripped and blood was filling the space between the young girl's brain and the inner wall of her skull. Her body began to jerk in spasms and Biker began to laugh.

"You knocked her cold Bruno my man, two shots and she's on the mat."

Bruno said nothing. He looked mutely as her sister knelt beside her and began to cry. The new pimp who had been sitting on the couch with Annie Mae moments before got up and walked out of the apartment without acknowledging Biker or Bruno.

"Get some water," was all he said to Annie Mae's sister. His only concern was that she be revived before neighbours called the police.

Annie Mae's sister didn't hear him. She was glaring at Bruno, tears streaming down her face. "She's not breathing any more. My god, you killed her. You bastard, you killed Annie Mae."

Biker grabbed Bruno by the arm and pulled him back toward the stairs and out of the apartment building. As Bruno walked toward Biker's car the friend he had left at the poker game came running toward him.

"Bruno. What happened? What did you do?"

"I think she's dead," was all Bruno could manage as Biker pushed him into the passenger side of the car and sped away.

Bruno's friend ran upstairs where he found Annie Mae's sister and another young prostitute who had arrived on the scene. Both girls were crying and trying to raise Annie Mae into a sitting position. Bruno's friend decided he would have to act fast if he was to save his friend from a murder charge. He bent down, swept Annie Mae up in his arms and ran full speed down the hall toward his waiting car. Annie Mae's sister and her friend followed; the new pimp walked back into the apartment and closed the door.

Doctors at the nearby Dartmouth General hospital were able to revive Annie Mae but they realized something was seriously wrong inside the young woman's head. Annie Mae was transferred to the Victoria General Hospital across the Halifax Harbour. There a neurosurgeon recognized the symptoms of the hemorrhage inside her skull, but it was too late; Annie Mae was dead.

The police were called to the hospital where they interviewed Annie Mae's sister and her friend. Bruno Cummings was arrested and charged with murder. He pleaded guilty to a reduced charge of manslaughter and was sent to prison for just under ten years. The judge accepted his claim that he had not intended to kill Annie Mae.

Annie Mae's family and her friends—most of them other prostitutes—attended her funeral in a tiny church in Dartmouth. For Annie Mae the pain of life on the street was gone forever.

Annie Mae Wilson never really had a life, although at nineteen she had had more life experience than most people could ever dream of, no matter how vivid their nightmares. She had visited and worked in most major Canadian cities, earning tens if not hundreds of thousands of dollars, although she died without a penny. Annie Mae had either been beaten by and or had sex with more men than most women meet in a lifetime. A high school drop-out who had slipped through the cracks, Annie Mae ended up a piece of society's trash. She was just another dead hooker; one of twenty-two prostitutes murdered in Canada in 1992.

Annie Mae Wilson was one of the hundreds of young Canadian teens who chose to play the deadly game of prostitution. Statistics Canada figures show the vast majority of street prostitutes arrested in Canada are young teenage girls. In 1984 a federal study into sexual offenses against children in Canada uncovered some startling facts. At that time a large number of male and female prostitutes were interviewed. Fifty per cent of those prostitutes had entered the sex trade before turning sixteen years old; almost every one of them had taken to the streets before turning nineteen. That same study showed that most of the teens entering the prostitution trade had run away from home at least once in the past and that most had done so at a very young age. Being a young teenage runaway is just the first step toward becoming a prostitute. Entering The Game is usually a choice made for the girls by pimps with a keen eye for a profitable mark. Pimps chose young girls for two reasons: they are more profitable because they look fresh and attractive on the street, and they are easier to manipulate.

In many ways, Annie Mae Wilson fit the profile of a girl destined to become a prostitute. She ran away from home at a young age. She quit school because it made her feel inferior to the smarter kids. By age fourteen she found a pimp who convinced her she could be the smart one, that she already had everything she needed to be a success. Annie Mae followed the young man into the prostitution game and never looked back.

Annie Mae could have left the street without giving up her life. Only months before the teenage prostitute was killed, a special police task force had been established in the Halifax area, called into service when juvenile prostitution in Halifax suddenly became a high-profile social problem. But the public outcry that finally spurred Nova Scotia's law-enforcement system to take effective action against The Game came too late for Annie Mae Wilson. Her years in The Game had fostered a strong hatred and mistrust of police. Annie Mae knew it was the prostitutes, rather than their pimps, who were the targets of the criminal justice system. By 1992, Canadian police were filing ten thousand prostitution related charges every year. That was a dramatic increase from pre-1985 figures of about two thousand per year. The new figures did not represent a major influx of prostitutes in Canada's streets or a major crack down by police. It had its source in the inception of Bill C-49, an amendment to the Criminal Code of Canada that prohibited solicitation but failed to make a dent in The Game. The new law made it tougher for girls to work the streets; it did not deter the men who placed them there.

There are no accurate figures to indicate how many pimps are working in Canada. Calculating that number is made impossible by another rule the pimps enforce. When a prostitute is arrested she almost always tells the police she is working alone, and it is almost always a lie. Annie Mae Wilson was punished for not paying Bruno Cummings a leaving fee, a violation of the rules she was brave or foolish enough to risk. Annie Mae would never have risked telling a police officer she was working for a pimp.

Pimps in Canada take in millions of dollars yearly. They use the money to fuel their love of high living: fancy cars, fine clothes, expensive jewellery, while they shunt their young workers from city to city, stroll to stroll, degradation to degradation to maintain their preferred standard of living.

It was in the hands of the Scotians, the name given by police to the Metro Halifax–based pimping ring, that Annie Mae Wilson became a pawn in The Game. It was by the hand of one of its players, and only a peripheral one, that her involvement in it reached its tragic conclusion. Unlike the growing list of young prostitutes in Halifax, Toronto, Vancouver, and other cities, Annie Mae had rebuffed police efforts to take a new tack against the appalling trade in young people. That new approach had police targeting the pimping rings instead of their youthful victims.

Anti-pimping task forces had been fighting the battle against juvenile prostitution since the mid-1980s in Toronto and 1988 in Vancouver. They were making steady gains on the city street as officers slowly persuaded more and more young prostitutes to testify against their pimps. The key to their growing success was a dramatic change of attitude, deriving from a new police recognition that they were in a war to save young lives as much as to jail those bent on their destruction. Each one of these youngsters was somebody's daughter, and, often starved for nurturing family relationships, a young prostitute frequently turned to a task-force officer as a surrogate parent once she saw that the police were no longer intent on punishing her, but on rescuing her by putting her pimp out of commission.

But if juvenile prostitution preys on girls who fall through the cracks, who come from broken homes, or who are easily influenced for other reasons, it is also a predator that gives up its victims with great reluctance. Some cling to the heartbreaking belief in their pimps as "family." The vicious beatings those pimps often deliver are almost always accompanied by the reminder that the pimp/relative is only punishing a girl for her own good, however grossly inappropriate the lesson. Others turned their backs on the offer of help from the new police task forces in the belief that they can play The Game on their own terms, and that their lives will ultimately be better than their upbringing. That was Annie Mae Wilson's belief until Bruno Cummings showed her The Game is no place for an independent-mined working girl.

For police in Halifax, the death of a teenage prostitute could not have come at a worse time. Public outrage over juvenile prostitution was at an all-time high late in 1992, fuelled by media accounts of circumstances leading to the arrests of key members of the Scotians that summer. Graphic reports on the pimps' abuse of several Nova Scotia teenagers who had been located and returned home during a police raid in Toronto led to the highly publicized establishment of the joint-force anti-prostitution task force. It was set up in Dartmouth less than two months after the raid. The unit's office was only a few minutes by car from the apartment building where Bruno had killed Annie Mae, and it didn't take long for word to reach that police unit. The news hit the task force hard; its investigators, from the Halifax, Dartmouth, and Bedford police forces and from the RCMP, had spent endless hours trying to persuade local prostitutes to cooperate with them. The death of Annie Mae Wilson could cost the officers their credibility in the street. They knew the prostitutes might think their pimps still had the upper hand. The task force could not help Annie Mae because she would not let the officers get close to her. Before her body was even taken to the morgue for an autopsy, police were planning a news conference in an effort to exercise damage control. The message would have to get out that Annie Mae had not been under the protection of the task force, and that her death was unrelated to the struggle between police and the Scotian pimping ring. Senior police officers called a quick news conference on the morning after Annie Mae was killed. They explained to local reporters that her death had nothing to do with the work being conducted by the task force and that it would not stand in the way of their mission to run the pimps out of town.

Ironically, in her death Annie Mae did something she would never have done in her life. She provided a powerful boost to police in their attempt to successfully combat pimps who were running girls from Halifax-Dartmouth to Montreal, Toronto, and other major centres. Hearing that she had been killed, a seventeen-year-old girl she had befriended finally decided not only to stick to her decision to testify against her violently abusive former pimp, but to stay out of The Game for good.

Horror and Hope

That Stacey Jackson even survived to make those choices was, in large part, because of her friend Annie Mae's bravery. In August 1992, the two Nova Scotia teenagers were in Toronto, and in the middle of a real-life horror story that made even the worst experiences of their young lives seem inconsequential by comparison. Annie Mae stood numbly in a dingy downtown pool hall and listened as her pimp and Stacey's planned to "get rid of Stacey," a comment Annie Mae took to mean kill her young friend. The pool hall plan came the afternoon after Stacey had been beaten to within an inch of her life for planning to switch allegiance to another pimp. Her pleading calls home after that beating almost proved to be her undoing.

Praying the pimps would not notice, Annie Mae slipped out of the pool hall and found a phone booth nearby; she called the apartment she and Stacey shared with their pimps and told her to get out right away, without stopping to pack. Unknown to her, Anti Pimping Task Force officers had responded to a series of desperate phone calls from Stacey's mother and launched a sudden unexpected raid in Toronto that struck at the heart of the Scotians' powerful and seemingly unassailable pimping machine. Within a few hours, it was all over: Stacey and two even younger girls from Nova Scotia were on a flight back to Halifax; five key members of the Scotian ring were sitting in a Toronto jail. Among them was twenty-seven-year-old Manning Greer of North Preston, Nova Scotia—the Big Man, as he was known to Scotian players and prostitutes, and to those involved in The Game on both sides of the law across Canada.

That was only the beginning: less than three years after the raid, sixty Halifax-based pimps had been arrested through the efforts of the Halifax task force. All but three of them were jailed after convictions on charges ranging from living on the avails of prostitution to exercising control for the purpose of prostitution. The three men who walked away did so after the young girls they were accused of pimping refused to testify against them in court. Those who did not walk out of court were sent to federal prisons for terms ranging from two to seven years. Less than three years after the raid, Halifax, whose Scotians a Toronto police officer once described as one of Canada's most brutal pimping rings, was all but rid of at least the menace of juvenile prostitution. Officers patrolling the city's main stroll on Hollis Street rarely saw an underage girl there, nor were they turning up in other major centres.

In the fall of 1992, there were more than a hundred Nova Scotia teenagers selling sex on the streets across Canada and enduring the cruelties of their pimps. More than half of these young people responded, in some way, to task force members' efforts to get them off the streets and their pimps behind bars. Not all of the girls who sought help from the task force remained free of The Game, but many did. In the beginning the girls shared the belief held by Annie Mae—that police were not to be trusted. That gradually changed as the task force officers got to know the girls, chatting with them on Hollis Street and north-end strolls, sympathizing with their plight over coffee (or their preferred snack, a burger and fries), and finally offering them protection in exchange for their agreement to testify against pimps who had in some cases been brutalizing them for years. The assistance ranged from witness relocation programs—the girls could opt to change their identities and start new lives in a different city—to temporary accommodation in a safe house set up on the grounds of the Nova Scotia Hospital, located in Dartmouth just up the road from the apartment where Annie Mae died. The facility, which opened near the end of 1992, housed prostitutes whose decision to testify against their former pimps—"sign" on them was the phrase pimps used—made them vulnerable to the pimps who were still at large and were less than thrilled with these "betrayals" of their fellow players. Unlike youth facilities in the Halifax area, the safe house had no age restrictions. A seventeen-year-old, by any definition a heartbreakingly young victim of The Game, was considered too old for the protective custody of a juvenile training facility; yet such a girl, as well as much older women, desperately needed the security of a restricted environment. It was the age restrictions in many existing juvenile facilities that was in large part responsible for the establishment of the Dartmouth safe house.

The Sullivan House—the name given the safe house—welcomed a girl like Stacey Jackson who was too old to be accepted at the youth training school in Truro where other girls were sent: when the safe house opened its doors, she was the first to enter them.

Stacey hadn't been doing well in the months following her return from Toronto. She had agreed to participate in the task force program and sign on her abusive pimp, but her early experiences in rejoining the "straight" world, as players refer to any social structure other than prostitution, had been disillusioning. Tense, difficult weeks in relatives' homes; a brief and disastrous stint at school; sojourns in a women's shelter and a psychiatric unit, Stacey rebelled in all these environments, running away from the shelter and even considering a return to the streets. The safe house was a vast improvement, offering the reassuring and helpful companionship of girls and women who understood where she was coming from and shared her fundamental desire to make sure she wasn't going back. There were more regular visits with her task-force case officer, John Elliott, a Mountie who had been part of a 1990 investigation of the pimping problem in the Halifax area and who was deeply committed to helping its victims. Stacey had been living outside Halifax before moving to the safe house, and hadn't met as frequently with Elliott as she would have liked. She saw him as a father figure, even telling him so on their rare visits earlier in the fall. John Elliott had not even been the case officer assigned to Stacey Jackson; he was handed the file after it became clear she had quickly developed a strong bond with him.

The change that had come to Stacey's life in the more tolerable confines of the safe house made her days just a little less bleak, the possibilities for a real future just a little more credible. Despite that, she hadn't entirely closed the door on her old life when she stepped through the huge wooden door of the safe house. Some days, reminiscing with other prostitutes about street life, she succumbed to nostalgia, preferring to recall the closeness of her relationship with other girls than to remind herself of the man who had whipped both her legs into a solid mass of bloodied flesh. It did not help her resolve to put him behind bars when she received a death threat from one of his relatives, although police quickly stepped in, arresting and charging the pimp's nephew, whose voice she had recognized during the telephone conversation in which the threat was delivered.

In the weeks leading up to Christmas, Stacey found herself spending more and more time wishing she was back on the street with Annie Mae. They hadn't seen each other since Toronto. Stacey knew her friend had refused to get involved with the task force and was still working the streets, despite all that had happened. She had begun to believe it hadn't really been that bad, that maybe if they got together, they could somehow make The Game work for them. She was filled with a fear that her pimp had been right. There was nothing for her in the straight world; her real place was with her new family. The beating he had given her was severe but Stacey remembered how her real father had physically abused her mother for years, before she left him. She also remembered it was her father who had helped Stacey get her own place after the sixteen-year-old gave birth to a son, conceived in the dying days of her relationship with her childhood sweetheart. Debbie Jackson, now Debbie Howard, was happily remarried and obviously concerned about her daughter's welfare, but Stacey and her mother were like gas and fire—a very volatile mix. Stacey had been able to forgive her father for the abuse he dished out against her mother. When Debbie finally decided to end her marriage and walk away, Stacey and her younger brother chose to stay with their dad rather than give up the stability and friendships his home provided. If she could forgive her father maybe she should give that same chance to her pimp. Stacey had begun to believe all of her problems were of her own making and not the fault of the men she had been involved with. The custody of her own son was apparently going to his father's family. What difference did it make if she returned to the streets? That was probably where she belonged, she thought, and as for the violence, well, it probably would not have happened if she had not broken the rules.

Stacey was in the common room of the safe house, so lost in her thoughts that she didn't hear John Elliott approach; he was suddenly there, looking very serious. "Why don't we go for a drive and talk, Stacey?" he suggested. "I've already signed you out at the desk." She always looked forward to their conversations, but he seemed upset, his compact, muscular body held rigid as they walked towards the car. They sat in silence as the car pulled out of the hospital grounds, and then he told her. There would be no reunion with Annie Mae.

Elliott was prepared for the angry tears, the shock, the string of obscenities, and finally the sullen silence of the emotionally devastated teenager. What he didn't expect was the vehement fury against all pimps that poured out of her when she began to speak again. He knew Stacey would always detest the man who killed Annie Mae, but because she had been hinting to him so strongly that she could be back on the stroll soon, he anticipated a defensive reaction: not all pimps are alike; it's possible to beat the odds, anything to justify going back to the streets despite what happened to Annie Mae. All Stacey could think about was how her friend had always been there for her, even when it meant jeopardizing her own life, back in that summer of horror they had experienced. Now she was dead, and it was with a sudden jolt of comprehension that Stacey realized it could as easily have been her, or any of the dozens of other teenagers she had met in her brief but hellish career as a prostitute. They had all been brutalized, regularly and often without provocation; it was a wonder any of them were still alive. A very powerful memory she had washed away in her self doubt sprang to the front of Stacey's mind— it was her, lying on a bed stained with her own blood, pleading in agony to be allowed to die.

Stacey Jackson made a commitment to herself and to John Elliott in that car. She swore she would never again work the streets and she vowed to get even with the pimps who had very nearly ended her life and who had now taken away her closest friend. John Elliott sat quietly in the car; he was happy to have Stacey back on side but he knew her moods could swing and he could lose her again.

A happy ending, or was it? For Stacey Jackson, and for many other Nova Scotia teenagers, it certainly seemed to be. Stacey did testify against her former pimp, Michael ("Smit") Sears, who was sentenced in 1993 to six years in prison. She did leave The Game and rejoin that straight world. Today Stacey derives great satisfaction from talking to high school students about her experiences. She has seen how young people readily accept a lesson learned in the school of real life. When Stacey visits a school she does not see that glassy eyed expression of teenage boredom that often greets a guest lecturer offering advice—even if that advice is something the teens really need.

Stacey paid dearly for her involvement in the deadly game. She lost custody of her son to his father's family. She also lost her home after realizing she could not stay in Halifax, as she had wished. For two years after her court appearance, she insisted on living in a small north-end apartment and maintaining her friendships with the young women she had met as a prostitute but who, unlike her, had been unable to break free. Perhaps she hoped to steer them away from The Game; certainly she felt they deserved at least her support and sympathy, but in the end she yielded to pressure from her family and from police. In early 1996, as the date for Smit's possible parole neared, Stacey Jackson moved to another part of Canada. That the location, like her name, must remain unknown is another painful consequence of her experience with the world of violent crime.

Yet Stacey Jackson was one of the lucky ones. Other young prostitutes, like her friend Annie Mae Wilson, had paid the ultimate price. Still others stopped being juvenile prostitutes only because they turned eighteen. The Game is still being played on the streets of Halifax, although now the rules have changed. The task force has all but disappeared; before it fell victim to the budget cutter's knife it sent a ringing message to the pimps who still ply their trade in Halifax. The brutal treatment of prostitutes, whatever their age, is not to be tolerated. Tough new federal anti-pimping legislation, carrying much longer prison sentences for pimps who prey on juveniles, has enhanced the message. Violence had been touted as the key to a pimp's success. Today it is seen as a weakness. The Game is played for money and the players adjust to rule changes quickly. If beating girls means going to jail, then beating girls is not a smart man's way to play. One jailed pimp recently joked about this trend, saying his colleagues now had to buy ice-cream cones for their girls to keep them happy. That change in attitude may have made life safer for the young girls in Halifax it has not stopped the brutality elsewhere. The pimps know young girls are more profitable and they are not yet willing to give up that easy money. Police in Montreal and Toronto still report serious problems of violence against underage prostitutes, and task force members still point to the east coast as the source of that violence. The major change: the victims now tend to come from northern Ontario rather than Nova Scotia.

The anti-pimping task force was a success, but unfortunately that success has seen a return to the status quo. Prostitution has once again slipped to the back burner on the political agenda.

What the task force could not do, what it was never asked to do, was target the real source of the problem. In Nova Scotia, pimping is a complex, uniquely delicate problem with roots stretching deep into the province's history—a problem that is widely misunderstood and formidably challenging. In a word, the problem is racism.

Unfortunately, what happened to Annie Mae Wilson and Stacey Jackson is fodder for the racists. It is the kind of fodder that perpetuates the ignorance that lies beneath racism. Merely to state a single fact—that the vast majority of Nova Scotia's pimps are black men from a small community just outside Dartmouth—is to hold a lighted match under the powder-keg of racial politics past and present. If the discussion proceeds past this first danger-point, add a second fact: their "employees" are invariably white women and girls. Annie Mae Wilson and Stacey Jackson—white victims; Bruno Cummings and Michael Sears—black criminals. Those facts are enough for the racists.

Facts alone don't tell a story. People do. Statistics are a very dangerous tool that, in the hands of a manipulator, can appear to bolster an extremist's view. The statistics tell one story, all but two of the men charged with pimping by the prostitution task force were black and all but a handful of the girls helped by the task force were white. The people behind those statistics tell a very different story. It may be that politicians are more comfortable with prostitution on that back burner because they are afraid to walk into the minefield those statistics present. What they fail to see is the minefield is not what it appears to be. It is ridiculously ignorant to apply a racist view to the facts presented by prostitution in Nova Scotia. Only a tiny proportion of white females become prostitutes, just as a small minority of black men become pimps. People who understand even a scrap of the history behind the image of the jive-talking, gold-laden Cadillac-driving black pimp would no more consider this caricature an accurate reflection of a racial group than they would picture white women—as a group—in stiletto heels and leather miniskirts, cigarettes dangling from their scarlet-painted lips.

The trouble is that many people know nothing, or very little, about the history of black people in Nova Scotia—let alone the factors that influenced the rise of pimping in the ranks of a very small minority of young men in one of the province's several black communities.

This community, North Preston, traces its roots to the end of the U.S. War of Independence, when the first large influx of Loyalist blacks arrived in Canada, to be joined in the eighteenth century by a large group from Jamaica. Often highly skilled trades people, they worked on many of the building projects in the quickly growing town of Halifax, including the reconstruction of Fort George on Citadel Hill. The early black settlers had been promised land grants, but they were not expecting the rocky, hilly territory they were give, over-looking the lakes and woodlands that would demarcate the city of Dartmouth. This was thin, unyielding soil from which it was almost impossible to coax a decent crop; and the area, now only a fifteen-minute drive from downtown Halifax, was a journey of many hours on foot or by horse and wagon. An equally daunting challenge to the settlers of what would become North Preston was the exodus of more than one thousand black residents of Nova Scotia and New Brunswick to Sierra Leone, West Africa, in 1791. Many of the best-educated and most influential community leaders believed there was no future for black people in Atlantic Canada, and those who remained were hard-pressed to prove them wrong.

Incredibly, the many obstacles they faced only seemed to forge a stronger bond among the settlers, united by spiritual values, an abid-ing belief in the importance of education and self-sufficiency, and a deep sense of community loyalty. These remain the principles of the vast majority of North Preston residents today, people who have had to fight for just about everything they have, from adequate schooling for their children, to decent jobs at times when unemployment could soar to 80 per cent. Unlike other communities facing some of the same problems, the people of North Preston have had to fight the deep-set racism blocking them from achieving many of their goals. Integration helped improve educational standards for young black people, but it also exposed them to a barrage of racial slurs that seri-ously undermined the focus of their early teaching, tolerance based on equality.

Racism, and the frustration and anger it evokes, is cited by social scientists studying the source of criminal activity, along with poverty, high unemployment, inadequate education, and the breakdown of family. All these factors, except the last, were at play in the proliferation of pimping among young men from North Preston in the 1980s. Ironically, the very importance of family unity they had learned as youngsters became twisted into the Scotians' most valuable weapon as a criminal ring. Loyalty to "family" members (relative or not) against other pimps, or against the police was the key to the Scotians' success. By 1992, more than one hundred young people from North Preston, a community of five thousand, were identified by the police as being involved in the prostitution game; a deeply concerned community group was formed to examine the underlying causes. To the list of sociological triggers for crime was added the powerful influence on these young men by the handful of "pioneers" who paved the way for them in the 1970s.

Miles States was one of these men. Born into a military family that moved frequently, he lacked the strong sense of community that had such a positive effect on most of the residents of places like North Preston. Like them he learned early on that racism was a reality he would face all his life. States was only seven years old when a white boy at the military base where his family was stationed called him "nigger," and he never forgot how the cruel taunt made him feel singled out for ridicule, contempt, and hatred because of the colour of his skin. Many other such incidents fed his anger, and his growing sense of resentment towards all white people. That resentment grew slowly into anger and then rage. That was the makeup of Miles States personality when he returned to Halifax with his mother at age fourteen. In the late 1960s as civil rights activism took hold across North America, he joined the Black Panther Party, attaching himself not to the factions of the movement establishing programs for disadvantaged young people in inner cities, but to the more radical elements of the party. For three years, he helped smuggle his American comrades, denied entry into Canada because of their involvement in violent political activity, into Toronto from Buffalo.

For a few years States believed his membership in the Party and the work he was doing would someday make a difference. Gradually he became disillusioned with the movement. He began to believe white men would always hold the power and his midnight runs across the border were nothing more than a slight ripple against a tide he could not slow. When States met a young prostitute in Halifax, an experienced woman in her twenties who offered to teach him the trade on her home turf of Montreal, in exchange for his protection, he accepted. The thought of earning hundreds, maybe thousands of dollars by selling white women to white men was an irresistible irony to a man who saw his race as an insurmountable barrier to making it big in a predominantly white world.

During the 1970s, Miles States became one of Canada's most successful pimps, running a stable of as many as fifteen prostitutes in cities on both sides of the border. By the end of the decade, States was pulling in thousands of dollars a week, most of it going to support his taste for fancy cars, expensive clothing, comfortable apartments, and cocaine. It was the drug that proved to be his downfall; the cost of cocaine, on which he quickly became dependent, forced the high-roller to extend his criminal career to narcotics trafficking. In 1981, a drug deal went sour on him in Michigan when his contacts pulled their guns. States was forced to kneel facing away from the two men and began to believe his life was about to end. He knew the men were high and listened as they joked and taunted him. Fortunately Miles was not high. He slowly lowered his arms—the gunmen had forced him to clasp his hands behind his head—a move that made it possible to get to his own .22-calibre handgun. Miles States shot both men and then quickly grabbed their drugs and his money and fled the scene. The men were not dead. States had hit them in the legs and hoped the wounds would teach them a lesson. What he did not know was the police had been following the two men and had watched as the deal went bad. States raced back to his hotel room where he locked himself in a washroom and began to sample his drug cache. The police kicked in the door and his reign as a high-rolling pimp ended. States was sentenced to three years in Michigan State Penitentiary, and it was during his prison stay that he met a man whose influence changed his life. The change began when an older inmate made a statement that, at first, puzzled and angered States. "You'll never be a man because you won't let go of your toys." What Miles States thought was the most torturous ordeal he had ever faced, endless days of marking time in a cell, turned out to be the single factor that saved his life. States could not escape the older inmate turned philosopher and gradually the older man prevailed. When Miles States walked out of the Michigan Prison he believed his career as a pimp had been driven by a need to erase a self doubt he had fostered since the day that young boy called him "nigger." The older man convinced States that his drive to attain wealth and all the toys that came with it was a fight to prove himself to a world that didn't care who he was. States decided he would begin his new life by proving himself only to himself.

In the mid-1980s, States returned to Halifax and took a job as a janitor. Later he decided to seek a career helping others who were going down the same path he had traveled. Today, Miles States is a counselor of ex-inmates, and a keen observer of the trends that have led the young people of North Preston into such criminal activities as prostitution. States acknowledges his flamboyant behavior during the height of his pimping days—during visits to Halifax, he would flash a huge wad of bills to impress his friends—but he feels the significance of "role models" like himself on the next generation of pimps is slight. States believes the young men of North Preston increasingly turned to pimping because they were still facing extensive racism, as he had in his youth, as young black people still do. North Preston's parents, along with church and community leaders, still strive to instill in the younger generation a sense of pride in their history and of value in their potential. Institutions such as the Black Cultural Centre help provide information to students about their rich cultural heritage, there's even an Internet home-page devoted to the subject, and the annual Black History Month gives school-age children of every background the opportunity to meet together to discuss the black experience in Nova Scotia, past and present.

Still, many Nova Scotians, both white and black, acknowledge that racism remains prevalent in the schools and the workplace, and in society as a whole. Only a small percentage of the victims of racism turn to a life of crime as a response to the hatred they face. Some who do, and are able to break free long enough to enlighten others about the cause, point to racial hatred as the primary impetus. The hatred works both ways: one young man who grew up with several of the key Scotian players recalls using racist stereotyping as a weapon in the schoolyard.

If white students saw blacks as tall, tough and violent, that was the image they cultivated. "You could get their lunch money just by standing there, looking mean, and asking for the money," he remembers. "It didn't even matter if you knew how to fight." The same kinds of principles could be applied outside school and they were, as a growing number of North Preston teenage boys gave up on their education, another commonly cited characteristic of a young person headed for trouble. Angry, frustrated by their inability to get anything better than a minimum-wage job in a burger joint—or bagging groceries, like Bruno Cummings, and increasingly obsessed with revenge against "the system," a few of these teenagers began to follow their slightly older friends into the world of prostitution. The precious heritage of community loyalty, distorted by these pimps into a bond based on greed and violence, made the newly forming group of Scotians a powerful and dangerous force. "We could do anything, it didn't matter," recalls one jailed member of the ring. "You always knew you had the family behind you." Like Miles States, these young men saw a certain irony in running white girls on Hollis Street to attract white buyers to the apparent indifference of a mostly white police force, which in the early 1980s did not view pimping as a serious problem. And, like States, these young men enjoyed the cars, the clothes, and the money.

But, unlike States, the new breed of pimps showed a decided, and disturbing, penchant for violence against "their" girls as a disciplinary measure and a method of exercising control. This, and the Scotians' preference for underage girls—even preteens—went completely against the experience of States and other successful pimps of his era. He rented well-appointed apartments for the prostitutes he controlled—not run-down hotel rooms where regular beatings, verbal abuse, and repeated rapes were all the young women had to come home to. "A girl must respect her man." States says "and violence will only drive her away." States knew some brutal pimps in his day, and took their girls away from them easily, but he says the extent and level of violence seems more pronounced now. As for the pimps practicing that violence, they have convinced themselves that it is the girls who want it. "Many of these girls come from homes where they were abused," explains a jailed pimp. "They really think a beating is the only way to be sure a man loves them. We didn't teach them that, their fathers did."

One thing is certain, the violence was self perpetuating. Pimps began to brag to one another about the beatings they handed out. In that light the group dynamic played its part—Biker's taunting of Bruno Cummings was a common example of the kind of peer pressure exerted on a pimp reluctant to dole out a beating. The violence was a yardstick of success in the Scotian hierarchy; if a young player wanted to get closer to the Big Man and his core group of pimps, he would have to show that he commanded his girls' respect. Many of the Scotians believed respect was instilled with a fist. In the case of Michael Sears it was instilled with a wire whip. Dehumanizing the girls, referring to them a "dumb 'ho" or "stupid bitch," made it easier for these men to lash out in increasingly sadistic ways. Miles States was wrong about how at least some young prostitutes responded to their pimps' violence. It didn't drive them away, some believed it was all they deserved.

Millions of dollars have been spent on police operations like the

Metro Halifax task force yet, every night men drive their cars to the local strolls and offer cash for sex; and every night girls like Stacey and Annie Mae make the trade. This full and tragic account of the lives of Annie Mae and Stacey and the others caught up in the prostitution game during the early part of this decade is not offered as a recipe for solving the problem of prostitution. Instead it is offered as a window for parents, teachers and others who should know the warning signs that signal a child's entry into that dangerous world. The Game has a life force of its own; a life force fueled by millions of dollars and the greed that kind of money can create. While The Game has its own energy it cannot play itself. The Game needs somebody's daughter and somebody's son to stoke its cash starved furnace. Understanding its rules may help you keep your children from becoming its pawns.

Part Two:
Stacey and Annie Mae

In the spring of 1992, Stacey Jackson was seventeen years old. She was a shy, attractive single mother—and a perfect candidate for the pimps recruiting young women in Nova Scotia. She had just taken a small apartment in the Highfield Park area of Dartmouth. She was sharing it with her six-month-old son, Michael. They were alone because Stacey had just ended the relationship with her boyfriend, Michael's father, Roger Morgan. Highfield Park overlooks the McKay Bridge, one of the two bridges linking Dartmouth to Halifax. It is a mass of high- and low-rise apartment buildings where people live in close quarters but for the most part don't bother to get to know the people living in the next building, or even on the next floor. Stacey loved its bustle of early-morning activity. She and Michael would sit in the window of their apartment and watch the parade of strangers leave for work each day. The mornings were the busiest time for Stacey; it was when Michael seemed to need the most attention. After lunch, there'd be a knock on the door as her friend Rachel Williams came over to visit. Her visit meant an afternoon of TV and chatting, more time with Michael, supper, and then bed. That was the routine and Stacey was comfortable with it. She had dreams of going back to school someday, maybe even college, but that would be someday, not today. Life here was a lot better than it had been at home for the now seventeen-year-old mom. Home was a place filled with bitter memories of violence and hatred.

For years, Debbie Howard had tried to hide the violence from Stacey and her younger brother. When their father started drinking—a sure sign that trouble would follow—Debbie would play games of hide-and-seek with the kids. It was fun at first, but they soon got tired of squatting in a broom closet or kitchen cupboard, and they were frightened at the sound of their mother screaming and their father throwing things. Stacey's earliest memory is the confusion she felt during a "game" with her mother. "I remember we were running up the street, away from the house, and he was chasing us. I remember wondering where we were going and why we were running." Mrs. Howard also recalls the incident: "Stacey must have been about three. Her father came home from work and the trouble started right away. When I couldn't calm him down, I took her and ran to a corner store just up the street. I can still see him behind us with a baseball bat, cursing and threatening me, and all I could think was, 'My God, the neighbours.' "

The incidents of abuse continued until in 1989 Debbie Howard decided she had had enough. She left her husband and began the job of putting her life back in order. Stacey and her brother, by this time young teens, refused to come along. Within a year, Stacey was pregnant, and a few months after the baby was born she had her own place. Her father helped her find the apartment in Highfield Park, and the Nova Scotia Department of Social Services helped her pay the rent and fill the apartment with a few pieces of used furniture.

Stacey still carried the scars of her troubled childhood, although not physically. Slim-waisted, five-foot-four, with long, curly blonde hair and bright blue eyes, she was a pretty girl who had been asked out on dates as often as many of the popular girls at school. She had always felt awkward though, and lacked confidence, especially around boys. Roger was different simply because she had known him since she was ten years old; their physical relationship had grown out of adolescent curiosity rather than deep passion. Stacey's insecurity was a feeling her mother understood—only after years of loneliness had the forty-three-year old Debbie Jackson finally met Gordon Howard, a man with whom she could finally have a rewarding relationship. She hoped that her own positive experience would influence her daughter to get out a bit more—enjoy dating some nice boys her own age—but it seemed Stacey preferred her rather insular life. Little did Debbie Howard realize how far Stacey would go when she finally did "get out," and what it would take to bring her back.

Stacey's desire to get out came through her relationship with her new neighbour and friend, Rachel. Rachel was eighteen but to Stacey she was a woman of the world. The two became friends before Stacey had even finished unpacking her things in the new apartment. The two teenage girls very quickly developed their afternoon routine, and it became the highlight of each day for Stacey. It was Rachel who introduced Stacey to a world that would change her life for ever. Rachel was a prostitute and she told Stacey how she'd started working the streets of Halifax at age thirteen and how she had travelled to Montreal and Toronto with her pimp. Stacey was fascinated by the life Rachel led and every day asked her about the activities on the Hollis Street stroll the night before. Rachel lived with another teenage prostitute in an apartment paid for by their pimp, but before long Rachel moved in with Stacey so the two could spend more time together. That was how Stacey met Kenny Sims, the younger more attractive cousin of Rachel's pimp, Terrance.

Kenny told Stacey to call him K-bar, the street name he'd chosen for himself. He picked K-bar because Terrance had been given the name T-bar. Terrance liked that name because it linked him to his pride and joy; his black Pontiac Trans Am sports car with its smoked glass T-bar removable roof panels. Kenny also told Stacey she should always refer to him and his cousin as "players." They did not like the term "pimp."

They were players, he insisted—and Stacey had no idea that she was destined to be the latest object of their game. The Game, as they called it, as if there could be no other.

In the evenings, when Terrance came to pick up Rachel, Kenny would always take time to talk with Stacey or play with Michael. Terrance tended to stay quiet around her; he was polite, but never initiated a conversation. Kenny paid a lot of attention to Stacey and sometimes stayed behind with her after the others had gone downtown. Kenny had a serious interest in Stacey and it shocked her. The seventeen-year-old pimp often told her how pretty she was, even suggesting she dye her hair an even brighter blonde to bring out the blue of her beautiful eyes. Stacey was a little embarrassed by all of this; but she told Rachel it was a nice sort of embarrassment. One afternoon, the two girls decided to dye Stacey's hair to see what Kenny would say. Rachel had become somewhat of an expert in hair care having changed her own colour and style on more occasions than she could remember. With the new colour added, a curling iron and some gel tamed the wild curls, and when the two pimps arrived, they were both impressed.

"Whoa, look at you, girl," Kenny commented, running his hands over her hair. "You look fine tonight. T, man, doesn't this girl look fine?" Stacey blushed at the men's obvious approval. Even the taciturn T-bar agreed, laughing: "Stacey, I might just make Kenny take the girls down, so I can stay here with you." Stacey had rarely heard her father compliment her mother on her appearance; it gave her an odd feeling to hear such open approval, especially from men she liked, but she also felt she could easily get used to the attention. She never thought there was anything other than honesty behind the remarks made by the young pimps.

"Listen, Stacey, I got some work to do," Kenny said. "Mind if I come back in an hour?" Stacey didn't mind at all, and she told Kenny she'd see him soon. On the way down to the car, Kenny asked Rachel what size blue jeans Stacey wore, then asked Terrance to drive him to the mall. Terrance covered the distance to the mall in minutes and Kenny ran in to a designer blue jeans shop just before the clerk closed the doors. He quickly picked out a pair of pre-faded jeans and a bright red shirt.

After driving Rachel and her former roommate to the Hollis Street stroll, the two pimps headed back to Dartmouth, stopping just before the bridge to buy burgers, fries, and milkshakes at a fast-food drive-through restaurant.

Stacey had just put the baby to bed for the night when she heard the knock on the apartment door. Her heart raced a little; she was excited and happy that Kenny had returned, and her strong emotions surprised her. "Hey pretty lady, I brought us some food—hope you're hungry," and Kenny thrust the bag of burgers into her hands. "I've got a little something else here for you too, but let's eat first." Stacey was intrigued at the thought of a gift from Kenny, but she was too shy to tell him she wanted to see what was in the shopping bag and didn't care about the food. Kenny ate his burger and fries, then picked up the bag from the floor beside his chair. "Here," he said. "This is to celebrate your new look."

When she opened the bag and saw the expensive clothes, Stacey flushed. "Kenny, what did you do?" "Nothing. I just figured a pretty girl should have pretty clothes. Besides, I have money and you don't so try 'em on for me and let's see how you look." Stacey grabbed the bag and headed into the bedroom. At the sight of the new outfit, she started blushing again—the jeans were much tighter than the pants she usually wore, and the bright shirt made the pants seem loose. She was still looking in the mirror when the bedroom door opened. "Sorry, I couldn't wait any longer," Kenny said, then took in the picture. "Hey, that looks good, Stacey. Really good."

"Don't you think it's a little tight?"

"Hell no, girl. You got the curves; you should show 'em." With that, he grabbed her around the waist, pulled her close, and kissed her; she felt a thrill of excitement and anticipation she had never experienced before. Within moments, the T-shirt was on the floor and Kenny was kissing her chest. Later, in bed, Stacey ran her hands along Kenny's body, marvelling at how white her skin looked against his.

Then she began to giggle. "What are you laughing at, girl?" "Well, now I know why my mother is so happy all the time," she said, explaining that Gordon Howard, her mother's husband, was an attractive, muscular black man who treated his wife very well.

Kenny came back to the apartment at about two o'clock the next afternoon; he was taking Stacey to the mall he announced, and rather peremptorily told Rachel to stay and watch Michael. Stacey didn't seem to find it strange that Kenny simply instructed Rachel to look after the baby, instead of asking her—or that Rachel simply complied. She was too caught up in the thrill of her new "relationship" to notice the subtle changes in the behavior of those around her. At the mall, Kenny insisted on buying Stacey a denim jacket to go with her outfit. "I want my girl looking good," he said, looking her over with satisfaction. "You know, we should get outta here and go to Toronto to do some real shopping sometime." Stacey's eyes lit up at the very idea. "God, Kenny, that would be great! I've never been to Toronto— what's it like?" From the glowing picture painted by K-bar, the naive teenager got the impression that all people in Toronto did was shop and have a good time. She was still daydreaming about the trip when they returned to the apartment to find that Stacey's mother had shown up for a visit.

Debbie Howard immediately noticed the tight clothes and the new hairstyle, but she didn't comment. She just introduced herself to Kenny, who mumbled hello and walked into the living-room to sit with Rachel and the baby. The reaction surprised Stacey, but she thought Kenny might be a little nervous about meeting her mother. Mrs. Howard didn't mind the mumbled greeting she was more concerned that the young man seemed so ill at ease, even avoiding her gaze when they met. She was impressed with two things she noticed about this young man. Stacey's new boyfriend was a good-looking fellow and, judging by his expensive clothes and jewelry, he had a good job.

Kenny quickly became part of Stacey's life, dropping by most afternoons and evenings. The new clothes and the bright-gold hair were just the beginning—with Rachel's help, Stacey began using more make-up before going out; her bearing and even the way she walked became more provocative and she actually began to think of herself as sexy. The subject of prostitution often arose, and Kenny openly promoted The Game as a plausible alternative for any woman considering her career options. Better than collecting welfare, he said—and it would provide a solid financial foundation for other goals she might pursue later in life. It all sounded so practical, so serious. Stacey, thought she might like to become a lawyer someday and began to think prostitution might be the best way to earn the money that kind of education would require. Kenny enjoyed hearing Stacey talk about her dreams, her plans. Like most pimps he was a very good listener. He wanted to know everything there was to know about what made Stacey tick.

The trouble struck one evening, when Debbie and Gordon Howard dropped by to find Kenny, Terrance, Rachel and Stacey listening to music and chatting. For Gordon Howard, the alarm bells started ringing almost as soon as he walked through the door. The first alarm sounded when Terrance and Kenny would not make eye contact or take his hand when it was offered—and then they quickly left the living-room to sit in the kitchen when Debbie and Gordon sat down on the sofa. Ten minutes later, they left, and Howard Gordon walked to the window to watch as they jumped into Terrance's sporty Trans Am.

A hard-working man all his life, Gordon was fairly certain he had just seen an example of one of the biggest problems plaguing the black community in the Halifax area. Members of the community were concerned about the number of young men who had abandoned the struggle to find employment and make a decent life for themselves, opting instead to make big bucks—or try—by becoming pimps. Gordon Howard did not want to prejudge Terrance and Kenny: he knew how common it was for white police officers to assume that any well-dressed black man in a fancy car was a pimp. He had faced that kind of prejudice himself. A sharp dresser, he liked to wear gold jewelry and his car was less than conservative—bright yellow, with contrasting stripes and silver rims. One day he was pulled over by a police cruiser, and the officer asked where Howard worked. The question was not all that unusual but Gordon could hear an accusing tone that quickly disappeared when Howard said he was an offshore fisherman.

Well, maybe he could find out a bit more from Stacey.

"What do those boys do?" he asked, calmly.

"Nothing, really. Kenny is a student, and Terrance doesn't have a job right now."

"Really? That's an awful nice car for someone without work."

Stacey blushed and didn't offer an explanation. Gordon didn't need to hear more. "Debbie, those boys are pimps." No dissertation, a simple comment that brought the house down around him, as mother and daughter launched into a heated argument. Stacey became defiant and angry, as was her habit in arguments with her mom, and she bluntly conceded that Terrance and Kenny were pimps, even defending their choice by repeating Kenny's assertion that prostitution was better than living off "the system." Her frustration mounting, Debbie Howard demanded to know if Stacey was working as a prostitute. Stacey accused her mother of mistrusting her as her anger grew. She was Kenny's *girlfriend,* she insisted; his "working girls" were an entirely different matter. At that point Gordon Howard offered an opinion. "If a pimp is spending that much time with you, he plans to turn you out. Those boys don't spend time on a girl unless they believe they will get it, and more, back."

An infuriated Stacey asked the Howards to leave—probably because Gordon had hit the nail on the head. Earlier in the day, Kenny suggested that the planned shopping trip to Toronto would happen sooner if Stacey could help him raise a little money. She had balked at the idea of working on Hollis Street, where her friends or relatives could see her, but was contemplating his idea that she work at a local escort agency—no-one would see her, and he could arrange everything. Kenny had worked fast: Stacey was really wondering if she could sell her body for money—only a few weeks after meeting Kenny Sims, the pimp who, unbeknownst to her, was only pretending to be her boyfriend. Stacey had hoped her mother would agree to pay for her ticket to Toronto—she didn't want to ask Kenny—but now Gordon Howard had gone and screwed that one up. How did he figure out what K-bar and T-bar were doing? He even knew the language; "turn you out," he had said, referring to a prostitute's first foray onto the stroll after her pimp considers her ready to handle herself. Gordon knew much more about prostitution than Stacey ever imagined. Years earlier he had befriended a local pimp. Gordon didn't like what the man did, but he didn't judge him either. The two were only casual acquaintances but the pimp often bragged about The Game when they met at a local bar.

Stacey believed Kenny loved her and that he would not let her become a full-time prostitute, but if turning a trick once in a while would help them out.... Besides, these escort agencies were listed in the phone book, as Kenny had shown her; they sounded quite legitimate. She would definitely be able to earn enough for the trip to Toronto, and she'd be doing something positive for her future, and Michael's. Rachel had made even street prostitution sound like a fascinating life—such a variety of people, the companionship of other girls. It also sounded frightening.... All night the teenager tossed and turned, trying to decide what to do. Debbie Howard had left Stacey when her daughter needed her most. The anger of the moment had driven them apart but the moment was the most important so far in Stacey's young life. She felt she had to make a decision, and she made it alone. By dawn she was already preparing herself mentally for the first visit to the escort service where she would work.

Stacey's reasoning might seem unbelievably naive even for a girl with no exposure to prostitution, but that gullibility was exactly what Kenny was counting on, along with any adolescent's natural rebelliousness against the adults in her life. Other than the Howards, there was no-one in Stacey's life who would offer her a warning. Her friends could not help, because they were caught in the same trap: Stacey was spending all her time in the company of young prostitutes and their pimps. Even her son was being tended by a fledging pimp. When she and Kenny went out for the evening, he provided the baby-sitter. The sitter was his fourteen-year-old cousin Vincent; a "bubble-gummer" trying to prove his value to experienced pimps by offering them a variety of services, from baby-sitting the children of young mothers, to running errands and keeping an eye out for possible recruits, preferable teenagers.

While Vincent looked after Michael, his mom usually accompanied Kenny on one of his outings to a colleague's apartment for a card game. There would usually be a group of them gathered at the table, cellular phones at the ready so they could keep in touch with the girls on the street. Occasionally, one or more of the men would drive down to Hollis Street to check on their charges and collect some money from them. The other pimps tolerated Stacey's presence; they were polite and offered her compliments. A few wondered why K-bar was playing this girl for so long when he could be making money from her. The pimps all knew K-bar was in the process of turning this girl though and didn't interfere. It was his business and they allowed him the freedom to conduct it his way. The more experienced players considered Kenny a minor pimp who spent too much time playing his girls and not enough working them.

Roman Neville was one of the more experienced players whose place Stacey visited with Kenny. He was the first pimp Stacey had met so far whose street name seemed to fit him perfectly. He stood five foot three and was almost as wide at the shoulders or at least he looked that wide to Stacey. Tank was short, stout and as strong as an ox. He was a human tank who had chosen not to work girls in Montreal or Toronto. Even the most successful pimps who had left Halifax for the profitable cities respected Tank. At age thirty he had been flirting with the prostitution game for fifteen years. He began in the mid 1970s as the "eyes" of an older pimp who did not want to drive

The pay phone, the link between the girl in the street and her pimp
with his cellular phone. [Print from ATV video tape]

downtown to check on his girls every night. The older pimp gave his
sporty car to Tank who would cruise Hollis street like a player and
watch the girls. He even took it on himself to copy down license numbers as girls went on dates. He figured he could use the information if
someone tried to rip off or rough up one of the girls.

That protective instinct stayed with Neville long after he struck
out on his own, Tank set his own rules: he stayed away from juveniles,
often encouraging then to change their minds and leave The Game.
Once he informed the police that a thirteen-year-old who had been
playing on the edges spending time with local pimps was in Montreal, where a pimp had taken her against her will. Tank even helped find
her and get her back to Halifax, and her family—all in all, a dangerous move that could have cost him the respect he had earned from
other players and even ended his career. Not to mention that he
continued to operate his sideline business—running a small gang of
teenage boys who were pulling B&Es for him—breaking into people's
homes and bringing stolen goods back for him to sell. Avoiding any
contact with the police should have been his main priority but Tank's
ego would not allow that. He wanted people in square society to
respect him as well. He helped the police in the hope they would look
up to him. Tank's unwavering belief that he would not get caught was

shared among the Nova Scotian pimps. The men had been playing The Game for more than a decade with little or no interference from police and they felt immune to the laws that govern prostitution. Whenever there was a crackdown on prostitution the girls took the brunt of it as police charged them and not their pimps. Tank was confident but part of him wanted out—maybe his natural protective instinct would make him a good prospect to become a crisis counselor for troubled adolescents.

Tank considered trying out his skills on Stacey the first night they met—taking her aside and advising her to stay away from the crowd she was now moving with—but he was deterred by her obvious excitement at the prospect of going to Toronto. "You could tell she wanted to be in The Game; she was in my front room, just bouncing, telling me where she was going," he recalled years later. "I figured she knew what she wanted, so I ignored her." Of course a trained counselor might have wondered if Stacey was being manipulated into believing the trip really would be an innocent shopping expedition, but Tank never took the courses. His recollections of meeting Stacey emerged during an interview in a federal prison, where he was sent in the spring of 1993. Tank's dreams of leaving The Game and becoming a respected citizen were put on hold for three years as he served concurrent sentences for living on the avails of prostitution and running a common bawdy house.

Stacey's time to work in the escort service arrived in early July. Kenny came to the apartment to get her and then drove to a small older home in the South end of Dartmouth. Stacey's image of where and how prostitutes worked changed the second she saw the old gray house that served as a brothel and escort service. She had expected to be in a plush apartment with a well-stocked bar. She thought she would sip Champaign and wait until well-dressed customers came to her. The escort service was about as far from plush as you could get and still have a roof over your head. The run down old house needed a paint job both outside and in. When Stacey walked in the first thing she saw was a filthy, tattered old sofa that had been shoved up against the wall in the entry hallway. A girl about Stacey's age sat silently in the middle of the sofa and paid not attention as Stacey walked in with Kenny. The girl didn't smile, she didn't even bother to look up. It was as though she'd been shoved there along with the beat-up old piece of furniture.

The hallway opened on one side to a large room that probably had served as a family room when the building had been a home. Now the room was an office with a desk, a phone, some cabinets and a couple of chairs. The man seated at the desk looked up when Stacey walked in, his eyes skirting past her to Kenny who walked into the room without waiting for an invitation. Kenny and the man spoke briefly, and then Kenny gave Stacey a kiss and promised he would be back later. Stacey sat next to the young girl on the sofa and waited for the man to call on her. Kenny had already explained the workings of the house to her.

Clients calling the escort service could ask to have a girl come to them or they could arrange to come to the house to meet with a girl in the private bedroom at the end of the hall. Inside the bedroom there was a single bed, a night table with a lamp on top, and a small waste basket. The night table had one drawer; inside were an assortment of condoms. The waste basket beside the bed was half filled with discarded condoms and their wrappers. Stacey would not be asked to leave the house on her first night. She was there for in service customers only, as part of the deal Kenny made with the owner. On that first night Stacey had either oral or straight sex with four different men. Two of those men promised they would be back to see her again. Stacey was polite to the men and while she did not like what she was doing she was proud of herself for having the nerve to do it. She couldn't wait to swap stories with Rachel when she returned to the apartment.

Kenny returned to the Escort Service shortly after midnight. The old man behind the desk opened a cash box and pulled out an envelope which he handed to Kenny without comment. Stacey pulled herself up from the uncomfortable sofa and silently followed him outside. Back in the car Kenny kissed her and asked how it went. Stacey told him it was okay but Kenny wasn't really listening. He was busy opening the envelope and counting out just over two hundred dollars stuffed inside. He pulled out twenty and gave it to Stacey.

"Just in case you want to get some cigarettes or something. I'll keep the rest for the trip. Two or three more shifts and you won't have to go back there any more."

Stacey sat quietly in the car as Kenny headed back to her apartment. She didn't really want to go back to the old man and his dirty little house but she was happy Kenny knew it was just a temporary thing. She was sure Kenny would understand when she told him she would never go back to the service after they returned from Toronto. Kenny may have known that was what Stacey wanted but it was not what he had planned for his new recruit.

In the days that followed Stacey could detect a slight change in the way Kenny treated her. He was still attentive and still talked about the trip to Toronto but he didn't spend nearly as much time with her and rarely took her to the mall anymore. A new routine developed almost overnight. Kenny would pick her up at the apartment, take her to the escort service, pick her up at the end of the night, give her twenty dollars from the envelope and then take her home.

It was the same way T-bar shuttled Rachel back and forth from Hollis Street—just as every pimp controlled the every movement of his girls, not out of concern for her welfare but in order to keep track of the money. His money, not hers; Stacey Jackson had become a commodity, and the "trip" was just a come-on K-bar had used to obtain that commodity. She had no emotional significance to him, and never had.

Stacey didn't have time to reflect on the change in Kenny's behaviour or what it might mean. She was too busy fighting a running battle with her mother, as Debbie Howard begged Stacey to stop seeing Kenny and start looking for some new friends, while Stacey defiantly insisted that it was her life to do with as she wished. The arguments gradually eased off, neither one of them was going to change the other's mind. Mrs. Howard's anger created another difficulty for Stacey as she planned her trip. Her mother refused to look after Michael, hoping somehow this would stop Stacey from going. She hadn't counted on Kenny's resourcefulness; the pimp suggested Stacey contact her ex-boyfriend, Roger, whose parents adored their grandson. With her child-care problem solved, Stacey was free to head to the big city.

In the week before leaving Halifax, Stacey met a young prostitute who quickly replaced Rachel as her closest friend. Annie Mae's "Choosy Suzy" routine of switching from pimp to pimp had brought the nineteen-year-old into T-bar's stable—she'd heard he and Kenny were going to Toronto, and even though neither of them was a major player, the trip sounded like just what she needed. She met Stacey soon afterward and the experienced prostitute took a liking to the naive beginner. As for Stacey, she found it impossible not to like Annie Mae, a fast talker who filled the younger girl's head with stories of her travels and exploits telling her about the bars she would visit in Toronto and Montreal. Annie Mae promised to show Stacey the heart of the big city.

Annie Mae's upbeat personality, and her excitement about returning to Toronto, made Stacey begin to feel good about herself for the first time since Kenny had dropped her off at the escort service that first night. Neither of the two girls had ever had a best friend in high school—Annie Mae never made it that far in school, while Stacey, who quit early, kept to herself most of the time. High-school chums were indeed what they resembled; they played off each others' strengths and seemed to know almost from square one how to make each other laugh.

Annie Mae was the kind of person who lived in a world of tunnel vision where there was only one path to follow. She had chosen prostitution several years before meeting Stacey and had never looked back. Despite all of that, Annie Mae liked her life and was a great cheerleader for anyone wanting to give the streets a try. Stacey did not suffer from tunnel vision because she lacked any vision at all. The teenager had no life plan, no ambition to speak of and absolutely no idea where she would be in five months let alone five years. That lack of general focus resulted in Stacey's lack of problem solving skills. Like many young women recruited by pimps Stacey had no strength when it came to finding solutions to the problems she faced. When Stacey hit a road block she could see it clearly but she could not see any way around it or over it and she could never see it coming. A serious problem would stop Stacey in her tracks or cause her to try to run backwards. Annie Mae would see the obstacle and not even bother looking for a way around preferring to charge ahead no matter the consequence.

Annie Mae had no money of her own; she had been beaten by pimps and robbed by customers; and she had been arrested a number of times. Yet her zest for life was unmistakable, and The Game was to her liking. Annie Mae told Stacey she had nothing to fear as long as she kept her head up and knew how to have fun. Stacey figured that if Annie Mae could go through all that and cheerfully continue to identify herself as a "lifer," then she, Stacey, had little to worry about. After all, she wasn't going to be in The Game long enough for any of those bad things to happen to her. She was going to Toronto with Kenny and she had a wonderful new friend who was clearly delighted to take the younger girl under her wing. The rest could wait.

For Kenny, on the other hand, the presence of Annie Mae had an entirely different significance. This was one of the best girls working out of Halifax when it came to training new talent—she knew more about the streets than most pimps—and Kenny hoped that with her help, he could turn Stacey into a real money-maker and also earn himself a lot more respect among the major players.

Kenny, Terrance, Annie Mae and Stacey arrived in Toronto late in July, and on their first night in the city Kenny stopped "playing" Stacey and started working her. Stacey, typically, could not, or would not, see it coming. There were six of them staying in the small apartment—another pimp and prostitute from Halifax had joined them. While Annie Mae and the other girl, a heavy-set redhead named Stella Daniels, began to dress for work, Stacey sat down in the cramped bathroom to chat with them, as she had done so often in Halifax. Annie Mae was applying a heavy dab of make-up above her eye, and Stacey was digging around in the small cosmetics bag the girls shared, when Kenny walked in. "Get dressed," he said curtly. "You're going with them."

Stacey was shocked, and started to protest, her voice rising with anger. "Kenny I can't do that. I don't do that. It's not the same. No, I'm not going with them." When she saw the expression of the face of the young man she thought was her boyfriend, her anger turned to fear. Gone was even the polite indifference of the past few weeks. This was a stranger, his face a mask of fury, his voice a venomous hiss as he moved threateningly towards her: "What the fuck did you say to me? Are you disrespecting me, girl?" Annie Mae quickly intervened. "Relax, K, I'll get her ready. Stacey, you just be quiet, girl. I'll look after you down there—you got nothin' to worry about."

Kenny left the room, and Annie Mae grabbed Stacey by the shoulders. Clearly, she would have to explain a few ground rules to this new comer. "Honey, you knew why we were coming here. I hope you didn't think you'd be hangin' at the mall while the rest of us worked. That just ain't gonna happen, so get it out of your head *now*, okay? Listen to me when I say this, girl, or things are gonna get real hard on you real fast. You never, never talk to your man that way. They hate it. If T-bar had been in the room, Kenny would have been forced to beat you for back-talkin' like that; so don't let that mouth of yours get you in any more trouble."

"Annie, this isn't why I came here, and he knows it."

"He doesn't care what you thought your were doing, Stacey, so just get ready and we'll go downtown. It's a warm night and we'll make some good money."

Stacey suddenly understood that her relationship with Kenny was nothing like what she had been hoping against hope it might still be. He hadn't used the word love in weeks, though she had, and now she knew it had been completely one-sided. She couldn't go home— Kenny had all the money she had earned and Stacey never even thought of calling her mother to ask for help. She decided to accept Annie Mae's advice and go downtown with her friend; working the street in Toronto couldn't be any worse than working the escort service back home. As she began to apply her make-up, Stacey suddenly felt excited, as fear and adrenaline heightened her senses. Then, just after nine o'clock, the three girls piled into the back of T-bar's Trans Am, while Kenny and Terrance sat together up front.

Kenny laid down the law as they drove towards the stroll. "This is not like the escort service, Stacey. No one books your dates—you have to hustle the man from the curb. A car slows down, you make sure he sees you first. You walk over and see what he's shopping for. Do not talk to a black man on the stroll, ever. There are some players up here trying to move on our women, and you don't want to get mixed up with them, so just stay away from any black guy who approaches you."

That last rule sounded stupid: Why couldn't black men buy the services of the Nova Scotia girls? Stacey didn't get the point—that the players were unwilling to take the chance of having their girls scooped up by pimps who weren't part of "the family," as they called themselves. As long as she did what she was told, she'd be keeping up her end of the family compact, and that was all the pimps cared about. A "dumb 'ho" couldn't be expected to understand loyalty. Kenny continued to talk, but Stacey tuned him out as the car turned onto Yonge Street. The teenager stared out the window, taking in all the people and all the stores—clothing boutiques, stereo shops, jewellers, gourmet food emporiums.

As the car got closer to the heart of downtown Toronto, Stacey craned her neck excitedly, searching for the fabled CN Tower. Was that it, that thing that looked like a lit-up spacecraft in the sky? She wanted to ask—maybe they could all go visit it sometime—but she thought that would sound stupid.

The two men dropped the three girls on Gerrard Street, just east of Yonge and only a block or so from the stroll. The Metro Toronto Police Juvenile Task Force was paying closer attention to Nova Scotia pimps, so they avoided driving near the stroll when they had their own vehicles in Toronto, knowing their plates could give them away. This meant a bit more freedom for the girls than in Halifax. There the pimps patrolled Hollis Street frequently and picked up "their" money at regular intervals; but Kenny and Terrance, like most of the Scotians, insisted on staying in touch by cellular phone, as they sometimes did back home as well. Kenny had told Stacey to phone him right after she "broke" (serviced her first client) and to keep calling regularly until he had decided that she had earned enough for the night. Such anxiety was a perfect example of what distinguished young pimps like Kenny and Terrance from experienced players operating in Toronto and other big cities—the leeway they gave their girls on the street. Major players often sent prostitutes to another city on their own for days or weeks, and rarely supervised them on the stroll; they were confident that the girls knew better then to try to pull one over on them.

Stacey was a walking contradiction as she headed toward the stroll. She was dressed like a woman of the night but she was every bit the awestruck kid in the big city for the first time. She walked awkwardly in her heels and tight miniskirt. The stumbling gait was not improved by her tendency to look everywhere except where she was walking. Stacey could not get enough of the city sights and she asked Annie Mae about everything she saw, the big buildings down toward the harbour and the manicured courtyard at Ryerson Polytechnical Institute.

The three girls reached Annie Mae's favourite corner shortly before ten o'clock—a prime slice of the section of Church Street referred to by the prostitutes, the pimps and Toronto police officers as the Scotian Stroll, so named because the pimps who had laid claim to it years before were from Halifax. The girls came not only from the Maritimes but also from Quebec, Ontario and many other areas of the country. Teenagers from small towns out west; young women from Montreal; girls from rural Ontario—they were all lined up next to their Maritime "sisters" in the Scotian Stroll, hoping to earn enough to keep their pimps happy. For the first time, Stacey Jackson of Dartmouth, Nova Scotia, was one of them.

Young girls work the Scotian stroll a block from
Annie Mae's favorite corner. [Print from ATV video tape]

Stacey had been on the stroll less than five minutes when a man in a blue Jeep crooked his finger and signalled her. Terrified, Stacey turned her back and walked away, hoping one of the other girls would approach him instead, but Annie Mae blocked them, making sure no-one moved on her friend's first date. "Stacey turn around girl, that man wants you," she hissed, grabbing Stacey and spinning her back towards the curb and the waiting Jeep. The man behind the wheel was much more attractive than any of the guys who frequented the escort agency; in his mid-thirties, he had a slim build and a handsome face.

"Well, are you going to say anything?" The man leaned across the seat and smiled at Stacey, obviously attracted by her youthful nervousness.

"Hi—um—" What should she say? The other men had always told her what they wanted. "Can I help you?" He smiled again: "I sure hope you can. How much for a blow?"

Well, at least he'd come out and asked—and Stacey knew the answer, too, because Kenny had told her. "Eighty dollars, she said, more confidently.

"Fair enough. Get in." Stacey jumped into the vehicle and the man pulled away from the curb, keeping up a steady stream of conversation as he turned a few corners. She wasn't watching exactly where he was going, intent as she was on paying attention to the stranger by her side. Years later, as she recalled the incident, she shook her head at her own naiveté. "I was pretty stupid; I mean, he could have taken me anywhere and killed me. As soon as we left the curb, I was lost. I couldn't tell him where to go, and I didn't know if he was taking me somewhere dangerous." Luckily, her first customer wanted "only" what he'd asked for. They pulled over in an alley, and he promptly parked the Jeep and unzipped his jeans. Stacey pulled a condom from her purse; the man placed it on his penis, and she leaned over, her hands shaking. She could barely catch her breath; she was so nervous. This apparently excited him all the more—before Stacey thought she had actually started, he was finished.

Back at the stroll, as he dropped Stacey off, the man suggested he would see her some other night. She nodded numbly, looking for her friend. "Hey, girl, welcome to the club!" Annie Mae shouted. "Better call Kenny and tell him you broke." Stacey couldn't believe the difference in Kenny's tone; he sounded like her boyfriend again, and even apologized for cursing at her earlier in the evening—the drive from Nova Scotia always left him tired and cranky, he said. Despite his better mood he told Stacey she couldn't come back to the apartment just yet, she had to pull in a lot more money first: five hundred should do it. Five hundred dollars! How could she possibly earn that much? Slowly returning to the stroll from a nearby phone booth, she told Annie Mae what Kenny had said. "Don't you worry about that," her friend consoled. "You'll make more than that before midnight. These guys know when there's new talent on the stroll. Annie Mae knew what she was talking about. For the next two hours, Stacey barely got her feet back on the sidewalk before another man was asking her to step into his car, and by midnight she had more than seven hundred dollars in her purse. Minor players like Kenny usually asked an experienced girl like Annie Mae to collect the cash from their other girls and hand it over at regular intervals to one of the players working the stroll in a rental car, but Kenny hadn't made such arrangements. Stacey was getting tired and cold, but she didn't want to go back to the apartment without the others. Annie Mae only had four hundred dollars and Stella was lagging behind, at one hundred—so she offered to get them all a hot chocolate at a nearby Harvey's while the others tried to catch up. The Harvey's on Gerrard Street was in the area where Terrance had dropped them off earlier in the night so Stacey walked back that way. On the way she noticed a Tim Horton's coffee shop but decided against going in. It was crowded and she felt awkward dressed in her sexy outfit. When she arrived at the Hamburger spot there were only a couple of young people inside so she headed up to the counter and ordered three cups of hot chocolate. Although she felt nervous, no one seemed to notice what she was wearing nor did they appear to care what she was doing out at that hour. Stacey walked back to the stroll in time to see Annie Mae pull away in a car again. She handed Stella her hot chocolate and the two girls sat on the edge of the step back by the building. Stacey was finished working and Stella didn't appear to be overly interested in attracting any attention at the moment. Stacey was not sure how old Stella was but she was fairly certain she was a lot older than Annie Mae. Stella was twenty four years old, ancient by street standards. The red headed woman was about twenty pounds too heavy for the outfit she was wearing and the haggard angry expression on her face seemed to scare more customers away than it did bring her business.

As Stacey wondered how Stella would ever get any dates unless she made an effort to at least smile occasionally, Annie Mae re-joined them, gratefully accepting the cup Stacey handed her. Stella slowly walked back to the curb, and Annie Mae sat down.

"She been here the whole time I was gone?" Annie asked the question over the lip of the cup as she sipped. The chocolate wasn't very warm but the sugar would help keep her awake.

Waiting for a date, one girl enjoys a hot drink on the stroll.
[Print from ATV video tape]

"Yeah, why?"

"Well, she's not trying very hard, and I don't think her man will let her come home. She can't say the stroll was dry if we both hit our limits."

"Should I give her some of my money?"

"Stacey, don't ever even suggest that. Do you know what would happen if you started working for two men at the same time? That's what you'd be doing, and one of 'em would call you on it, and you'd be forced to choose, so don't play any games. You earned your money—keep it." Her harsh tone softened, and a smile lit up her pretty young face. "Speaking of money, I just went around the world, and now I can take my tired butt home." Stacey wasn't sure she wanted to know, but she asked anyway, and Annie Mae gladly explained. Most men came to the stroll looking for oral sex, she said; some wanted straight sex; and then there were a few who preferred a bit of both—"around the world," in the ever-colorful parlance of street sex. The journey didn't come cheap: in Toronto, Annie Mae was charging $125, which put her total well above the magic $500 that meant she was home free, or more appropriately—free to go home.

Stacey made the call, telling Kenny that she and Annie Mae were ready, but Stella wasn't having much luck. After a pause, the pimp came back on the line—she and Annie Mae were to meet him back on Gerrard, while Stella remained on the stroll until she had met her quota. Stacey was surprised at how much she had enjoyed her evening, not so much the dates, but the feeling of closeness to Annie Mae. When the men arrived, however, Stacey's mood altered drastically. She suddenly felt dirty and embarrassed—Kenny was a guy she liked *so* much, and now what would he think of her? The first inklings of what *she* thought of herself were rising in Stacey's mind. She quickly pushed back the stirrings of conscience when, back at the apartment, Kenny (after counting the money and handing her the usual twenty), took her in his arms and kissed her passionately, telling her how incredible she was, and how proud he was that she would do this kind of work for him. The pimp explained that in his eyes Stacey was now a real woman, he said, not just some kid trying to impress him. That did it: if Kenny still loved her, everything was fine with her. In one night, the month of work Kenny had put into recruiting Stacey had paid off; she had gone from reluctant participant to eager working girl. The seven hundred dollars more than covered the money Kenny had spent on clothing for his new recruit. Now with his cash balance looked after, it was only a matter of time before Stacey earned enough to cover the valuable time he had spent turning her. Kenny was satisfied with himself and relaxed as Stacey rushed to take a shower and tumble into bed with him.

The apartment was quiet the following morning, and Stacey slept until almost noon. When she awoke, she padded out to the living-room where Annie Mae was watching TV.

"What time did Stella come back?" Stacey asked, plopping down on the couch next to her friend. "She didn't. Kenny went to get us some food, and he's going to pick her up now. When they get here, there's gonna be trouble, Stacey, so you just sit quietly. Stella didn't earn her money and you saw she wasn't tryin' very hard. We made more than we were supposed to, so her man is furious at how he looks in front of Kenny and Terrance." Stacey could not believe the three men had forced Stella to stay out all night and were now planning to punish her; and her outrage turned to fear as she began to imagine the same thing happening to her. The mood of the night before evaporated in a rush of terror and confusion, and a clear single desire suddenly emerged from the murk of her thoughts. She wanted to go home, and quickly told her friend so. "We can't talk about it here," whispered Annie Mae, who, truth be told, also thought this trip was not going to be the fun romp in the city she was looking for. "Let's see what we can do tonight." Stacey was about to say more when she heard the door open.

It was Kenny, carrying the girls' breakfast—burgers and fries—and

Stella, who walked in with her head bowed and stood listlessly as her pimp came in from the kitchen. Without saying a word, he lifted a leg and kicked her in the stomach, hard. Stella fell to the floor. "That's right, bitch, you lie down, 'cause that's what you been doin' all night. Don't you come up here and lay your lazy ass on the sofa. You got work to do and you better get to it. I wanna see some serious cash tonight, girl, you understand that?" He kicked her again, not quite as hard this time, but with enough force to elicit another muffled grunt from the exhausted girl. Stacey shot up off the sofa, her burger and fries tumbling to the carpet; but before she could say anything, Annie Mae grabbed her—just as the violent pimp turned her way, demanding, "What the fuck do you want, bitch?" Then, to Kenny: "K, you better settle this 'ho before I have to."

Grabbing Stacey by the arm, Kenny led her into the bedroom. Furious, tears welling in her eyes, Stacey said she had never seen anything like that in her life, and begged him to take her home. Kenny took the pimp's side and told Stacey to mind her own business; what went on between Stella and her man had nothing to do with her, and as long as she behaved herself, nothing like that would ever happen to her. Challenging another player for beating a girl would not be considered good behavior, he warned, and if she tried it again, he would have no choice but to beat her. Otherwise, his fellow player would see that he lacked control over his girls; he would lose his respect, which meant no turf and no prostitutes to run. K-bar did not tell Stacey that Stella's pimp had beaten her in front of the other players—and their girls—quite deliberately, to demonstrate his control over Stella and thereby solidify his respect. Nor did he explain that the word *respect* means something quite different in The Game than it does in the "square" world. "Respect," to a pimp, is not simply determined by one's ability to do a job well—and certainly not by demonstrating kindness or generosity—but primarily by superior force of will, enforced violently. In the street, money is the primary goal but respect is the real currency of The Game. Stacey held her tongue, but that didn't mean she had accepted Kenny's explanation for what had happened to Stella, or that she believed his assurances. She stayed in the bedroom for the rest of the day, not out of fear of Kenny, but because she didn't want to look at the other pimp; he disgusted her. He also frightened her.

That night, between dates, Stacey tried to comfort Stella—taking time to encourage the older girl and comment on how pretty Stacey thought she was—when she wasn't pleading with Annie Mae for a way the two of them could go home.

The way back to Halifax presented itself in the form of two pimps heading east themselves; Annie Mae knew both men and had previously worked for one of them, so when she saw them driving around the stroll, she motioned them over. Anne Mae always broke the rule about talking to black men while she was working, and her pimps had long since given up trying to stop her from shopping around. It was the perfect opportunity—Stacey could get home, and out of The Game if that was what she really wanted, while she could take up with the Peanut Man again. Reginald "Peanut" Cleary would be a safe escape for both girls. Terrance knew that Peanut was much closer to the centre of the family than he was, and would never challenge him. Peanut often traveled with the Big Man—Manning Greer, one of the most powerful pimps in Canada and in many ways the leader of the younger breed of Scotians. Just knowing Greer elevated your status in The Game. Annie Mae had hoped to spend a little more time in Toronto but, like Stacey, she felt the enjoyment had gone out of it—and very quickly. Unlike Stacey, however, Annie Mae knew the situation would only get worse: there was Stella sitting on her ass again. She'd get it from her pimp again—unless she got the lead out, or just got out of The Game entirely. There was nothing Annie Mae could do about it, but she didn't have to hang around and watch. So it was time to hit Hollis Street again, and there were worse ways to go than with a major player like Peanut.

Annie Mae had three hundred dollars she had earned so far that night so she handed it to the pimp driving the car. Peanut accepted the money—and it was as easy as that; by taking the money, Peanut was taking on Annie Mae. Terrance would just have to deal with Peanut if he had a problem with Annie Mae's choice. Annie Mae knew a small-timer like Terrance would have no problem—or at least he would claim he had none. Now they had to get Stacey settled: Annie Mae called her friend over to the car, and this time the passenger spoke up. Michael ("Smit") Sears was only twenty-one—not that much older than Stacey—and she couldn't help notice what a good-looking young man he was. But that didn't matter. She wasn't interested in anyone associated with prostitution. Stacey explained that she wanted to give up working and asked the men if she could get a lift back to Halifax with them. That was no problem, Smit said, smiling slyly at his partner. A smooth talker, he was sure he could persuade this slender young blonde to be his girl; anyway, he would have hours in the car to try.

The men told the girls they wouldn't be leaving for a few hours yet, and while they were gone, Annie Mae warned Stacey that during the trip Smit would lobby hard to get her to "choose" him (take him on as her pimp, as Annie Mae had with Peanut). "He's still earning his respect, but he wants it faster than anyone else ever got it," she said.

Indeed, Smit was the kind of guy who threw himself into any endeavor he became involved in. He had worked at the Black Cultural Centre in Cherry Brook, near Dartmouth, on a summer grant after finishing high school, impressing the staff with his energy and enthusiasm, though they noticed he had a tendency to lose interest in a task before it was completed. He always seemed to want a new challenge, and he didn't have to wait long before one presented itself.

While he was working at the Cultural Centre, Smit took a unique baby-sitting job—for a group of prostitutes. The girls considered him a charmer and marvelled at how he enjoyed playing with their children, and his association with Manning Greer, at whose behest he had started the job—their parents were good friends—immediately raised his stock with some of the young men he was spending time with. Smit could see for himself how successful Greer was: only in his early twenties, the Big Man made more money than anyone else he had ever known. The money was only a small part of what attracted Smit to The Game. The young man really liked how his friends treated him after they saw him driving Manning Greer's car. Smit wanted people to look up to him the way they admired Greer. That was three years before; Smit helped to recruit some high-school friends into The Game, continued baby-sitting for the players, and waited for his chance to strike out on his own. Stacey looked like just that chance.

Peanut Cleary was another story. Peanut had already achieved a high level of respect in the street and was a man born to The Game. The only child of a single mother, Peanut had been raised by his grandparents, or so they thought. The truth is Peanut very quickly fell under the charismatic spell of his uncle and he decided at age eleven that he would be just like him. Peanut's uncle was a pimp, one of the first to enter The Game from North Preston. Peanut's only real memories of his childhood home were of the regular visits made by his uncle. The older pimp would stay with his parents—Peanut's grandparents—whenever he was in the Halifax area. For weeks at a time Peanut would cruise the streets in the pimp's fancy car and listen to the stories of the wild city life. Peanut left home and moved to Montreal with his uncle when he was only thirteen; he'd been playing The Game now for fifteen years. When pimping became a career choice for so many young men from Nova Scotia there were those who thought Peanut would be their leader. Peanut had no desire to set himself up as anyone's leader; he was only in The Game for the money—a lesson his uncle had taught him. Peanut had been a pimp longer than Manning Greer and had probably made more money; but Greer's size and his fierce temper had made him a leader by default. Peanut was one of many Nova Scotia pimp's who had been in The Game long enough to know how it really worked. He was close to Manning Greer and the two often watched out for one another but they also shared a degree of mutual respect. Peanut was an associate—not a follower—and Manning Greer was okay with that.

The drive back to Halifax took almost two days, and it seemed to Stacey that she spent every moment of it trying to fend off the charming but aggressive Smit. Finally, just west of Nova Scotia, Smit relented and told Stacey he accepted her position—but if she changed her mind, he'd be waiting. He made it clear she would have to work for him; he was owed *that* much for giving her the ride home; that was his reason, anyway. Stacey wasn't paying attention. She was strictly square now.

It was almost midnight when Peanut and Smit dropped the two girls off at Annie Mae's apartment in Halifax, and just after they waved good-bye in the parking lot, they heard someone call to them. Annie Mae peered into the darkness and suddenly saw a tall figure approach. "Shit, it's Terrance's brother Toddy," she whispered. "He musta been waiting for us.... How the hell did he know when we would be here? Shit, Stacey, this is gonna be trouble. You just be quiet and let me talk."

Toddy Anderson was only seventeen, but he was very strong, very nasty, and very angry. He walked straight up to Annie Mae, grabbed her by the hair, threw her to the ground, then started kicking her, telling her between the kicks and curses that she was working for him until T-bar got back from Toronto. Stacey screamed, and Toddy turned on her, too, slapping her across the face: "You're workin' for me now too, bitch!" Stacey defiantly insisted she was square now, and would straighten things up with Kenny when he got home. Just as Toddy was readying a response to this arrogance, a car pulled into the lot, forcing him to back away. Stacey lifted Annie Mae to her feet and helped her inside, locking the door behind them. Annie Mae was more angry than hurt; how could she have allowed some seventeen-year-old bubble-gummer to do it to her—and, worse, leave convinced he had some claim to her. Well, Toddy would back down soon enough, when he found out she was working for Peanut again. Not that her new man would punish Toddy; the two of them would call it a misunderstanding, caused by that "Choosy Suzy" routine of hers. So what? At least she wouldn't have to work for that big, mean baby; and if he was stupid enough to try forcing the issue—demanding she hustle for him despite Peanut's new claim to her—then Toddy Anderson would be the one with sore ribs and a bruised pride. Come to think of it, that wouldn't be a bad idea.

Stacey wasn't spending much time on thoughts of revenge. She decided not to return to her apartment or pick up her baby from Roger's parents; not just yet. She needed some time to clear her head and figure out how to deal with this tangled web of players trying to say they owned her. After spending the night at Annie Mae's, she borrowed clothes from her friend and headed out on the bus to the Annapolis Valley. Maybe a few days with her Aunt Jean would help her. The visit seemed to be just what Stacey needed—some rest, good food, some heart-to-heart talks about her hopes to go to college. Stacey had only said there'd been some bad arguments with her mother (whose sister had had a few of those herself), so there was no cross-examination when Stacey, who looked very drawn and tired, said she just needed a bit of space. Her aunt even agreed to keep their visit a secret, after Stacey promised to call her mom when she got back to her apartment in Dartmouth. By the time the bus was on the outskirts of town, Stacey was ready to reclaim her life: she'd get a job, and she'd avoid these pimps, refusing even to talk to them if they called.

Debbie Howard was so delighted to hear her daughter's strong new resolve to stay away from the pimps and prostitutes she'd been calling friends that she immediately forgot her disappointment in Stacey's decision to take off to Toronto without telling her—and spend three days in the Valley before calling.

Stacey thought she had managed to break away from the nightmare that Kenny had introduced her to, at least for a couple of weeks as she began to see her life return to normal. As the Labour Day weekend approached it became clear her plans did not take into account the priorities of the pimps she had become involved with. When Toddy called Toronto to tell his cousin the news about Stacey leaving The Game, Kenny Sims was furious that he'd spent so much time on this girl without seeing any serious return on his investment. True, Stacey had earned enough in one night to cover his financial investment in her; but his time was worth more and he wanted compensation. Bad enough that T-bar had lost Annie Mae—but at least he could console himself that she did that to everyone. This was different. He was going to get his money's worth out of this bitch, and then some; Kenny told Toddy to find Stacey and send her, or a leaving fee back to Toronto immediately. The younger pimp kept an eye on the stroll for a week or two; fully expecting to see Stacey there. When she did not return to work he simply went to her apartment and pounded on the door, ignoring her tears and pleas and calmly informing the terrified teenager that he would knock down the door and beat her severely unless she either came up with her leaving fee—eight hundred dollars—or returned to Toronto. With no job and no education that would bring her anything but minimum wage, Stacey knew she couldn't come up with that kind of cash—and Toddy wasn't interested in arranging a pay-back schedule. Stacey considered asking her father for the money, but that would mean telling him what she was doing. She just *couldn't* talk to her mom, who'd been so thrilled to hear of her new plans. No, she would work for Toddy; and she persuaded him to promise he would give the money to Kenny and then leave her alone. It wouldn't take long and then she'd be free.

*W*hy didn't she call the police? It's a good question, and one most people in Stacey's position might have been expected to ask themselves at about this point in the sequence of events. Unfortunately, Stacey would never even have contemplated making such a call. She hadn't been in The Game for very long, and she badly wanted out, but Stacey Jackson had spent long enough in the murky world where respect means fear to have absorbed some of the twisted thinking characteristic of the prostitution business. Girls like Rachel and Annie Mae, who had been prostitutes for years, truly hated all police officers; indeed, Annie Mae had even told Stacey she'd been beaten and sexually assaulted by cops. Although she had never been more than vague about time and place when Stacey asked, enough of her anger against the law seeped through her friend's equally vague doubts—policemen didn't do that kind of thing, did they?—to plant the seeds of hatred in the younger girl's mind. Never mind that both of them knew from personal experience how pimps behaved towards their girls. That was different; players were *family,* and both Annie Mae and Stacey knew the words *family* and *violence* often went together. They did in their families, anyway. But the police? They were, quite simply, the enemy. They stopped you from working and they treated you like dirt, besides. Stacey was also afraid she would be charged and sent to prison, she knew what she had done in Toronto and in Halifax was illegal. No, the police were to be avoided, always.

Not an assessment with which either Constable John Elliott or Constable Brad Sullivan, Halifax-area RCMP officers, would entirely

RCMP officers Brad Sullivan and John Elliott.

disagree. At least, not considering prevailing attitudes to prostitutes at the time they began a fact-finding mission in February 1990 to identify pimps working in Halifax. The assault accusation would make them shake their heads in exasperation, but they would understand its origins. As John Elliott expresses it today, many of the people in positions of power—law-makers as well as law-enforcers—saw prostitutes, even those younger than Stacey, as "sluts who are out there every night doing what they want to do."

The two officers' involvement in juvenile prostitution had its origins in the August 1989 disappearance of a Halifax girl, eighteen year-old Kimberly McAndrew, whose fate remains unknown. Kimberly finished her shift at a local Canadian Tire store and left for home; she never got there. Halifax police were considering two theories: either she was a runaway, or she was a victim of murder, possibly at the hands of someone she knew. Kimberly's father, a former RCMP officer, insisted his daughter had not run away—she just wasn't the type to leave without contacting her family or her boyfriend. This was a teenager with plans for her future, and there was nothing in her behavior before the disappearance to suggest a problem so terrible that she had to run away without leaving a trace.

In January 1990, the investigation into McAndrew's disappearance was faltering when a third theory surfaced. An informant who claimed to have information about Kimberly met with Elliott, an investigator with the Cole Harbour RCMP, and told him the girl had been picked up by a pimp not far from the store where she worked. This man had met Kimberly on several occasions when he came to buy auto parts, the informant said; and though it was difficult for Elliott to accept that Kimberly McAndrew might have been abducted and put to work as a prostitute in another part of the country, he decided to at least share the information with another Mountie.

Brad Sullivan and John Elliott were teammates in the Metro Halifax Police curling league—and they had become close friends. Elliott knew that Sullivan, an investigator at RCMP headquarters in Halifax, had a keen interest in the McAndrew case and had been monitoring its progress since the beginning. It was only logical for the two officers to discuss the possibility that Kimberly had been abducted, and Sullivan thought they should try it out on the Halifax police investigators. The reception they received was cool—at the time, police did not believe there was a serious pimping problem in the city and considered the idea of an abduction far-fetched. Brad Sullivan was not to be put off that easily; he asked for time to pursue his theory, and although this was not an RCMP case, he was told to go ahead. Anything relevant could be passed on to the investigators handling the file.

As Sullivan and Elliott began questioning informants, they started to hear some disturbing stories about large numbers of pimps operating in the Halifax area; abductions, they were told, were not at all uncommon. The more he heard, the more Sullivan became convinced that, quite aside from the McAndrew case, it was imperative to determine how big a problem pimping was in Metro Halifax; he proposed a fact-finding operation, and he won approval. It was only natural that John Elliott be assigned to work with him, Sullivan argued: the Cole Harbour detachment covers North Preston, and North Preston was the name Sullivan's informants were mentioning as the home base of the pimps.

The name for the investigation, fittingly enough, was Operation Heart; it could as easily have been called Operation Eye-Opener. Within weeks, Sullivan and Elliott realized they had uncovered a major problem. After only a month of interviewing prostitutes, following leads, and talking with informants, Operation Heart had revealed there were more than fifty pimps working in Halifax—and they knew many hadn't yet been identified. As the officers moved onto the street to tail a few or their subjects, they were shocked at how blatantly these men operated, picking up their girls every evening, stopping at a pharmacy for condoms and at a fast-food restaurant for the prostitutes' usual dinner of burgers and fries, and finally dropping them off

KIM McANDREW
reward offered   call police
or CHILD FIND   1·800·387·7962

MISSING

Eighteen year-old Kimberly McAndrew, whose fate remains unknown,
disappeared in 1989.

on Hollis Street as casually as a cabby dropping off a fare. These passengers would be paying for their ride all night. Some of the pimps parked near their girls and spent the night there—after each date, the girl would walk over and give them the money—while others preferred to cruise the stroll, passing their girls every few minutes and stopping once or twice an hour to collect. Either way, they were practicing what the men of Miles States' era derisively called "popcorn pimping"—they popped down to the stroll to oversee their cash flow—a procedure later supplanted by the cell-phone method favored by the likes of Stacey's jilted pimp Kenny Sims. On a busy night, Sullivan and Elliott counted more than thirty young girls—they would later learn how young some of them really were—working on Hollis, and almost as many fancy cars hovering around them or parked nearby. Two emotions began to build as Elliott and Sullivan continued their operation; one was anger and the other was guilt. The two officers knew what they were watching had been going on for a long time, it was too organized to have happened overnight and they knew that they—like virtually every other Halifax area police officer—had ignored what was right in front of their eyes.

As Operation Heart widened, the officers began to earn the trust of several young prostitutes, who agreed to talk with them once they realized these policemen neither threatened their livelihood nor saw them as "sluts." The girls described their difficulties with abusive pimps; their grim existence; their frequent trips to Montreal, Ottawa, Toronto, Niagara Falls, Calgary, and even some American cities. It was the unexpected mobility of the sex trade that made Sullivan and Elliott begin to wonder whether Kimberly McAndrew really might have been taken to another city—or cities. The officers got in touch with police forces across Canada, and sent McAndrew's photo to the morality squad personnel most likely to deal directly with prostitutes

In March, an officer from Calgary who had agreed to keep an eye out for Kimberly asked Sullivan and Elliott to do him a favor. Calgary police had issued a warrant for the arrest of a seventeen-year-old Nova Scotian who had jumped bail after being released pending his trial on pimping-related charges. They asked around, and found out that the youth was running a couple of girls on Hollis Street. It didn't take long to find him: the officers had a description of his car, and when they saw it circling the stroll in the now-familiar pattern, the Mounties knew they had their man—or boy, rather. For the first time in their lives, Brad Sullivan and John Elliott were face-to-face with a pimp: it was an encounter neither of them would forget. When they tried to question him at the lock-up, he simply laughed, openly admitting he was a pimp and challenging the officers to give him a reason to quit The Game. "Look, man, when they arrested me in Calgary, they took my clothes, my jewelry, my car, and my money. Look at me now. I got clothes, I got jewelry, I got a car, and I got money. I'm seventeen and I make more than my father. What else am I gonna do to make this kind of money? Forget *you*, man—you do your thing and leave me alone. I got a good thing going." There was no point asking this walking attitude problem about Kimberly McAndrew. His infuriating arrogance did serve one purpose: it stuck in John Elliott's mind with such force that he promised himself to help find a way to target these pimps, who saw the police as an inconvenience, or a joke.

The guilt the two officers felt at having ignored the prostitution trade in Halifax was made worse when they realized other police officers across Canada were well aware of the problem in Nova Scotia. A routine call for help to the Metro Toronto Juvenile Task Force turned out to be an embarrassing incident for the Nova Scotia Mounties. The officer they talked with knew more about the pimps working in their area than they did. Fortunately, that officer was more than willing to share information. Elliott and Sullivan had been told by more than one prostitute that Manning Greer was the worst pimp and they had hoped he would have information about the missing McAndrew girl. The Toronto officer informed them that Manning Greer was not someone who would be willing to talk with them about anything—let alone a girl they thought had been abducted by pimps. Greer spent most of his time in Montreal or Toronto and police in both cities considered him a serious player. The Toronto officer said he believed Greer ran girls in both cities, and in Halifax; that he had first come to the attention of the Toronto Task force in 1989 when a turf war spread from Halifax to Montreal and then Toronto. The Toronto Task Force had been unable to get a girl to make a statement identifying Greer as a pimp but they had heard enough street talk to know he was feared by the prostitutes—and a good number of Ontario based pimps. That police in Toronto and Montreal knew of a problem that originated in Nova Scotia strengthened the resolve of both young Mounties—they wanted to clean up the mess in their own back yard.

In the final days of Operation Heart, the officers received a frantic call that heightened Elliott's determination to strike back at the pimps. The girl on the phone, who had provided them with information before, was a juvenile prostitute working for a particularly violent pimp from North Preston. She was in a house in North Preston and said she was being held against her will; when Elliott asked how many people were there, she replied: "No-one." No-one? Why not just leave, then? She was just too afraid, she said, her pimp had too many friends in the neighbourhood, and he'd asked them to watch for her, and if she tried to escape she would be captured, and he would beat the shit out of her. The terror in her voice was palpable: Elliott asked her to describe the house and said he and Brad Sullivan would be there in twenty minutes; she was to run out of the house and jump into their unmarked police car.

The rescue was like a scene from a movie, Elliott recalls—the teenage girl bursting through the front door, slamming it against the outside wall of the house as she scrambled across the yard and jumped into the back of the car. The hysterical screams for the officers to drive, to get her out of there. The squeal of the tires as Sullivan accelerated down the street, circled back, and headed out of North Preston. No-one had apparently paid the slightest attention to the car or the young girl; that wasn't the point. The point was the level of fear the pimp had instilled in this child.

On the way back to Halifax, the officers tried to persuade the girl to give them a statement; they would arrest that pimp, they said, and help her break away from The Game forever. No, she said. He'd have her killed. Sullivan and Elliott agreed to take her to a friend's house. Both officers felt bad as they watched her walk away from their car. It was the first chance they had to press a charge against a pimp and they had let it slip away. Later, they would learn it was the wisest decision they could have made, under the circumstances. The girl told several other young prostitutes that Brad Sullivan and John Elliott could be trusted; they weren't like other police officers, and if the girls needed help, these were the men to call. Eventually, they would start calling.

Sullivan and Elliott faced some frustrating setbacks when Operation Heart wrapped up in the spring of 1990. Police were no closer to locating Kimberly McAndrew, and Sullivan was turned down when he made a formal proposal to expand the operation's mandate into a full-scale, Metro-wide crackdown. He wanted the four area police forces—Halifax, Bedford, Dartmouth and the RCMP—to work together to catch and jail the pimps openly running the sex trade in downtown Halifax. Sullivan and Elliott knew those pimps were running the trade with a large number of under-age prostitutes—*girl* was the street term regardless of age, but many of them were under eighteen. Tight budgets were the problem, the officers' higher-ups said, but Elliott felt that the politicians and policy-makers just didn't see prostitution as a priority or prostitutes, even very young ones, as worth bothering about—except as an eyesore to be dealt with through existing anti-solicitation laws.

Elliott and Sullivan considered this view narrow and short-sighted, but they realized that only when—if—there were a wide-ranging change of attitude towards prostitutes would an effective attack on pimping be launched. During the two years that followed, they often discussed the growing need for a major push to stop the pimping. They were hearing more and more from their contacts, especially Dave Perry the young well-informed Toronto police officer who had been so willing to share his information. Perry was a member of a unit that was doing exactly what Sullivan and Elliott wanted to do—he was fighting pimps and helping young girls. Perry knew, and he shared his belief with the two Mounties, that he could not stem the tide of Maritime girls flooding his streets without the help of police in Nova Scotia. It was a constant source of embarrassment for Elliott and Sullivan that Nova Scotia pimps—the Scotians, as police started calling them—were making their presence felt on the streets of big cities like Montreal and Toronto and being ignored at home.

Dave Perry had an enthusiasm for his job that was contagious—he loved arresting pimps. He welcomed the information Sullivan and Elliott were able to provide, the names of the fifty or so pimps identified during Operation Heart. Perry also had a goal that both Elliott and Sullivan adopted; he wanted to arrest Manning Greer. It was Perry who first used the term Scotians to describe the Halifax area pimps to

Dave Perry of the Metro Toronto Juvenile Task Force.[Print from ATV video tape]

Sullivan and Elliott. He told the officers he was not certain how big an operation it was but he did know Manning Greer and his associates were a powerful force in Canada's sex trade. They were powerful because they were violent and no one involved in their operation would talk to police about it. That single fact had kept the Toronto Task force from breaking the ring—as they had several other pimping rings active in that city. Perry told the Nova Scotia officers that Police in Montreal were also looking for a chance to nail the Scotians who were as active in that city as they were in Toronto. The problem faced by the police was simple—until they had a statement or something solid to go with, Manning Greer was a ghost. He was haunting them and taunting them but they could not touch him.

The myth of Manning Greer infuriated Brad Sullivan but every time he tried to revive his proposal, he got the same response: great idea, but no money to implement it.

Elliott and Sullivan kept in contact with the prostitutes they had met during Operation Heart, and helped when they could. They couldn't do a thing unless a girl knew enough to approach them—and Stacey Jackson hadn't spoken with the teenager they'd rescued from the house in North Preston. If she had, she might just have decided to call, and she might have avoided the nightmare that was just beginning.

As for Stacey, she was sinking in deeper and deeper every day. Toddy Anderson was nowhere near as patient as his cousin Kenny had been about playing Stacey as a way to trick her into loyalty; when she protested against working the Hollis Street stroll—someone might recognize her, she said—the less-than-sympathetic young pimp told her to buy sunglasses and get ready for work that night. His only concession, and it was less consideration than practicality, was to allow Stacey to work only three hours a night so that she could pick up Michael and go home without touching off her mother's suspicions. Stacey called her mother and asked if she could drop the baby of for a few hours, while she went for a job interview at the mall; Debbie Howard was so eager to see her daughter start taking responsibility for her life that she pushed away her doubts—what kind of company conducts interviews at ten o'clock in the evening?—and went along with Stacey's explanation.

If Stacey thought she was going to earn eight hundred dollars in a few hours and walk away from prostitution just like that, she had a lot to learn. Prices in Halifax were much lower than in Toronto—only fifty dollars for a blow job, eighty for straight sex, or one hundred dollars for both—and it seemed there were more girls and fewer customers. As Stacey looked north from a corner near the Hotel Nova Scotia, a choice spot near the end of the Hollis strip, she could see more than twenty prostitutes, some even younger than she. The girls congregated at the intersections, leaning on almost every power pole or storefront in sight. That hot August night gave Stacey her first real sense of the extensive sex trade in Halifax, and she realized there was no way for her to buy back her freedom in one night. She would have to make up another story to tell her mother—oh, well. It wouldn't take long.... Oh, there was Annie Mae! Stacey was delighted to see her friend, and Annie Mae stayed close by, providing a running account of the personalities, the cars carrying the pimps and their friends who came and went in a steady rhythm. It never even occurred to the two girls that Annie Mae's man, Peanut, might consider telling his young pal Smit that the girl he'd tried to recruit, all the way home from Toronto, had been turned out by a seventeen-year-old bubblegummer.

Smit was playing cards in an apartment in the north end when Peanut arrived to tell him the news. Smit was furious; he would never get any respect if he let that happen, and he promptly dealt himself out of the game and went downtown to see for himself. Stacey had just left with Toddy, and the enraged Smit uttered a string of obscenities before driving off, to a cacophony of revving engine and protesting brakes. Tomorrow he'd find her for sure, Smit told himself, already starting to work out a plan. Back in Highfield Park, Stacey too was doing some quick planning: she called her mother and asked her once again to mind Michael; once again she said she was going to look for work in the mall; and once again Debbie Howard agreed without question. The following evening, Annie Mae came with Stacey to drop off Michael; the older girl had made arrangements for Peanut to pick her up nearby, and Stacey who had told Toddy she would be at work on time. The inexperienced young pimp had yet to develop the habit of exercising total control over his girl. He would learn the reason behind that pimping habit that night. Mrs. Howard liked Annie Mae, but was fairly sure she was a prostitute; she wanted to ask Stacey, but told herself there was no reason her daughter shouldn't befriend these girls. No reason to start an argument—as long as those pimps didn't show their faces. She had no idea how close those pimps were to her home: as Stacey and Annie Mae walked through a schoolyard on their way back to the Howards' from the pharmacy—Stacey had bought a few things for the baby—Peanut pulled into the parking lot.

It was Smit, who jumped out, striding past a shocked Annie Mae and grabbing Stacey by the throat. Stacey screamed and Annie Mae protested but Smit would not let her go. He backed her towards the car and pushed up on her chin, lifting her against the door, forcing her head to the side. Then he relaxed his grip, letting Stacey slump against the car as he finally began to speak: "I thought we had an understanding and now you go and make a fool out of me for being kind. What are you thinking? Everyone knows I tried to become your man, but you said no. Now you're on the street for that clown Toddy. I'm being laughed at, girl, and no one is gonna laugh at me because of you. You understand that?"

Stacey tried to explain her predicament—how Toddy had forced her to work on Hollis Street to settle her debt to Kenny—but Smit wasn't interested. Stacey had a bigger debt to him for taking her home from Toronto and letting her go so graciously. "Well, that treatment is over, girl. You are coming to Toronto with me, and you're payin' the freight on this trip. You're going downtown *now*, to work for *me*, so everyone here can see whose woman you are. Once Toddy gets the message, we'll be leaving—and you better have enough money to pay for the gas and the food. Is that clear?" Tears welling in her eyes, Stacey tried to protest, but Smit angrily ordered her to shut up and get in the car. She was surprised when he agreed to allow her and Annie Mae to take the baby supplies to her mother before they went down to the stroll. The car would be parked at the corner of the street where the Howards lived; Smit wasn't willing to let Stacey get out of his sight for long.

As the two girls walked, they considered their options. Stacey felt she just *couldn't* tell her parents what she'd been doing, and she just *couldn't* stay in Halifax until everything with Kenny and Smit was cleared up. Utterly unaware that she was digging herself in even deeper, Stacey made up her mind to return to Toronto, earn the leaving fee that would now have to be paid to Smit, then break away from The Game. Annie Mae promised to help Stacey find another man in Toronto—a man who would not be a threat to Smit and his vision of himself; a man who would accept only a portion of her earnings, so she could save enough to buy her freedom. Annie Mae didn't tell her friend she had never encountered such a man in five years in The Game, but she needed to persuade Stacey she could find one. That way, Stacey would behave herself—not make waves—until Annie Mae could find a realistic way for them both to get away from Smit. Annie Mae trusted Peanut—she had worked for him enough times to knew she didn't have to be afraid of him—but she also knew pimps acted differently when they were trying to impress each other. Smit worried her; there was something very dangerous in his eyes. Maybe it was because he was rising so fast. Prostitutes working in the Scotian family believed the really serious players belonged to a secret club of sorts, to which admission was only granted when they had killed a girl; and Annie Mae didn't want Stacey to be one of them. The pimps did nothing to dispel this belief—whether the club existed or not it was good for the girls to believe in it.

Back at the Howard house, Stacey's mother finally had to admit to herself something was seriously wrong. To begin with, there was the red patch on Stacey's neck and chin; Debbie Howard had been an abused wife, and she knew perfectly well that those marks were—despite Stacey's assurances that she'd bumped into a wall. In no time, Stacey was accusing her mom of not trusting her, and when Annie Mae told Stacey not to yell at her mother, Mrs. Howard turned on the older girl, shouting that she should mind her own business. That did it; Stacey announced to her mother that she would be going back to Toronto in a few days. Her clothes and some gifts for the baby had been left behind in Toronto. She explained that she had left them when she and Kenny split up, and she wanted to retrieve them. Grabbing Annie Mae's hand, she stormed out of the house and they got into the car waiting to take them down to Hollis Street.

That night on the stroll, Stacey learned for the first time that she had a whole other group of men to fear. She had been so absorbed in the confusion and terror of dealing with pimps that she had overlooked the danger of getting into a car with a strange man and demanding money from him in exchange for sex acts. Ironically, however, it was a lesson that only reinforced the odd excitement she had sensed in The Game—the thrill of its dangerous edge, which she had a sense of the first time she met Rachel, and which was pulling inexorably at her despite the fear. Or maybe because of it. On this busy Thursday night, the girls had so many dates that some of them were making use of the parking lot behind a restaurant off Hollis Street. They ran the risk of being seen by diners returning to their cars, but the location enabled them to service their clients and return to the stroll with very little delay, so they took the chance.

Stacey and Annie Mae

Heading to work on Hollis. [Print from ATV video tape]

Stacey was standing nearby, chatting with Annie Mae, when the two girls heard screams from the parking lot. A large blue car sped out of the lot and headed down Hollis past the girls. Annie Mae tried to make out the license plate, but the car was moving too quickly and the street was too dark. A sudden fear filled Stacey as she saw a prostitute stagger out of the lot with her hands up to her face; as Stacey and Annie Mae ran towards the girl, they could see blood pouring out between her fingers. "Oh my God, Viki, what happened?" It was only the night before that Stacey had met Viki, a very funny and pleasant fifteen-year-old with one serious problem: she was trying to hide her crack addiction from her pimp. A piece of tissue pressed to her lips, Viki haltingly told them the story: her date refused to pay her, and when she made a grab for his wallet, he pulled out a hammer and struck her in the mouth. Stacey and Annie Mae tried to stop the bleeding while another girl called her pimp, who arrived in only a few minutes to take her away—to a hospital, Stacey hoped.

The description of the blue car spread up and down the stroll in a matter of minutes; girls who had been with a client were told there was a bad date out; and everyone got just a little more careful. It was Annie Mae's view that Viki, an experienced prostitute, should have had the street sense to recognize trouble when she saw it coming— and she would have, except that her drug habit probably addled her

Watching the cars, hoping to avoid a bad date.
[Print from ATV video tape]

judgment. The only problem with developing a street sense—and Annie Mae didn't mention this part—is that many prostitutes only start paying close attention to their dates after a bad experience. Stacey probably didn't need to get that message; she had already decided to be much more cautious from then on. If that wasn't enough education for one night, only a few hours later Stacey watched another bad date unfold before her on the street.

The drunken client was cursing a prostitute who had approached him—she was too ugly to charge that much money, he said, and he should get a discount just for talking to a girl like her. If he hadn't been so intoxicated, he would have known better than to argue with a prostitute in public, especially with that big black car with the darkened windows parked only a block away. Tiny Simms was leaning on that car, talking to one of his girls.

One of two Halifax pimps using the street name Tiny, this one was 5'8" and maybe 145 pounds—Real Tiny—as the girls called him to distinguish him from his namesake, who was a little taller and a lot heavier. Unlike other pimps, Tiny enjoyed hanging out with his girls and spent more time chatting them up on the stroll that he did cruising and watching the action. Some of the other men had asked him to stop the chit-chat lest he scare away customers, but he didn't care what the others thought of him—another distinguishing characteristic. Tiny did, however, care a great deal about how the girls felt about him; hearing the commotion up the block, he went around to the driver's side of his car, opened the door, and picked up a baseball bat. Tiny Simms might have been an exception to the rule when it came to some aspects of pimping etiquette, but he was a player and he knew what he had to do in this situation. The girl being hassled was not one of his, but she was a part of the family, so Tiny had to defend her.

The drunk was getting louder and pushing the girl, and a few other prostitutes had gathered to curse at him. They could see Tiny passing by on the street side of the man's car, but he only saw what was happening after Tiny had circled around the front of the car and come back towards him. "I suppose you're gonna hit me with that bat, are ya?" the belligerent drunk demanded. "Why don't you just fuck off outta here and leave me to my business?" Without a word, Tiny pulled back and swung the bat, striking the man in the side of the face and sending him to his knees. Blood poured from a gash above his cheekbone.

Tiny remained silent, and his victim wasn't saying much either. Calmly, the pimp lifted him by the arm and led him to his car; the man managed to get his keys in the ignition and drive away. Good riddance: Tiny didn't agree that his own presence on the stroll was a deterrent to customers, but he knew for sure that a bleeding date at the side of the road would not be an incentive to others. Tiny did not talk to the prostitute whom the drunk had been pestering. She could thank him by choosing him, and moving over to stand with his girl; if she didn't, he had no business talking to her. This was a pimp with his own style, but he was still a pimp; attacking the unruly date was a courtesy to a fellow player, but so much the better if his action gave a girl—or girls, preferably—the message that he was the man to be with. Tiny walked back to his car, tossed the bat inside, lit a cigarette, and returned to the conversation he was having with his now very excited young employee.

Tiny's girl was not the only one turned on by what had happened; all the prostitutes began talking and joking about the man who learned the hard way not to mess with them. Stacey felt an adrenaline rush, and she quickly forgot about Viki and her injury. Once again, she began to feel she was involved in something adventurous and wild, and she liked that feeling. She would remember it all the way to Toronto, she promised herself—and maybe she didn't need to worry about leaving The Game if it was going to be like this.

Part Three:
Taunya and the Big Man

In the spring of 1992, Manning Greer was out cruising in his yellow Corvette one night, enjoying the sight of Montreal coming to life as winter released its grip. The comfortable warmth in the air meant more to Greer than the sheer pleasure of the season, however. The warmth meant Montrealers were once again venturing from their homes and apartments having survived the cold of another winter. Greer looked around at the pedestrian clogged sidewalks and smiled at what they represented. More people meant more business for his family of pimps. Most of all it meant more money—and that was something to *really* be happy about. The screech of car tires on pavement as he turned a corner startled pedestrians; a few looked up, but the heavily tinted side and rear windows prevented them from seeing who was making all the ruckus. It wasn't just the tires, but also the Corvette's dual exhaust, spitting and crackling with the firing of the engine's eight cylinders—not to mention the deep bass thud of the powerful stereo, which could be heard half a block away.

In a way, it was a shame he'd had the windows tinted, because the Big Man presented quite a spectacle behind the wheel of his 'Vette. The gleaming yellow sports car sparkled as he moved along the street. The car came alive as it passed beneath the amber street lights, their warm glow bouncing off the long sleek hood and catching another equally polished array of yellow metal as they danced over the swept back windshield. Seven sparkling, jewel-studded rings adorned his fingers; as he clasped the steering wheel, they seemed to fight for attention in the amber wash of the street lights. As he shifted gears, the flash of an expensive white running shoe could be seen below the car's dashboard. His powerful, muscular frame was draped in a deep-green, low-necked T-shirt tucked into trendy, baggy jeans secured by a belt with a buckle of real gold. Around his neck, he wore a massive gold chain, below which hung, fittingly enough, a solid-gold dollar sign. The three thousand dollars in his wallet was what the Big Man would call "chump change."

Money and power were Greer's gods: he had utter contempt for most of humanity, and only really cared about one person outside his Scotian family of pimps. That person was his mother, Rose.

At the age of twenty-seven, the youngest in a family of two boys and three girls, Manning was Rose Greer's baby boy. The Greers, like many other hard-working families in their North Preston, Nova Scotia neighborhood, had high hopes for the bright, energetic Manning, a natural leader who possessed that special quality—charisma, as it's sometimes called—of someone who could exert influence over others. Rose Greer believed her baby was working in Montreal as a delivery driver for a large furniture company. Aside from his personality traits, Greer's size and strength meant he could handle the toughest physical labor and Rose was happy he was not afraid of hard work. Her own husband, Manning's father, had worked hard all of his life and Rose was happy that very important ethic had been passed on to her son. She was equally happy that Manning had been able to find work in Montreal for his older brother. There simply wasn't enough work for the boys in Nova Scotia and she was thrilled that they had the sense to move away and make a life for themselves. She did wish the boys would visit more, but they came when they could and she had to be happy with that. That was the life Rosy Greer thought her youngest child was living; hard working delivery man with an eye to the future. It pleased her that the high-school drop out had managed to make it after all. There was a time when she was afraid he would fall under the influence of the wrong crowd: and she spent many a Sunday on her knees in church praying that would not happen.

Rose's prayers were not answered—although she really believed they had been. By the age of sixteen, Manning Greer had fallen in with the wrong crowd; he had become a pimp.

The man who was probably the key to young Manning's career choice was his uncle, Garfield ("Popeye") Greer, a dynamic, outspoken, and very successful North Preston player in the style of Miles States. The elder Greer made his money and achieved his dubious fame in the 1970s. Like Miles States, Popeye had a large stable of young women working for him and was not shy about showing his burly young nephew what those girls had done for him. Popeye loved to flash his cash and watch as Manning's eyes popped at the sight. He filled the young Greer's head with his own romantic interpretation of life on the streets. The sight of all that cash had a profound affect on

Manning Greer. His hard working father kept food on the table and a roof over the family but there was rarely extra cash kicking around to offer the kids. Popeye on the other hand always handed Manning a twenty, or even a fifty, before he left town to return to the city and the life Manning wanted for himself. Like many pimps, Popeye Greer liked the idea of having an apprentice, so he agreed to introduce Manning to The Game when the young Greer asked him in the early 1980s. The student soon outstripped the master. Manning Greer jumped from bubble-gummer to full fledged pimp in less than a year. He was too big and ambitious to settle for the menial jobs the other young pimps accepted. Popeye Greer saw in the young man the potential to make some serious money and he encouraged it. Manning had not been successful in school not because he lacked intelligence but because he lacked motivation. He resented what he perceived as the racist attitude of the white school system and he could see the fear in the eyes of the other students when they looked at the angry young Greer. At age sixteen Greer was already approaching six feet, a height he would pass within two years. In his uncle's tutelage Manning was motivated by the quick return he saw for the time invested.

By the mid 1980s Popeye Greer had been in The Game for most of his life and he was content to settle down and reap the rewards. Manning, on the other hand, was just beginning and he wanted to see everything Popeye had seen and do even more. When Popeye Greer explained the rules of The Game to Manning one rule stuck out in the young recruit's mind. "We're the lords of this game man, the streets are ours, the rules are ours. We make 'em and we break 'em." Manning Greer very quickly started playing by his own rules. He began recruiting young men from home to help him find girls to work the streets. Greer never trusted the other pimps he met in Montreal because they were not from home. He preferred to do business with the people he trusted. Gradually Manning Greer surrounded himself with a core group of close friends and relatives that he called "his family." These young men enjoyed the life and the money the Big Man offered so they followed his lead. Greer spent most of his time working with that close knit group of friends but he also dealt with almost any pimp from his home town and by the end of the 1980s there were close to one hundred of them.

When Toronto police first began to hear about the Big Man they wrongly assumed he was a kingpin and that all the Nova Scotia pimps answered to him. Greer's vicious temper had earned him the fear and respect of the other pimps but the family was not as organized as police first believed. "Everything we did, we did because we learned it the hard way. There was no big plan to it," one jailed pimp remarked. There was no master plan driving the Scotian pimps, they worked together when they had to and apart when it suited them. Greer was a firm believer in fear as a great motivator so he used the threat of a large number of pimps working as a unit to keep girls in line and keep competition at bay. A girl working for Greer in Toronto might think she could break free while he was in Montreal, but the thought that the other pimps working in Toronto would stop her kept her in line. Other pimps might think about raiding Greers stable but short of all out warfare with the Nova Scotians there was no way to move on the Big Man. Manning Greer was a re-active pimp not a pro-active one. When Jamaican pimps began to hassle the Nova Scotia girls in Montreal, claiming the prime corners as their own, Greer reacted quickly and decisively. He used brute force, and the number of loyal friends he had welcomed into The Game, to teach the Jamaicans a lesson. After beating one pimp and ordering him to take his girls out of town, Greer decided to claim sections of the stroll as his own, or as Scotian territory. He did the same thing in Toronto. Interestingly though, the loyalty of the Scotians did not extend to their business activities in Halifax. Greer and the others shared their territory in Montreal and Toronto and watched to make sure other pimps did not place their girls on the family's turf. Back home in Halifax, Greer, who was the biggest, claimed the best turf and his associates claimed their own in a trickle down fashion.

It is still unclear how much money Manning Greer was making as a pimp; he never shared that information with anyone. Police believe he made millions of dollars during his career, an estimate based on the belief that Greer ran a stable of five to fifteen girls depending on the season. In peak season—the summer when he needed as many as fifteen girls to meet the demand in Halifax, Montreal and Toronto— his girls would all earn a minimum of five hundred dollars a night.

Like other pimps from North Preston, Greer lied to his mother about the widespread criminal activity he was involved in; as far as Rose Greer was concerned, Manning worked for that trucking company in Montreal—his favorite of the three cities he most often visited in his actual profession. To explain the elegant attire and flashy jewelry he always wore on visits home, he boasted about how his great strength made him such a valuable asset to the company that he earned twice what the other shippers could generate. He made more money, he explained, because when a late shipment had to be delivered the company would ask him to do it alone. He worked all that overtime and his company rewarded him handsomely. Rose Greer was very proud of her son's success; she knew other boys from North Preston had been drawn into prostitution, and held up her Manning as an example of what they should be doing with their lives. The few neighbors who knew the truth didn't have the heart to disillusion her.

The streets are a dangerous deadly place where fear is a fact of life. The streets are also a pipeline of criminal information where legends grow bigger with every telling. It was fear that placed Manning Greer at the top of the heap. He was big, he was mean and would stop at nothing to defend his turf—that was the legend and legend is as good as the truth in the street. Manning Greer *had* become a leader, known across Canada as one of the most-feared, most-powerful players in the business—a man who, only in his mid-twenties, had reached the top of a profession he was too ashamed even to identify to his mother. She would have been shocked to hear the real story of his "progress"—from popcorn pimp to violent kingpin who used fear and unpredictability to control his girls in Montreal, Halifax, and Toronto. The Big Man didn't bother cruising the strolls regularly to collect cash: he was far too important for a job better suited to a bubble-gummer. He thought nothing of jumping on a plane to Toronto or Halifax so that he could ensure the young prostitutes were toeing the line. They never knew when to expect him, and that's just the way Greer wanted it. Greer did nothing to dispel the myth, that he was the boss. He reveled in it, and like every other opportunity that came his way he took advantage of it. If impressionable young men wanted to work for him, instead of developing their own stables, as he had done, that was fine with him. Greer knew he could not expect real players to follow his orders and he never asked them to. Popeye Greer, and the others who came before the new king of the street, worked with Manning when it was profitable and did their own thing when it was not. The following of impressionable young bubble-gummers helped Greer exert his force without ever raising a fist. He was not reluctant to order one his henchmen to administer a bit of physical or psychological discipline if a girl strayed out of line; the definition of "straying" altered according to his highly volatile moods, as did the criteria for determining when a particular prostitute required his personal attention. He had no qualms about exacting these punishments—it was just part of doing business, whether wrangling with rival pimps, or teaching a " 'ho" a much-needed lesson.

This was not a popular approach to pimping in Popeye Greer's era, and Manning Greer didn't start out by regularly and brutally beating his girls; but the Scotians learned in their efforts to hold onto their territory—the blocks demarcating a prostitution stroll—that muscle means power. Largely unchecked by the police, who concentrated their efforts on the girls, the Scotians' penchant for the punch could be indulged at will, in battle with their equally aggressive and well-armed enemies, or for domination over vulnerable teenage girls. Violence had always had its place in The Game; as Popeye explained the rules to Manning, there were those times when a girl "needed a beating." The difference between the two men was that Popeye and his generation of pimps used violence sparingly, believing the threat of it was enough. Manning and his generation of pimps used violence constantly, believing the reality was more effective than the threat. A girl who thought she might be abused might still risk violating a rule but a girl who knew her friends had been savagely beaten for the same violation would think better of it.

Manning Greer was not thinking about the past as he cruised through Montreal on that warm spring night. He was there and he was content. Greer glanced down at the speedometer—seventy clicks, a little over the posted limit but not enough to interest police. Still, why take a chance with those fools? Greer let his foot ease off the accelerator and watched the needle drop; as the car slowed to fifty kilometres per hour, he reached down and touched the handle of the dull-gray .9-mm Beretta handgun tucked between the bucket seat and the shifting console. He tapped his ringed fingers on the wheel in time to the blaring music. Police? The Big Man didn't care about the police, and he was confident they didn't care about him, either. One of Manning Greer's greatest assets in The Game—along with his personal magnetism—was a remarkable ability to quickly assess and act on just about any situation presented to him, almost always to his benefit. Even the Big Man had a blind spot though, and Greer's blind spot was the police.

If anyone told Greer there were police officers in three provinces and the state of New York who were aware of him and his activities and just waiting for a chance to put him behind bars, he would simply have laughed. The police were just an annoyance, to be avoided as easily as lifting one's foot from the accelerator every once in a while. The fact was that police had been monitoring the activities of Greer and his family of pimps for some time. For example, Halifax RCMP officers John Elliott and Brad Sullivan had been told by some of the young prostitutes who opened up to them in 1990, during Operation Heart, that although Manning Greer was the acting leader of the Scotians, his uncle remained the highly respected family figurehead—the only player to whom the Big Man would defer. That kind of information was probably the single reason the police were unable to stop Manning Greer. The police really were chasing a ghost; they had accepted the street myth surrounding Greer and did not focus on the reality.

The police believed Greer headed a highly organized crime family on par with the Hell's Angels biker gang. They had also heard the street story about the turf war between the biker's and the Scotians. That story, like most in the street, was part truth and part myth. The Hell's Angels had left the stroll in Halifax after a clash with the Scotians, but not because the Scotians were a serious threat to the Angels. The truth was the street trade in Halifax was not worth the police attention a turf war would bring and the Angels knew a turf war was the only way to chase the locals off the stroll.

There was a large number of Nova Scotia pimps but they were not, in the traditional sense, an organized crime family. The Scotians were more like a blowfish: blowfish can double in size when threatened. The fish does that by ingesting water or air and distending its stomach. It's a trick, but it often scares off predators in the deep. When Manning Greer or one of his friends was threatened, or when they were all threatened by another pimp or some other perceived problem, they joined forces: distending the stomach and exaggerating their size. It worked for them as well. When the threat was over, most of the pimps would go their own way and do their own thing until the next threat was encountered. Greer did stay in close contact with his core group of friends but even they did business their own way. The pimps were just friends from the same small town sharing a wild adventure. The young bubble-gummers who followed Manning Greer's orders were just naive and he and his friends took advantage of that. There was another problem that kept police from isolating and arresting Manning Greer. Unlike the Scotians, the police did not join ranks to solve a problem. Police in Montreal wanted Manning Greer arrested, or moved out of their town. They did not care if he worked in Toronto or Halifax. The same could be said of police in those cities. By 1992 that was beginning to change. The change started when Brad Sullivan and Dave Perry began to share notes following Operation Heart.

Greer was unaware of that subtle change in policing and he continued to believe the police were no threat as he whipped the 'Vette over to the curb and clambered out. Even without the flashy car, Greer turned heads as he headed along the busy downtown street. His 6'3" frame carried 225 pounds in well-distributed proportion—a big man not only by reputation. The glowing gold jewelry; the expensive yet casual clothing; the smooth, dark face framed in thick black curls weighed down with styling gel: an extremely attractive package—except for the dangerous distance in the moist brown eyes. Manning Greer rarely met a gaze directly; his mind seemed perennially occupied with something other than what—or who—was right in front of him. On this night in early June, though, he was just enjoying the smell of the city, and he inhaled deeply as he walked towards his favorite club. Montreal smelled just a little like home. There was a hint of moisture in the air as the breeze from the waterfront worked its way into the downtown core, and he thought nostalgically of the Hollis Street stroll, only a block away from the busy Halifax harborfront; the sickly sweet scent of raw sewage and petroleum products—lifeblood of the ships slipping into and out of port—was a powerful trigger for memories of home. A trip back east was just what he needed—and he could also use the time to fill a vacancy in his stable of prostitutes. Lynn, one of the Big Man's favorite girls had disappeared and he was looking for someone new to fill that void. He was also still looking for Lynn. Greer's favorite club was a small, dark street-level bar popular with Montreal's pimping community; two pool tables on one side of the room, a few small, round tables and a long oak bar on the other. Greer walked to the Scotian family's usual table near the back of the bar where he sat with his back against the wall. The satisfied smile he had worn out on the street was beginning to fade, though. It was just after 11:30 P.M., and the Big Man had expected two of his cousins to be in the bar, but they hadn't shown up. After ordering a Coke—Greer rarely drank alcohol—he pulled out a cellular phone and punched in a number. "Yo." The single-syllable greeting was delivered in an impatient tone. "It's B.M. Where you at?" Only Greer's inner circle referred to Greer as B.M. instead of the Big Man; and it was a privilege that had to be earned. It was shared by that small group he spent most of his time with.

"Shit, man, it's Glenda. Dumb 'ho got herself busted again."

"Deal with it."

"Yeah, later."

Greer clipped the folding phone to his belt and sipped his drink, looking around the room and quickly deciding there was nobody worth hanging around for. On his way out he noticed five men at a table near the door; one of the three facing him looked familiar. It was a Jamaican player from New York; one he'd diss'd. Two weeks earlier, the Big Man had taken a girl from the other pimps stable and refused to pay the leaving fee of eight hundred dollars demanded by the

Jamaican, who called himself High T. He'd done this deliberately as part of his continuing effort to drive the Jamaicans off what he considered Scotian territory—a pimp without respect would be unable to hang on to any of his girls, or his turf—but now Greer was beginning to wonder whether he had made a mistake. He locked eyes with High T., who stood, met his glance, and walked out the door, followed by his companions. Greer was being challenged; if he stayed in the bar, he would be announcing that he was afraid, and there was no way he could do that. Pulling out his phone, he hit the re-dial button, but his cousins were at the police station bailing out the busted prostitute and they'd shut off their phone and left it in the car. *Shit, and the gun is in the 'Vette!* Well, he'd just give that fool High T. his money and catch up with him later.

Outside, the five men had gathered at the edge of the sidewalk near a gray van; when Greer walked out of the bar, High T. stepped away from the others. "B.M., you'd better be carrying my money, fool." Well that was different: High T. could not call him B.M., and *nobody* called him a fool. The Big Man's powerful leg shot out in a lightning-fast kick, and High T. was out of the picture. "Anyone else gonna dis' me here?" The other men seemed confused. Greer's challenge was not what they'd expected. One of them rushed over to the fallen pimp, who was still clutching his groin. "Fuck, T. You okay?" Greer prepared to kick this second guy in the head as the side door of the van slid open and two more men stepped out, one carrying a baseball bat. He tried to fend off the blow but only managed to slow it down with his raised arm. The bat glanced off the arm and struck the side of his head. He felt the sidewalk disappear beneath his feet. Then came flashes of light and mumbled sounds as a flurry of kicks battered his head and face.

Greer could feel the force of the blows, but not the pain, and he tried to force himself up. One of them stepped on his back and pushed down, and somebody else shouted: "Stay down, motherfucker, or we'll kill you!" Greer tried to ignore the threat, but the guy with the bat struck him hard in the right shoulder, and he suddenly was unable to push against the sidewalk. Finally, the beating stopped. The Jamaicans picked up their fallen comrade and helped him into the van. As High T. was led past Greer, he spat on the fallen Nova Scotia pimp, gasping: "Get your ugly ass out of my town or you're dead."

Laughter echoed down the street as the Jamaicans drove off; certain they had seen the last of this so-called Big Man. They would have been surprised to learn that Manning Greer was furious, not at all cowed by the savage beating he had taken. Within a few moments he had pulled himself up on a parking meter and begun making his way back to his car. Passersby glanced away at the sight of the bruised, bleeding man—probably because of the look of sheer rage in his eyes—but he didn't care. They were just chumps. Safe behind the wheel, he reached for his phone, using his left hand—the pain in his right shoulder made it impossible to use that hand—and told his cousin to find him. No way he could drive; he needed his shifting arm.

"Shit, man, we shoulda been there. Fuck."

"C.C."

"Yeah, man, what?"

"Beat that 'ho." Greer hung up, knowing his cousin would punish the girl who was foolish enough to get herself arrested, leaving him in a bar without back-up. It didn't matter what went wrong in the family business; ultimately one of the girls paid the price. Greer tossed the phone onto the passenger seat and reached across his lap with his left hand. He pulled the Beretta out of its hiding place and slid the safety on and off as he contemplated revenge. The weight of the deadly weapon was reassuring—as reassuring as the Big Man's knowledge that he would be able to count on his family in the next battle with the Jamaicans. They had been there before, and they would be again. It was time for the Blowfish to inflate.

The first war between the Scotians and the Jamaicans began late in 1989, when Nova Scotia pimps were already running girls in Halifax, Montreal, Toronto, and Ottawa, but not at the level they would attain by the 1990s. One aggressive Jamaican-Canadian working in Montreal took a liking to the pretty, fresh young Nova Scotia girls he was seeing and—deciding the Scotians were country hicks who didn't deserve his respect—he planned a trip to Halifax to find some girls for his stable, which he ran in New York as well as Montreal. What the man lacked in common sense he more than made up for in nerve: on his first visit to Halifax, the pimp took his shiny Cadillac down to Hollis Street, opened the door, and asked three likely looking girls to get in. When they hesitated, he placed a gun on the seat beside him, and the request became an order. Then he simply headed out of town and back to Montreal: the Nova Scotia pimps had no idea who had pulled this bold manoeuvre.

The information pipeline worked quickly; within weeks, the girls had been traced to a stroll in Buffalo. Meanwhile, the Jamaican decided to go back to the well, this time in the company of some protection; an enforcer reputed to be a member of the Hell's Angels. The Nova Scotia pimps had been keeping close watch on their territory; in particular, Tank—the man who would later predict Stacey Jackson's attraction for The Game—was spending hours on end in a parking lot near the stroll, monitoring the action and recording the license numbers of suspicious-looking cars. He would have been hanging out there anyway; Tank liked The Game and spent as much as time around it as he could. His beat-up old Caddie didn't even draw a glance from the raiders as they cruised the stroll—but their gleaming car, with its darkened windows, certainly attracted Tank's attention, and he phoned the home where several of the North Preston players were involved in a card game.

The word spread like wildfire, and a convoy of more than ten cars and trucks soon left North Preston for downtown Halifax. The New York pimp probably would have gotten away, but he was being more selective on this trip and he cruised the stroll repeatedly eyeing the girls as they worked. He wanted the busiest girls if not the prettiest. He wasted valuable time shopping the stroll for the best catch—just enough time for the contingent from the country, as Scotians liked to refer to North Preston, to get into town. Tank cut him off at the corner of Hollis and Prince streets, and while he was cursing at this fool, whoever he was, there was another car, positioned behind him. Suddenly there were men jumping from their vehicles, surrounding him. The pimp's enforcer didn't even get the chance to threaten anyone: the first blow, from a wooden club, came from behind; it broke his forearm. That was enough for the muscle man: "Get me the fuck out of here!" he ordered, jumping into the Caddy. The young men from North Preston weren't quite finished—they furiously pounded on the fancy black car, denting it badly and cracking a couple of windows before the pimp managed to force his way past Tank's Cadillac and make for the nearest route out of town. A few of the Scotians gave chase, but most just celebrated the easy victory. The response showed the strength of the Scotian group: this was a family unit, whose members trusted each other and were ready to fight for each other. It didn't matter whose girls the pimp was trying to steal: if he was raiding a Scotian's stable, he was raiding every pimp working in Halifax.

That fierce loyalty was characteristic of the Scotians' rise to dominance on the strolls of Toronto and Montreal by 1992. Now a new breed from New York was showing some muscle, and Manning Greer was not about to sit back and let these Jamaicans walk all over him all over again. When he heard that these jerks had actually had the audacity to scoop one of the family's girls, only weeks after his beating at the hands of High T. and his friends, the Big Man figured it was pay-back time. This looked like a job for Bullet he figured—the enforcer. Not everyone in the Big Man's family was a pimp; occasionally, he relied on a very special friend from home to handle trouble with other players or to provide that little extra incentive for girls who weren't convinced of the error of their ways even after their pimps beat them.

A cousin and childhood friend of Manning Greer's, Cam "Bullet" Greer was neither bright enough nor patient enough to be a player himself, but he was unquestioningly loyal and uncompromisingly violent. The twenty-eight-year-old enforcer split his time between Montreal and Halifax, and was occasionally parachuted in to handle a problem in Ottawa, Toronto, or Niagara Falls. He too was part of the street myth that surrounded Manning Greer. The Big Man did not need an enforcer; he was simply loyal to a cousin who wanted to spend time with the other players. Greer found a role for Cam to play and Cam, or Bullet, remained a loyal soldier as a result.

Bullet's street name originated in his bizarre habit of playing with his ammunition before loading his .9-mm handgun, a predilection he parlayed into a sick game that his friends always enjoyed watching him practice on any girl in need of a lesson. At 6'1" and about 250 pounds, Bullet never had to pull a gun to scare a young prostitute, but if he had even half an excuse to take out his toy and play, he would.

While Greer and three of his fellow Scotians were parked on the stroll in Montreal on a warm night in early July waiting for their Jamaican target who thought he could steal one of their prettiest young prospects, Bullet filled them in on his latest exploit, involving another young prostitute who was giving the Scotians some trouble. This girl, Clara Ferguson, was a sixteen-year-old working for the family in Halifax—yeah, the one with the crack habit, Bullet said, and they all rolled their eyes in disgust. Crack cocaine was a serious violation of the rules set by the Scotians for their young "employees"; contrary to popular belief, no serious pimp allows one of his girls to even experiment with drugs, not out of any concern for her health, but because a prostitute with a drug habit costs—the money she could be giving him is going into a crack pipe, and up in smoke. Crack pushers were impossible to control, but the pimps could, and did, use any means necessary to keep the girls away from the highly addictive drug. Clara, who had made a lot of money for the family since being turned out at the age of thirteen—another runaway from an abusive home—was beginning to look like a lost cause, she might even have to be shuffled out of the deck. A girl with no value in The Game was dropped by the serious players. If some other pimp wanted to pick her up he would have to pay a fee; if not Clara would be relegated to working the crack stroll with the other addicts. The girls working the crack stroll had no pimps, they just worked to get high and they were not considered a threat to business since they charged only twenty five dollars for a blow job and most men avoided the crack stroll anyway. Clara had been a profitable girl though and the Big Man knew that if anyone could scare some sense into her, it was Bullet; he and the others were more than willing listen to his story. Clara was being held at her pimp's house in North Preston and had been there for a couple of days before Bullet paid her a visit. Her pimp had done his best: Bullet laughed as he recalled that the man even went so far as to dangle her off a highway bridge by her ankles in an effort to scare her off the drug, but she somehow contrived to get some more crack even after that. When Bullet arrived at the house, Clara had been locked in an upstairs bedroom; she was taken downstairs to the big enforcer. He was sitting in the kitchen, rolling several bullets across the table, his palm grazing their smooth, round surfaces. He called Clara over and asked her to look closely at the shells—they weren't all the same, he said. *Every bullet is slightly different, girl, and one of these is very, very special—because it belongs to you. Hold it in your hand, he said. Look at it real close.... Now, give it back to me.* He set the bullet aside, then delivered the punch line: the one she chose was the one he would use to kill her. Clara never forgot the encounter; years later she still talked about "her" bullet, and her fear that it is out there waiting for her. She needn't worry, the pimps have long forgotten her, knowing well enough the crack would kill her for them. The men all had a good chuckle listening to the story, but now it was time for bullet to deliver another lesson in the etiquette of The Game. They had spotted the arrogant Jamaican's car pulling away from its parking spot on the downtown stroll; at the wheel was the New York pimp who had scooped their girl. The Big Man leaned forward in his seat: "Drive," he ordered. First they would show these fools whose city Montreal *really* was; then he, personally, would take care of that little bitch Taunya.

Taunya Terriault had just celebrated her fourteenth birthday, in 1992, when she decided to give The Game a try—a choice that, to the three-time runaway, seemed the only option. Taunya's childhood in the Cole Harbour area outside Dartmouth was not a happy one—although she quickly grew into an extremely attractive child, with glistening blue eyes and nut-brown hair framing classic, delicate features; and although she and her sister Gwen, four years her elder, were very close, Taunya herself had difficulty in school and at home. She had no interest in anything her teachers had to say. For her school was the place you met the people you could have fun with. At home Taunya's problems were of her own making. Her parents loved and cared for her. Taunya was just a rebellious teen who did not like following anyone's rules.

Her parents blamed Taunya's problems on that rebellious streak, which they thought too "cure" by imposing arbitrary rules on their daughter. Her early life was marred by sexual abuse, the first incident occurring when she was only three years old. Her attacker was arrested and convicted after he grabbed the child, who was playing in his neighborhood backyard, and forced her to touch his penis. The Terriaults never dealt with the issue through family counseling; preferring to try to forget the attack had ever happened. Then, when Taunya was thirteen, a close friend of the family began making suggestive remarks to her: the response of her mother was to tell her to wear less provocative clothing. A few days later, the "friend" left a party he was attending with Taunya's parents and, under the pretext that her mother had asked him to make sure she didn't have any friends visiting her—one of the rules imposed after the teenager's first attempt to runaway —walked into the Terriault home. There, he assaulted Taunya, forcing her into an embrace and grabbing her breasts when she tried to resist the kiss. When she threatened to tell her parents what he'd done, the man left. Taunya said nothing to her mother and father; her actions spoke volumes, though—a few days later, she took off again. Her sister had already moved out after finishing high school and the two girls shared a dingy little apartment in a converted older home in north end Dartmouth. Gwen had a job at the Mic Mac mall, in a shoe store. It paid minimum wage, which meant the sisters could barely pay the rent, and were having trouble scrounging enough money for food. This was particularly hard on Taunya, who loved to party with her friends; she needed a job, and she needed one fast.

The idea of trying prostitution came from a new friend, Jennifer Kennedy, a twenty-three-year-old single mother and prostitute who lived in the same building. While Gwen went to work in the mall, Jennifer filled Taunya with tales of street life—which she had left behind, although she still worked for escort services once in a while. Taunya's ears perked up at the sound of such easy money—maybe as much as a couple of hundred dollars for a few hours' work—and asked how she should go about getting such a job. Her friend offered what advice she could: "When you go, they'll want to make sure you know what the business is all about, but they won't come right out and say it, and you shouldn't either. Otherwise, they'll tell you that you're wrong, and you won't get any farther than that.

A few days later, Taunya glanced through the escort services listed in the Yellow Pages, chose one with a nice-looking ad and phoned. She was told the agency was looking for a few girls and she could come in to talk about it; someone would come to pick her up in about an hour. The someone was a man in his mid-thirties, who drove her to the office of the escort service in Dartmouth and conducted the interview, asking her several times—as Jennifer had predicted—if she fully understood what would be expected of her. Yes, she knew what it was all about; and Taunya did know. She had had sexual intercourse already, with one of her friends; unlike Stacey Jackson, she was keenly aware that men found her attractive. She figured she might as well take advantage of that fact, and make a few dollars while she was at it.

Taunya's first exposure to The Game came in a different arena than that preferred by Manning Greer and his fellow pimps. Escort services offering prostitution to clients do so beneath a thin shroud of legitimacy. That shroud was the reason Taunya could not openly explain to her interviewer that she wanted to sell sex for money and he could not ask her to. It is legal to operate and advertise an "escort service" that offers men, and women, companionship. Brothel/escort services claim to fill a necessary role. They offer clients someone to take out to dinner or to a formal occasion when the client cannot find a date. They offer hostesses, not hookers. Their Yellow Pages advertisements offer up dinner dates, not blow jobs.

The woman Taunya met when she showed up for the work the next day suggested the teenager would do very well—but she could use a look that was a bit more *dramatic*. "Go on into the sitting-room, dear, and ask one of the other girls to help you with your make-up." Wearing more make-up than she liked and with her hair teased and sprayed Taunya headed out on her first assignment. She was told to meet a businessman staying at the Lord Nelson Hotel in Halifax, just across from the Public Gardens. A man in his mid-twenties drove her to the hotel and told her he'd be waiting outside in case anything went wrong. "You make sure he gives you the money as soon as you arrive," he reminded her. "A lot of these guys try to hold out and then refuse to pay you. And remember, as soon as you have the cash, you call the office so they know everything is okay. You don't make that call, and they'll page me—and I'll be up before you know it."

Taunya did not even notice the group of teenage girls walking in the Public Gardens as she arrived at the hotel. The June flowers were in full bloom and the girls were enjoying them after finishing an afternoon of shopping on busy Spring Garden Road. Taunya was just like those girls, but she was about to enter the hotel and begin a career that would separate her from them forever. By the time she got out of the elevator on the fifth floor, the bit of paper that told her what room number to find was clutched in her sweating hand; her heart pounding, she opened the door in response to a slurred "Come in." The naked man sprawled on the bed had gray hair, a big paunch, and pasty-looking skin; he was in his mid-fifties, but to Taunya he looked about two hundred years old. Grabbing his penis, he ordered the disgusted girl to "come and get it."

"You have to pay me first." Taunya hovered just inside the doorway and waited, and as the client got up and staggered towards her she could see—then smell—that he was drunk. Without a word, he grabbed her and threw her onto the bed, then started pulling at her clothes; Taunya pushed him off her body, and he rolled off the bed. Before he had a chance to haul himself off the floor, Taunya dialed the agency and breathlessly pleaded for help. Then the line was disconnected and the drunken businessman was looming over her again. Tears of fright and anger springing to her eyes, Taunya shouted that she had a bodyguard in the hallway—"and if you don't leave me the fuck alone, I'll get him in here." The man nonchalantly reached for a glass on the bedside table and sipped, then offered her a drink, laughing noisily when she glanced past him towards the doorway. The only way she was getting out that door, he said, was by doing the job she was hired for. Just then came a loud knock, and Taunya flung open the door, pushing the man aside. Her driver stomped into the room and a relieved Taunya scooted out into the hallway. She could hear her "bodyguard" yelling and the drunk laughing. There was a moment of silence; when the younger man joined Taunya in the hallway, he handed the girl five twenty-dollar bills, which she pocketed without asking any questions. Nor did they chat on the way back to the agency. After handing over the cash, Taunya said she wouldn't be coming back—this was just too much for her. "Give it some thought, sweetie," the woman urged. "It's not always so bad"—and she gave the surprised teenager fifty dollars, her share of the hundred. Taunya hated the job but had to admit she liked the feel of money in her pocket as she returned to Gwen's apartment.

Gwen Terriault was furious when Taunya told her sister what she had done: "How could you even *think* about becoming a prostitute?" Don't worry, Taunya insisted, it'll never happen again. Two days later,

Taunya called the agency, ready to give it another try. That fifty dollars had soothed her bruised feelings and besides, she had been perfectly safe, with her "bodyguard" downstairs on Spring Garden Road.

In two days of work, the fourteen-year-old serviced eight clients and earned nearly five hundred dollars—then quit the agency altogether and decided to return home. Taunya liked the money but at age fourteen she wasn't ready to commit to a life of prostitution, not yet. A few weeks later, the need for parental concern and guidance won out over the fear of being lectured and reproved; Taunya confided in her mother, telling her all about the escort service. Brenda Terriault, shocked and outraged, pleaded with Taunya to stay away from the agency—and for a while, she did. She even promised to try harder in school when it resumed in September. It was too late for her to do anything about the disgraceful marks she had earned in the preceding months. That was the promise but Taunya was not ready to keep it. Within days Taunya resumed her habit of showing up at home on Sunday afternoon after a Friday night party; she skipped more classes than she intended, and when her parents persistently asked her what she was planning to do with her life, her usual response was, "I don't know."

The only bright spot for Taunya was the job her mother found for her after she returned home: Taunya worked afternoons at a vacuum sales and service outlet owned by a family friend. She had worked a few days there over the winter and now it looked like she had a full time job. Taunya was already planning to find a way to drop out of school when the fall rolled around, and if she could work at the shop she could support herself.

The frustrated Mrs. Terriault tried once again to impose some discipline on her daughter, and fell into the unfortunate habit of needling Taunya about her episode with the escort agency. After one all night party she even accused her daughter of trying prostitution again. The worried mother hoped her approach would act as a deterrent, but it had the opposite effect. In the final week of June Taunya left home again and returned to the service; but this time her mother knew where she was working—the furious Mrs. Terriault phoned the office and scathingly informed the manager that she had hired a fourteen-year-old. When Taunya returned from her "date," she was fired. Running juveniles was not part of the legitimate image that escort services attempt to convey.

Brenda Terriault thought she had put an end to her daughter's prostitution career. She was mistaken. Her intervention only served to drive Taunya into the dangerous world of street prostitution, where younger is better. Taunya's first exposure to pimps came through a friend, Teri MacDonald, another fourteen-year-old runaway from Dartmouth. Teri and Taunya had developed a bond in school and it strengthened now that they found each other alone and away from home. One of four children, she and her siblings had been repeatedly beaten by their alcoholic father; the MacDonalds had separated in 1991, when Teri was thirteen and she had been living on her own ever since jumping from one foster family to another.

Teri was not a prostitute, but she spent a lot of time with the pimps from the North Preston area, in particular a man named Jeremy "Slugger" Field, who was a cousin of Manning Greer's and a key player in the Scotian family. The thirty-year-old Slugger met Teri when she was hanging out on Spring Garden Road in the spring of 1991. He was home visiting family in North Preston and, as was his habit, he cruised Spring Garden Road and visited the local malls looking for new talent. After his visit, he returned to his apartment in Montreal, and the persistent pimp got on the phone to his now "girlfriend" several times a week, trying to talk her into joining him.

Slugger also began talking on the phone to Taunya; who now spent all of her time with Teri. Slugger hoped she would be willing to join him too and go to work for his elder brother Eddy, if both girls came to Montreal. Eddy was the reason Slugger had become a pimp. The older Field, Eddy was closing in on forty, had invited Slugger to join him in Montreal after Slugger finished school. Eddy was the first to join The Game but Slugger was a better looking, faster talking, harder working pimp. The two girls talked about the idea almost every day. As June drew to a close they decided they would just go check out this big city that Taunya kept referring to as "party central." After an uneventful hitch-hiking journey to Montreal, the girls landed in the east end of town and phoned Slugger from a small strip mall; he told them to hang on and he'd pick them up. About an hour later, a shiny blue Cadillac pulled up in front of the video store where they stood waiting. A tall, wild-haired man got out on the driver's side, and as the second man emerged, Teri whispered: "That's Slugger," and, waving to them as they approached, "the other guy is Eddy." Taunya thought Eddy's Afro hairstyle looked a bit weird, and although Slugger was a good ten years younger, she wasn't that impressed with his appearance, either. Still, they had a fabulous car.... "Hey girl, how ya doin'?" Slugger smiled at Teri; then greeted Taunya and politely picked up the girls' small knapsack. "Traveling a little light, aren't you?" If they wondered about the question, it wasn't for very long. Taunya couldn't help smiling as she sat in the back seat of the

Cadillac; it had to be one of the nicest cars she had ever been in—leather interior, air conditioning, and a really great stereo. She kept nudging Teri, who grinned excitedly at her friend. It was a longish drive through the city to a residential area on the west side, where Eddy parked near a three-storey building; the pimps led their two new acquisitions up a flight of stairs to an apartment on the second floor. The fun and games were over, though Taunya and Teri didn't know it yet.

Eddy and Slugger might have traveled in style, but their living quarters were sparse—to say the least. About the only furniture in the living room was a badly worn sofa and a mattress under a jumble of bedding; in the kitchen were a beat-up table and a couple of chairs. The place was a mess, especially the kitchen: hardened food formed a dark crust on dishes piled high in the sink; on the table were dirty cups and glasses, a half-eaten loaf of bread, and a small plate with a bit of butter melting on it. Slugger wasted no time in getting to the point: "Well, Teri, you did it—you're in the city," he crowed, as the two girls stood staring at the disarray. "I hope you're ready to go to work for me, 'cause I know we could make some real money. Taunya, you can be with Eddy."

After a long, dismayed silence, Teri finally found her voice. "Ah, we're not really sure what we're gonna do, we just wanted to come up and see you 'cause you were always inviting us.... I don't know if we're gonna work, though; we might just get square jobs or something." Slugger grinned, and exchanged a meaningful glance with his brother, who was jangling his car keys impatiently. "Well, girl, you just give it some thought, but I know you're gonna want the night life. No pressure, though—you think about it. Now, Eddy and me got some work to tend to with the Big Man, so do us a favor and clean this place up while we're gone." With that, they were out the door; the girls never even got the chance to question what was clearly an order, not a request.

Taunya had never met Manning Greer, but she knew how important the Big Man was thanks to the education Teri provided during the hours spent standing at the side of the road hitching a ride. Teri had also told her Eddy and Slugger worked closely with him—so they must be important, too. Taunya and Teri turned on the radio and cleaned the place then sat down to discuss sleeping arrangements. There was a bedroom, and then there was the mattress on the living-room floor. Teri made it clear she'd be sleeping with Slugger, whether or not she went to work for him, so they'd take the bedroom and Taunya could crash on the couch while Eddy used the mattress. It didn't quite work out that way. After Slugger and Teri had retired, Eddy clarified the situation. "Never you mind that couch, girl," he said, patting the space next to him on the mattress. "You come down here with me."

"That's okay, I don't mind the couch," the frightened teenager replied.

"I ain't asking you girl. I'm telling you. And I don't care what you mind or don't. *Now, come down here."* Taunya obeyed, and Eddy promptly crawled on top of her and began pushing off her panties. Taunya struggled at first, but she was afraid of Eddy, and didn't know what she'd do if he told her to leave; she'd be stranded, in a strange city, alone at night. So she gave in, and tried her best to pretend it was just not happening.

By the next morning, Taunya and Teri realized that Slugger's promise of no pressure, was a joke. When the brother pimps had finished their morning coffee, they started in again on their now familiar refrain about the girls getting to work. Well, they'd think about it. Slugger, winking slyly at Eddy, casually remarked that they were going out now, shopping for new clothes that two of their other prostitutes needed. Maybe they'd bring something back for Taunya and Teri. This was no simple act of generosity: men who worked closely with the Big Man had adopted his philosophy.

"Keep the 'ho lookin' sharp all the time. When a man comes downtown looking, he doesn't want to spend a lot of time at the curb. First bright, fresh-looking 'ho he sees, he's gonna choose her. A well-dressed 'ho is a money-maker." When Eddy and Slugger had left, the two teens discussed their limited options: they could only stay at the apartment if they hit the stroll, and soon; if not, they'd have to hitch a ride back to Halifax. Teri had heard stories, though; these guys beat their girls, and might even kill one if she got too far out of line. "It can't be any worse than the service," Taunya retorted. The fourteen-year-old had made up her mind: that night, Taunya agreed to go to work for Eddy.

Teri was still reluctant to give The Game a try. Slugger would have to continue to pressure her, a tactic that would—and did—work in time.

While Teri and Slugger discussed her future Taunya put on one of the outfits the two pimps had bought that afternoon, a tight denim miniskirt, a pair of black fishnet stockings, and a tight red sweater. She put on what she hoped was enough make-up, teased and sprayed her long, brown hair into a face-framing style, and set out with Eddy to a nearby subway stop. During the ride downtown, her man explained the rules of The Game to his newest recruit—just as K-bar had set out the situation for Stacey. One of the Big Man's more experienced girls would keep an eye on Taunya and show her the ropes; she would give him everything she'd earned at the end of the night—and she was never to talk to a black man, or even make eye contact with him. Undoubtedly he would be another pimp, and she was to turn and walk away. Taunya, like Stacey, found that rule unusual, but accepted Eddy's instructions.

When they got off the subway, Eddy stopped at a pharmacy, and purchased the prostitutes' usual nightly necessities: a supply of condoms and a pack of cigarettes. Next stop: dinner, at Harvey's on St. Catherine Street, where Taunya was delighted to see a girl she knew from school. Lori Campbell, a sixteen-year-old, who, like Teri, Taunya, Stacey, Clara, and just about every other teenager on the street, had run away from a difficult home life, was working for another Scotian player, whom she'd met about a year before. The two girls spent a few moments talking in the washroom, and Lori touched up her new colleague's make-up; when they returned to the table they saw a tall, striking young woman chatting animatedly with Eddy. Lynn Buchanan, a nineteen-year-old from Montreal, had reached the pinnacle of her chosen profession: she was Manning Greer's "main girl," a four-year veteran of The Game who had earned a great deal of respect on the street—almost as much as a player. It was a good thing Lynn had earned that respect because she had been the girl who was missing from Manning Greer's stable and only her long-term loyalty kept him from punishing her when she returned with the explanation that she had taken an unplanned vacation to visit her sister.

The first night for Taunya was a blur. She hardly blinked at the succession of nameless men paying her to blow them for eighty bucks a go. She could have been busier but she spent as much time talking to Lori on the sidewalk as she did approaching the curb when a car slowed. Before she knew it the night was over and she had more than three hundred dollars to hand over to her pimp. "Not bad, girl," he told the tired Taunya, "but it better be five hundred from now on." Eddy was threatening her not encouraging her.

It took Taunya less than a week to realize she had to get away from Eddy. "Doesn't matter what I do, he always hits me," she complained to Lori one night. "Yesterday I gave him, what was it, almost six hundred, and still he's like, 'You dumb bitch,' for no reason at all! Like I called at two-thirty instead of two, or something. I don't mind The Game, but I gotta find another player." It never occurred to Taunya that The Game itself was the problem. Unpredictable tempers and

Taunya and the Big Man

Waiting to go to work in Montreal. [Print from ATV video tape]

sudden unprovoked violence were just another part of the package. She never even considered making a break for home. Not yet anyway.

Lori agreed that Taunya should choose another man, but warned her to seek out someone the family respected—and, especially, someone willing to pay her leaving fee, which would undoubtedly be high, given young, pretty Taunya's bright prospects and Eddy's level of respect as a member of the Greer family. Could be seven hundred dollars, Lori suggested. Taunya though about approaching one of the Jamaican pimps from New York; they had several girls working the Montreal stroll, and one of them had told Taunya she would be welcome in the family. Not a good idea, Lori said, telling Taunya about the bad blood between the Nova Scotians and the Jamaicans. In the end, she decided to approach an older man, "the Coach," who monitored the stroll for the Scotian family but rarely took on a girl himself. When he was approached by Taunya Terriault, he decided to make an exception; when she was on her way over to his apartment, she found herself wondering, for the first time since she and Teri hit the road a week ago, whether it might not be better for her to return to Halifax and go square, after all. Maybe this old guy could be convinced to free her.

Taunya needed her clothes first, so she called Eddy's apartment and asked him to bring them to her. That was how she found out that the Coach had not paid Eddy his leaving fee. Nor, she deduced from her former man's barely controlled anger, did he apparently have any intention of ever paying it. "Please, Eddy, I just want my things," she implored. "I just want to go home." Maybe they could talk about it, he said; Taunya agreed, and about a half-hour later a van pulled up outside the apartment. She walked up to the driver's window—and suddenly her heart was in her mouth: Manning Greer was sitting behind the wheel.

"Get in," he said, and she obeyed promptly; exactly why he was there she didn't know, but she was fairly sure it didn't have anything to do with her clothes. She was right: Greer said it was time for her to get back to work and stop fooling around with that old man. He wasn't as angry as Taunya thought he would be, but even his mild tone conveyed that he was not there to discuss her options. She was with *his* family now, and she *would* take it back on the street. Greer drove Taunya to the stroll and informed her that Eddy would be picking her up at the end of the night.

Taunya had other ideas. Less than an hour had passed when she approached one of the Jamaicans' girls and said she wanted to join their family. Great, the girl said; Taunya could work with her and her "sisters" for the rest of the night, and then they'd take it from there. *Sisters,* Taunya repeated to herself; that sounded comforting. Although Greer's players were forever referring to "family" and "blood," the girls working for them rarely felt that sort of bond. Close friendships did form: Stacey and Annie Mae had become inseparable; Taunya herself was very fond of Teri and Lori. Teri had finally relented and began working the street for Slugger a few days after Taunya made her decision, and the street work helped intensify their strong friendship.

But Scotian girls often ratted on each other to the pimps about those who broke the rules, not out of meanness but because of their stress-induced fear: a prostitute who told her pimp about the "bad behavior" of another man's girl might get a little slack; that her colleague would almost certainly face a punishment was, unfortunately, something she should have considered before stepping out of line. That was just the way The Game was played, Nova Scotia style—and few girls knew that better than Lynn Buchanan. She didn't wait to speak to the Big Man: when she saw Taunya join the enemy, she walked over and ordered the teen to return to the Scotian section of the stroll. Three of the Jamaicans' girls, who were standing near the new recruit, retorted that Taunya was now with *their* man, Sweet Lou; unless Lynn was looking to join them, she should go back to her own beat. Ignoring their laughter, she fixed Taunya with a cool stare: "You just made one very big mistake, child"—and with that, she rejoined Lori and the others on the other side of the street. One of Taunya's newly acquired "sisters" headed to a phone booth to call Sweet Lou and moments later a sports car pulled up to the stroll to pick up the newest Jamaican property.

Indeed, Taunya's "betrayal" infuriated the Big Man and his family, still smarting from the incident with High T. outside Greer's club. They considered scooping Taunya off the stroll that night and giving her a lesson she'd never forget, but that could wait. The Jamaicans needed to get the message first. Contrary to High T.'s contemptible parting shot to the injured Greer; Montreal belonged to the Big Man and his Scotian family, not these New Yorkers. While Sweet Lou, a player who favored the seventies image of Hawaiian shirts, suede jackets, and snakeskin shoes, talked to Taunya in his car near the stroll, Greer his cousins, and the redoubtable Bullet waited and watched from their vantage point a few blocks away. As they had hoped, Lou returned to the stroll periodically to check on Taunya and the other girls—he knew the Scotians would be real pissed—but he didn't get a chance to pay a second visit. As Lou pulled out into traffic, Eddy eased the van over to follow: Bullet was beside him, and Slugger sat with the Big Man in back. Lou was out of the downtown area before he noticed the van following him: "We got a problem," he told his cousin and a friend traveling with them. In New York, Lou always carried a gun, but he never risked taking it across the border; his flashy tricked out Acura Legend sedan and loud clothes drew enough notice from Customs officials as it was and he had been searched more than once. His companions had no weapons, either. Well, there was no choice in the matter, as far as Lou was concerned. "I'm just gonna pull over and pay the fool," he said. Forking over a leaving fee was a lot easier than getting mixed up in a turf war. Sweet Lou had the same attitude Manning Greer had adopted when he was out numbered by High T. and his friends, and as in the earlier incident the issue was not so much money as it was turf. Unlike Greer, Sweet Lou had the advantage of better advice. His cousin, a Canadian at whose instigation Lou had expanded his thriving New York sex trade into Montreal, had a much clearer picture of the situation. "This ain't about no leaving fee, Lou," he said urgently. "These guys wanna bitch-whip you and take your stable, man. They're crazy, man! You pull over when we ain't packin', and it's gonna be pain city, man.... Keep drivin', okay?"

Lou had heard the stories about how the Scotians took over a stroll, whether in Toronto or anywhere else, and didn't want to get involved in that kind of scene; he did stay on the road, while Eddy and his family bided their time. As a long stretch of open road extended in front of them, Eddy floored the accelerator and pulled out to pass; the two vehicles raced down the road, almost in tandem. Bullet pulled out his piece and rolled down the window. "C'mon man, ice that fucker," Eddy shouted. "I'm runnin' out of road!" Just as they neared the sweeping curve, Bullet took aim, then pulled the trigger. "I nailed him, man!" Bullet pointed towards Lou's car as it veered to the left, almost forcing the van off the road. Eddy hit the brakes, and as the men watched, Lou straightened out his car and shot ahead again. Enough was enough; Greer figured they had at least managed to scare Lou, and they didn't need a running gun battle— even the Big Man accepted that the police, stupid as they were, would find their way to the scene. Eddy turned off the roadway, while Lou, unconvinced the crazy Canucks had actually left, kept speeding ahead while trying to calm his cousin, who had taken one of Bullet's slugs in the arm.

He also pulled out his cellular phone to get word of the chase back to his people. For the next half-hour, just about every Jamaican and Scotian player had been on the phone at least once. It was only an hour or so later that one of the New Yorkers arrived on the stroll to drive Taunya over to Lou's Montreal pad.

Sweet Lou knew she was the reason for the attack and decided he would get her out of the picture until things cooled off a little. The Jamaican car took Taunya away from the downtown stroll before Eddy returned in the van looking for her.

The apartment was buzzing with activity. One of the girls tended to the wounded pimp (whose arm, it turned out, had only been grazed), while another started tossing clothes into suitcases. Meanwhile, Lou paced from room to room, barking orders into his cellular phone. He was leaving town and he wanted his business looked after while he was gone and he wanted his girls in New York to get ready for his return there. As for the Halifax teenager who'd generated all this furor, she was helping the girl who was packing—and she was as excited as she'd ever been in all her fourteen years. Taunya Terriault was going to the Big Apple, for at least a week! There would be time later to think about getting out The Game and returning home; all Taunya could do was dream about New York. By midnight on July eighteenth, they were en route to the U.S. border, Lou traveling alone while the two teenage girls rode with his cousin, who had Canadian identification. The precautions proved unnecessary; officials at Plattsburgh, New York, couldn't have been less interested in either car. In town the tiny convoy stopped briefly to make an exchange—Taunya and the other girl joined Lou, and his cousin turned back towards

Montreal; he'd be looking after business until Lou got back—despite the Big Man's efforts, he was going to return, and this time he'd be well armed. With weaponry, at any rate: this child knew nothing about Manning Greer and his family, but that was all right. She was truly *fine,* and she'd make him some good money, more than enough to cover the expense of the trip—"ain't that right, girl?" She might have known it wasn't going to be a vacation; but by now Taunya didn't even bother protesting; she was learning quickly that a prostitute never travels with her pimp for free. She works to defray the cost for both of them.

Taunya didn't worry about that or anything else; she was having a great time so far. The chatty teenager fell into an awed silence as Lou drove through the streets of Manhattan, all glass and steel and concrete. She had never seen so many people in her life, or heard so much noise, from the blaring of hundreds of car horns, to the shouts of street vendors or the cacophony of outdoor entertainers, all vying, like Taunya Terriault, for a slice of the Apple. Taunya would soon find out that she might have been handed a slice that was less than appetizing; her first hint was Lou's house, which looked impressive on the outside but opened to reveal what she could only describe as a zoo. Taunya met seven young women who lived with Lou, and she gave up trying to count the children running around everywhere. The women were all in Lou's stable of prostitutes, and he claimed all the children were his. After clearing a pile of toys off the bed in a room upstairs, Taunya managed to sleep fitfully for a few hours before getting ready for work.

As she soaked in the tub, contemplating the scary yet exhilarating prospect of being a prostitute in New York, there was a loud knock at the bathroom door; it was Lou, cursing, and ordering her to open the door immediately. Taunya jumped out of the tub, wrapped a towel around herself, and let her pimp inside. He shouted at her furiously: "Girl, you never, never, put a locked door between you and me. I don't care what the fuck you do in here; you *do not* lock that door. You are my property, and if I want to come in here and watch you, I don't want to wait till you open the door. Do you understand that?" Taunya had never seen Lou angry before—was he going to hit her, the way Eddy did when he got upset? Lou took one look at her terrified expression and quickly softened his tone. "It's okay, girl, you're new. You'll learn. I'm the best man you ever want to work for, as long as you follow my rules. Now get yourself ready for work." He wasn't quite through; Lou wanted to have a good look at this girl he'd gone through so much to acquire. She complied, and after taking her in for what seemed an eternity, he let her in on another rule: he might decide to have sex with her, but there was only one way she could become one of his "wives." Lou wanted something Taunya knew she would not be selling on the street; when she was ready, he would have anal intercourse with her, and after that she would be his forever. Taunya knew with absolute certainty she would never be ready for that—being one of Sweet Lou's wives was an honor she would just have to forgo.

The stroll where Taunya spent her first night in New York was a litter-strewn, frightening filthy strip of pavement. It was also incredibly busy: the girls here didn't stand around waiting for customers, as they did in Montreal; a long line of cars stretched back along the curb, and the prostitutes walked from car to car, jumping in when a driver accepted their offer. A few moments later, they'd move along to the next car in line. Taunya couldn't help thinking of it as an assembly line for blow jobs. The price was twenty bucks, one-quarter the Montreal rate. The crowded, dirty stroll and bargain-basement prices sickened Taunya. It was one of the primary reasons the men from New York wanted in on the Canadian sex trade: not only was it a more appealing atmosphere, but is also provided prostitutes with more than double the income of their American counterparts. Not that Taunya was looking forward to retiring to the streets of Montreal; the longer she spent working the New York stroll, the more certain she became that she just had to find a way to get out of The Game altogether.

For Taunya, the week in New York was an accelerated education in life at its seediest. The fourteen-year-old could not even begin to guess how many men she had had sex with on the fist night alone. Nor was Sweet Lou's interference confined to the bathroom incident: he decided to provide Taunya with his "training program" in the prostitution trade, starting with the art of faking oral sex. None of his girls actually *performed* oral sex on the customers; it was done with what he laughingly called "sleight-of-hand"—and what the fashion industry terms "big hair." "You spray that hair up, and he can't see past it anyway," Lou explained. "You just make some noise and use your hands, girl." That part of the program was fine with Taunya—she could feel a little better about herself, and a little smarter than the men she was servicing, most of whom disgusted her. Amazing what men will settle for, she thought; none of them can tell they aren't getting what they paid for! Far less appealing was Lou's training in what he liked to call " 'ho loyalty." It had started with his order that she never lock the bathroom door. Lou liked to watch Taunya and the other girls whenever and where ever he could. He reasoned that they had to consider him a part of themselves if they were to be loyal to him. There could be nothing they wanted to do that he would not be welcome to watch.

Lou also decided that Taunya should wear his mark: a monogram bearing his name, with a flower below it; when he asked a tattoo artist to etch this creation onto Taunya's left breast, she didn't even flinch— not that she wanted the tattoo, but she never argued with Lou. If he was happy with her, Taunya thought he might let her go home once they were back in Montreal.

She was dreaming, she had no idea that Lou considered her a trophy that he would flaunt in the face of the Nova Scotia pimps. Releasing her would be the same as telling them he could not hold onto her either. He had to prove he was a better man then Manning Greer and Taunya would help him do it. Lou's respect was on the line: he had to keep Taunya out on the street to show the Greer family that he meant business—he also had a brand-new gun to put some muscle behind his demonstration of superiority as a player.

The night of July thirty-first, an angry, confused, and frightened fourteen-year-old was turned out again on the prostitution stroll of Montreal. Her friend Lori had managed to snatch a few moments with her in the washroom at Harvey's, warning Taunya that Eddy was still looking for her and that the Scotian girls had been ordered to contact him if she returned to the stroll. Back outside, Taunya became more and more frantic. Her life was a mess, all she wanted was to break free but she had somehow managed to place herself in the centre of a war with her as the prize. Tears welled in Taunya's eyes as she paced back and forth along the sidewalk, trying to figure out how to get off this treadmill.

Finally, Taunya did the first sensible thing she'd done in months; she went to a pay phone and called her mother—collect. She was working for a pimp in Montreal and she wanted to come home, but she was afraid; would her mom call the police? Would she tell them to come and get her? Of course, Mrs. Terriault promised; less than an hour later, a patrol car showed on the stroll and the officers began looking around. Taunya couldn't believe it; the car was right there but the officers were doing nothing, they just sat and looked at the girls. Taunya wanted to walk to the car, but then Lou might guess the truth and come looking for her; bad enough Eddy and the Big Man were after her; she didn't need trouble from Sweet Lou as well. The cruiser stayed only five minutes, then pulled away.

An hour later, with a coolness born of despair, Taunya called her mother back. This time she asked Mrs. Terriault to describe her outfit to the police so they'd know who to look for; once again her mother agreed, and Taunya turned back toward the curb. Just then, one of her regulars showed up, a businessman who had "dated" her a few times while she was with Eddy. Taunya saw to her client, and when she returned to the stroll twenty minutes later, there was the police car; but the officers still didn't seem to notice her. Her heart pounding, Taunya strode boldly up to the car, ignoring the girls' stares. "I think you're looking for me—my mother called," she said quietly but firmly. "I'm from Halifax, and I want to go home." The policeman in the passenger seat opened his door, then motioned her into the back of the cruiser. Taunya didn't even look back at Lori as they drove away. The following morning, an officer from the Montreal police juvenile division took Taunya to the airport and put her on a plane to Halifax. She had been asked to make a statement naming the pimps she was working for, but when she refused, no pressure was put on her.

The same could not be said for what she faced back in Nova Scotia: she was home, but not home free. Taunya was able to return to her old job in the office of a vacuum cleaner sales outlet, but she made the mistake of looking up some of her former friends, and it didn't take long for the family to find out she was in town. Within a week of her return, a sixteen-year-old cousin of Manning Greer's, Greg, tracked her down and told her bluntly that she still belonged to the family. She hadn't paid her leaving fee, and neither had Sweet Lou. There was no way Taunya could come up with the seven hundred dollars that would buy her freedom, and like every other pimp in The Game, from minor players such as Greg to the big guys of his uncle's level, he was not prepared to accept payment in installments. Her only choice was to work for him until she'd earned the fee. Like Stacey Jackson, Taunya pleaded with the young pimp to keep her off Hollis Street so that her mother wouldn't find out she'd gone back to The Game—someone might recognize her and call Brenda Terriault, who had made it clear that Taunya was only welcome at home if she worked at the vacuum cleaner shop and stayed away from prostitution. Greg's solution served his own needs more than Taunya's, but that was typical of a pimp. It seemed he had a cousin who had recently opened an escort service in Dartmouth, and she could work there strictly as an in-service prostitute; he generously added that she could service clients during the evening and hang on to her day job that way.

It seemed Taunya's problems would soon be over, but on her first day at the old apartment building in north-end Dartmouth, she learned that her freedom wouldn't come cheap. Greg began by introducing his cousin. Ricky, a short, stocky man with a salesman's patter and flare for hyperbole, informed Taunya he was not a pimp but a businessman; the escort service was one of his many enterprises. Taunya, who was aware of Ricky's activities, knew he ran girls down on Hollis Street—so much for his claim to legitimacy. As long as he paid her—and that was when Greg pulled another maneuver typical of his profession: Ricky, he said, would keep half the money she earned, and he would get the rest. When Taunya protested—what about her leaving fee?—Greg blew up and threw her to the floor, kicking her as she lay curled in a fetal position on the carpet. His teeth clenched in rage, he promised he would beat her worse if she ever dared to disrespect him in front of another man again. He told her she'd better work her butt off if she expected to buy her freedom. The next night was just as bad: Taunya thought it would be all right to ask Greg about her fee while they were alone in the car on the way to Dartmouth, but she was wrong—Greg struck her in the head, told her to shut up about "his" money, and kept driving.

This has to stop; Taunya told herself, and decided to ask her square boss for help. As a close friend of the family, he knew about her troubles in Montreal and had promised to do what he could if anyone tried to hurt her. True to his word, he arrived at the agency only a few minutes later. Taunya ran out to his van and Ricky followed her. Taunya watched as her boss stared down the owner of the escort service. If Ricky wanted to try anything he thought better of it after seeing the anger in the man's eyes. Taunya's boss drove her home. She was free.

By mid-August, however, Taunya was back on the treadmill. Lori was back in town, still working for the Scotians, and the two girls often hung out together before she went down to Hollis; but one afternoon, when her friend and a stranger picked Taunya up at work, she knew she was in big trouble, just by the way Lori said she was sorry—and nothing more—*after* the car had picked up speed. When the young man at the wheel told Taunya she was going to North Preston, where someone wanted to see her, she figured she was in for a serious beating for leaving the escort service. Taunya stayed quiet during the drive; and she and Lori sat in silence while the driver was inside the split-entry house where he had parked. He was gone a long time, but neither of the girls even considered trying to make a run for it. They were both feeling trapped; in the almost palpable stillness, Taunya reached out and touched her friend's hand, as if to say, "I understand; it's okay." Finally the girls were told to go inside; Taunya was directed and she very slowly made her way to the basement level of the house.

There, sitting near the bottom of the stairs, waiting for her, was Manning Greer. As she approached, he stood up, towering over her. Then he led the way outside to a beat-up Chevrolet parked in the driveway. She was surprised to see him driving such an old wreck when he had that fancy yellow Corvette in Montreal. As was his custom Greer had flown to Halifax and was borrowing this car for the visit. As Greer drove towards the main road out of North Preston, Taunya, feeling sick to her stomach, was wishing she had stayed in Montreal and stuck with Eddy. Where was he taking her? Was he going to kill her for running out on the family without paying her leaving fee? Just then he pulled into the rear parking lot of the old school, now vacant; the two of them sat silently for a time and watched a group of kids playing in a nearby street. At long last, the Big Man broke the silence: "You know why you're here?"

"I guess … I don't know … I'm not sure." In response, Greer pulled the rings off his right hand, placed them on the dashboard, and struck Taunya with a fast, ferocious backhand blow across the face. Her lip began to bleed immediately.

"Don't play stupid with me, girl. I asked you if you know why you're here."

"Because I left."

Greer slapped her three times in rapid succession. "You disrespected my family, girl, and that means you disrespected me. Now what are you going to do about it?" Taunya glanced down at the door as she turned her head away from the Big Man to protect her face. He slapped her again. "I said, what are you going to do about it, girl?"

"I don't know, what do you want me to do?" Greer slapped her again, and said again: "Don't play stupid with me. What are you going to do?"

"Go back to the escort service and work for Greg?" Wrong response; the Big Man slapped her yet again. "You better tell me what you plan to do to make this right, or I'm going to have to kill you," he said. "You understand that? I don't want to kill you, but unless you do the right thing by me, I will. You disrespected me—now what are you going to do?"

"You want me to go back to Montreal with Eddy?" Once again Greer struck her, and this time the pain didn't seem as severe. "You disrespected me. How's working for Eddy going to fix that?" Suddenly Taunya understood, and the slight dizziness became nausea as she realized that Greer wanted her to work for him. Why didn't he just say so? Why was he beating her? What Taunya didn't understand was that Greer wouldn't openly steal a girl from Eddy; they were family, and that would be wrong. If the girl chose him, that would be different; and the leaving fee, if any, would be modest. The girl would still be in the family, and Eddy would be able to maintain his own level of respect without challenging the Big Man. As Taunya sat there, sickened, hesitant, terrified, Greer pushed her head against the passenger window so hard she thought the glass would break; finally she said what she knew he wanted to hear: "I could go with you. I could work for you."

"Is that what you want to do?"

"Yes."

Greer put on his rings and took Taunya back to the house, a friend's place where he was staying while in Halifax. Inside, several of the pimps Taunya had seen in Montreal and at the escort service were playing cards. Neither they nor Lori, who was sitting quietly on the couch, looked up as Greer led Taunya into a bedroom. He sprawled across the bed, propped his head up on the pillow, and fixed her with a stare. "Okay, girl, if you wanna be mine, I gotta see what I'm selling. Take them clothes off." Taunya trembled as she pulled off her things and obeyed his command for her to turn around. "Well, whatcha gonna do? You just gonna stand there?"

"Can I put my clothes on, please?"

"Is that all you're gonna do?"

"Please, can I get dressed now?"

Greer would probably have forced Taunya to have sex with him, but something changed his mind. "Yeah, get dressed now," he said curtly. "I got things to do." He walked out of the bedroom and left Taunya to put her clothes on and join Lori on the couch in the family room. The cards were back in the deck, and the players were going back to their primary game.

"You two clean this house," Greer told the two girls as he headed for the door; Lori and Taunya scrubbed the place then spent a tense few hours waiting for the Big Man to return. When he did, after midnight, he told Taunya she'd be going to Montreal with him in the morning, then, to her surprise, left her to spend the night on the couch. Her sleeping was fitful and her dreams were lurid with images of the abuse and torture she was sure she faced if she didn't cooperate with him—although the real nightmare was what she had in store if she did. Her mind raced as she tried to consider her options. She considered calling her real boss from the vacuum shop again but discounted it. Greer would either kill her boss or kill her, if he tried staring down the Big Man as he had with Ricky at the escort service. Her mom couldn't help—anyway, *she* kept saying, these days, that Taunya was doing exactly what she wanted, and that her trouble was of her own making. The police hadn't been much help in Montreal. No, all she could do was return to Montreal with Manning Greer. Somehow, accepting her fate made it easier for her to go to sleep; and there were no more dreams.

What Taunya didn't know was that Greer had come back to get her not only because her flight from the family had been an insult, but also because his main girl had vanished, and he needed a replacement—someone fresh, young, pretty. It was a bonus that he had a "justification" for insisting she owed him the ownership of her body; even better, she was just so easy to terrorize. That didn't mean he had forgotten about Lynn—not that he cared about her as a person, but she had been an extremely profitable and dependable prostitute, and her disappearance angered rather than worried him. At first he thought she had taken another unscheduled vacation but he knew that wasn't it, he had not beaten her when she returned from the first but he had promised he would if she repeated the behavior. That she might have been killed by a bad date simply didn't cross his mind. Greer's constant obsession with the renegade Jamaicans was his only focus for the loss of Lynn, and once again he vowed to hunt down the pimps who had taken a girl of his; they would pay for messing with Manning Greer and his family.

Manning Greer had no trouble drifting off to sleep; he was safe in Halifax, where Jamaican pimps wouldn't dare to make a move on him. It was always enjoyable to come home, but the real game was in Quebec and Ontario and he couldn't stay here with the minor players, not for long. As usual, Greer's only concerns were with problems other pimps might create for him—not the police. As long as he kept his people in line, and no-one made any trouble for him, the cops would stay away. Greer was certain the police had better things to do with their time than chase him and a few runaway girls. Manning Greer had no idea that two police officers working within a few kilometres of him were very interested in his actions and would soon find out that he had returned to Nova Scotia, and why.

Brad Sullivan was nothing if not stubborn. He refused to let go of the theory that Kimberly McAndrew had been abducted by pimps and he continued to work that file whenever time permitted. He had failed to win the support of his commanding officers when he tried to have an anti-pimping operation launched but continued to enjoy their support in his pursuit of the McAndrew file. That pursuit kept him abreast of the movements of the Nova Scotia pimps. He continued to share information with Dave Perry and he and John Elliott continued to work with informants and prostitutes as they gathered information on the pimps working the Halifax area. There was still no solid bond linking police investigators in the three cities favored by Manning Greer but a strong bond was developing between two of them. Dave Perry continued to watch for Nova Scotia pimps on his turf and he continued to share that information with Sullivan. The Nova Scotia Mountie was beginning to believe Kimberly McAndrew might be dead, it had been two years since she vanished and he was loosing hope. His latest theory was that she had been abducted by pimps but that when media reports revealed the missing girl was a police officer's daughter she was killed because the pimps didn't want that kind of girl in their stables—she would be too much of a risk. That theory strengthened Sullivan's resolve to go after the pimps. He was patient and he was willing to wait and watch and when the time came he would be ready to jump.

Manning Greer did not know who Kimberly McAndrew was, or that her disappearance two years earlier had set of a series of events that was leading an angry and dedicated young police officer closer to the Big Man. The next morning, Greer visited his mother for a few hours before going to collect his property and leave for Montreal.

Lori accompanied them on the flight, and within hours Taunya was back on the stroll with Lori and Teri, who had become Slugger's main girl.

The mid-August weather was almost sultry, and business was booming; Taunya did well for her man that night, and felt safe in the company of her two friends. The Big Man wasn't impressed; he didn't trust Taunya, and let her know that she'd be punished if she even contemplated ripping him off. He had no reason to worry. Taunya was changing, fast; that moment of acceptance she'd felt back in North Preston had been cathartic for the teenager, who was no longer inclined to retreat within herself in cowed terror. Instead, Taunya decided to try some guerrilla action in an effort to win Greer's approval and increase her nightly take. She would rob some of her dates. Her first target was a drunk, who wandered onto the stroll late one night; Taunya walked up to him, put her arm around his waist, and started sweet-talking him, then ran her hand up and down his chest and grabbed him by the buttocks when he made a move to stagger away. The attention was so enjoyable that he didn't even notice when she pulled the wallet out of his back pocket. As he lurched off down the street, Taunya ducked into the washroom at Harvey's. Phew! She'd made just over one hundred dollars with almost no effort.

Back at the Big Man's apartment that night, she described her exploit; Greer liked what he heard, but warned her to be careful; drunks were a sensible choice, and she should stick with them. Greer was pleased and to celebrate he took Taunya to bed with him. For the first time, the teenager understood the full meaning of the term "main girl"—she was disgusted by the prospect, but she did everything he asked, without protest. His only criticism, and it was a serious one, concerned the flower tattoo on her breast; more to the point, the Sweet Lou monogram above it. His comment was delivered with a quiet venom that was even more menacing than an explosive rage would have been: "Get that fixed. If I see that bitch's name on my woman again, I'll kill you and him. I want my name there, 'cause you're my property and no-one else's." Taunya had become almost inured to Greer's death threats, made daily and for little or no reason, and then forgotten. This was different; she knew instinctively that he really *could* kill her if she didn't have the tattoo altered. Maybe she'd ask Greer, in a day or two, whether she could just get Sweet Lou's name removed, then get a banner or something for the spot above the flower; she certainly didn't want another name on her chest—especially not Greer's.

Her revulsion for the Big Man didn't prevent her from keeping up her efforts to make him happy: she was learning the survival skills necessary for a girl in The Game—which she had all but given up any notion of leaving. The fact was, she had to constantly be thinking of ways to please her man, or she'd be beaten. Greer had "only" hit her a couple of times since they returned from Halifax, but she believed the next blow was always poised just over her head; the only time Taunya could relax was when Manning Greer was happy—not just with her, but with everyone else—and that was rare. The Big Man's anger was legendary, and more often than not would be aimed at the nearest target, not necessarily the person responsible. If she had no other recourse, Taunya could always take refuge on the stroll. What Taunya should have feared, sex with strange men in strange places, she looked forward to as her only relief from the stress of life with Manning Greer. She began to look forward to going to work: Greer rarely showed up on the stroll, preferring to have Eddy or Slugger collect her money, or, more and more, have her bring it home herself—a test, Taunya thought, and vowed to pass. Most of all, there was the companionship of her friends Teri and Lori.

Taunya and the Big Man

The living arrangements in Montreal had changed since Taunya first arrived on the scene. Eddy and Slugger had given up their dingy apartment and now lived in a rented home with the Big Man. Greer had been sharing the home with Lynn but when she disappeared he told his two closest associates to move their girls into that one spot with him. It wasn't that Greer wanted company. He had decided the group should remain together until the problems with the Jamaicans were sorted out.

Taunya and Teri were especially close, and not just because they lived together; they had begun this journey together, and together they would endure its potholes and pitfalls. At the end of the night Taunya and Teri would shower or bathe together back at the house. It was their only opportunity to talk about their problems or gossip about Slugger and the Big Man, something they couldn't do on the stroll, lest they be overheard by a girl looking for the chance to gain favor with her man through such information.

In the confines of their shared bath they had created new street names for their pimps. Greer was the Big Mouth, Slugger was Slime Ball and Eddy was Shit Head. They laughed about it in the bathroom but were smart enough to leave it there.

There was a good deal of camaraderie on the stroll, despite the threat of informants; Taunya, Teri, and Lori always found time to share a smoke and talk for a few minutes.

Soon the trio became a quartet—Eddy had found a new girl, Gizelle Vachon, a seventeen-year-old Montrealer whom he had spotted near the stroll one evening. The slight blonde looked a bit lost, kind of frightened—just the air of uncertainty that makes a pimp sit up and take notice. He walked away from his car and started chatting her up, telling her she was "real hot" and that he'd love to be her man. Gizelle's averted gaze and blushing cheeks were Eddy's cue to keep going; he'd been in The Game for close to twenty years, longer than Greer or Slugger and long enough to recognize the diffidence that characterized an ideal recruit. Had she told him to fuck off, or looked around for assistance—or ignored him—Eddy would have backed away immediately. As it was, Eddy took only a half-hour to play his target, sympathizing with her complaints about an overbearing mother and father who forced her to meet an eight-thirty curfew, even on weekends. Usually he took girls who had already been turned out by a brother or cousin back home, but it was good to know he hadn't lost his touch—nor did his new look do any harm, he flattered himself, running a hand through his now-tamed curls and glancing down at the heavy gold jewelry around his neck and on his fingers.

Gizelle noticed, too—and she noticed the fine clothes, and she especially noticed the gleaming blue Cadillac whose passenger door he gallantly held open for her. Gizelle entered the car after Eddy invited her to join him for a burger. Before she had finished eating, she was hooked.

Eddy played up the image of a rich, successful businessman, describing his trips he made to Toronto, Vancouver, and Florida to a fascinated Gizelle, who didn't even ask what business he was in; just confided that she had always dreamed of seeing the world but still wasn't sure what she would do when she finished school. She hated her classes, she said, and wasn't doing very well; that didn't come as a surprise to Eddy. Gizelle seemed to be a very simple girl—simple and sweet, exactly what Eddy was looking for. He tried another test, flashing his wallet when he paid for the food, and smiled at the wide-eyed expression of the little blonde. This was gonna be a piece of cake.

Finally, Eddy told Gizelle what he did for a living—that he was a player in the prostitution game. Eddy talked about prostitution the way any salesman would talk about his product: this was a huge international business, and he was the man to see if Gizelle wanted to get in on the profits. He told her he and his partners were going to Toronto in a few days; she was welcome to come along if she was interested in the opportunity. He did not explain that her job would be to work herself to exhaustion every night, put herself in mortal danger, risk arrest or disease, and give him every cent of her earnings, in exchange for which he *might* decide not to beat her.

Gizelle didn't even hesitate: she was going to see the world, and this fast-talking stranger was her ticket. Gizelle Vachon was in the family—just like that.

Taunya, Teri, and Lori liked Gizelle, but quickly realized they would have to constantly remind her of the rules, or she wouldn't survive. This girl not only missed the point on most of the niceties of the stroll, but was also exceptionally nervous, afraid of everyone and everything. That made her ideal for Eddy—she always obeyed him—but the other girls knew she had to be more aggressive, projecting her own aura of danger, if she was going to avoid being victimized by dates.

The stress of the four girls' lives lifted considerably in late August, when the Big Man, Slugger, and Eddy took off for Toronto, leaving them behind to work in the Montreal stroll. For Taunya, this was a chance to enjoy what freedom she could, even though she still had to work the stroll. If anyone had suggested this was also an opportunity to escape The Game, she would have shrugged as she recalled her most recent attempt to go home. At least right now she didn't have Manning Greer to contend with and besides, she had a date with "Mr. Rogers," her favorite regular client; indeed, the favorite of every girl on the stroll. The prostitutes had given him that nickname because they said he brought sunshine to the neighborhood every time he dropped by. When his big red car pulled up to the curb, there would be a chorus of voices: "My turn, Mr. Rogers! My turn!" Invariably he chose Taunya, though, if she was available; she was prettier than the others and usually drew more attention on the stroll.

The allure of Mr. Rogers was what he liked to do on dates: he paid top dollar for, quite literally, the pleasure of their company. No sex when Mr. Rogers called; just pleasant conversation in a relaxed atmosphere. Sometimes he would drive around for an hour or so and chat with a girl; or they'd go to a café or restaurant for some dinner. This time, he took Taunya to a hotel and rubbed her feet until she fell asleep. She awoke hours later to find him sleeping at her side, still fully dressed; later, he told her that she looked like she needed the rest. Back on St. Catherine Street, he paid her three hundred dollars— a very expensive nap, Taunya smiled to herself. She often wondered about the life of this slim, well-dressed white-haired man, still extremely attractive despite his age, which had to be near seventy. The prevailing theory was that he was a university professor and a widower, but nobody knew for sure. The girls just knew that he brought a rare light into blighted young lives.

The freedom Teri and Taunya had enjoyed was short-lived, however; Greer phoned four days after leaving Toronto and told Taunya she and Teri were to join their pimps the next day. Gizelle had flown out the day before, and Lori was staying in Montreal with her pimp. Lori worked for a player who rarely went to Toronto, claiming he didn't like the smell of that city. When they said good bye the morning before Taunya and Teri left it was their last good bye. Years later Taunya remembered, "Lori was pretty cool about it. She wanted to come but was okay with staying. As far as I know she's still working there. I haven't seen her since."

The trip to Toronto had been arranged by Greer. The Big Man was as familiar with flight schedules as a commuter would be with a bus schedule: Taunya and Teri were to show up at the airport at 2 P.M., and he would be waiting for them when the flight arrived in Toronto. He had one other bit of information for her just before he hung up: "If you don't have that tattoo changed yet, I'll have to kill you when you get here."

Taunya hung up and told Teri she was going to a tattoo parlor. There, she had Sweet Lou's name covered in a spiraling red ribbon, on which the artist inscribed "Big Man's Woman." It would still be bandaged when she arrived in Toronto, but Taunya knew it would satisfy Greer. She had forgotten her intention never again to have a pimp's name cut into her flesh.

Part Four:
From the Brink of Death

In the spring of 1992, Detective Dave Perry of the Metro Toronto Police Force was honing in on the Scotians with increasing intensity. As a member of the Toronto Juvenile Task Force since its inception in the mid 1980s, Perry was deeply committed to tracking down and bringing to justice the pimps who were luring, and in some cases, forcing, juveniles into prostitution. Like the other officers on the new police unit, Perry learned early how violent the sex trade really was. Within months of its formation members of the Juvenile Task Force had interviewed countless young girls whose horror stories were strikingly similar. The girls told Perry and his fellow officers of being wined and dined and promised love only to be turned out into the streets and savagely beaten if they tried to break away. More than one teenage girl came to Perry for help after being whipped or burned; some had even been thrown from moving cars. Perry learned that life on the street was no life at all; it was a prelude to an early violent death. By 1989, when he first became aware of the growing presence of the Scotians, and of Manning Greer, on the streets of downtown Toronto, Perry and his task force colleagues were already experiencing some success in persuading girls to turn away from The Game— and turn on the men who tormented and exploited them. That success was slow in coming but by that time the JTF—as the girls on the street called the task force—had a well-earned reputation. The JTF was the only real way off the street. That reputation was earned one case at a time. Word spread quickly and quietly on Toronto's prostitution strolls. Girls who said they were through with The Game and were ready to talk to the special task force disappeared from the street. Quite often their pimps disappeared soon after, having been arrested by JTF officers. The Toronto force adopted the same philosophy used in Vancouver where the Pimp Program was launched in

1988. The philosophy was simple, but differed dramatically from that adopted by the morality squads that policed prostitution strolls. The JTF officers did not consider prostitutes criminals. They were the victims of crime and the officers set out to help them, not arrest them. That simple philosophy earned JTF members the respect, and in some cases outright admiration, of the young girls they were trying to save.

Perry knew the task force had a long way to go before he could confidently say his city was rid of the menace that was destroying young lives; and he was particularly determined to target the violent Nova Scotians, who ignored the law with an arrogance that became a point of particular frustration. These men confidently conducted their dirty business in the knowledge that the girls they controlled would never betray them; Greer's family operated on the principle that the police sought out prostitutes, not pimps—and the prostitutes who worked for them had been so horrendously abused, physically and psychologically, that they would never rat on their overlords.

For a while, this was true. The work of the Toronto and Vancouver task forces were affecting the approach of the justice system to juvenile prostitution, and the attitudes of the young people being drawn into this netherworld. The Vancouver experience shows clearly how this change was taking hold. From 1981 to 1987 Vancouver police laid only 12 pimping related charges against only a handful of pimps. In 1989, a year after the Pimp Program kicked into high gear, 41 people were charged with a total of 104 pimping offenses. The days of free reign for pimps were coming to an end.

Dave Perry first learned of Manning Greer from a young Toronto prostitute he had befriended. The girl was not ready to leave The Game but she had become a valuable source of information for the officer. The girl told him about the Nova Scotia pimps and how they treated their girls, beating them for little or no reason. Perry did not like the sound of that and he decided these were the pimps he would target. The goal was admirable but proved difficult to achieve. It had been more than three years since he heard that first story of wanton abuse and he had heard many since, but he had yet to convince a girl working for the Scotians to give him a statement that would help put their pimp behind bars. By 1992 Perry began to believe his luck would change. He had a new advantage in his relationship with Constable Brad Sullivan in Halifax. The relationship had begun two years earlier and Perry had still not nailed one Nova Scotia pimp, but, like Sullivan, Dave Perry was stubborn and patient. He knew having a set of trained eyes in the Scotians own backyard would pay dividends eventually.

Perry was especially concerned about the scope of the Scotians' influence on prostitution in Toronto, and stepped up his daily conversations with the prostitutes whose trust he had earned after years of conversations over coffee and a smoke in downtown donut shops. By the beginning of the 1990s, these contacts were all saying the same thing: Nova Scotian pimps and Nova Scotian girls, most of them very young, pretty much owned the heart of the Toronto trade. Other players had moved to smaller strolls to avoid the Greer family's deadly serious approach to The Game. In short, what Perry was hearing, with alarming frequency, was that the Big Man and his family represented the most violent and dangerous pimping machine ever seen on the streets of Toronto. In a small way Dave Perry may have been responsible for the sudden strength of the Scotians on the Toronto strolls. The JTF had been successful in jailing some of Toronto's most vicious pimps; the very men who may have been tough enough to stop Manning Greer from taking over the streets of their city were in prison and could do nothing about his sudden rise to power.

As he observed the Big Man's ruthlessness and kept close touch with officers in Montreal and Halifax, Perry continued to chip away at the stubborn problem of juvenile prostitution, one pimp at a time. Early in 1992, he heard a remark from a pimp that gave him some hope for the task force's future. The man, whom Perry had arrested years before, was out of prison and attending a colleague's trial in Toronto provincial court. During a break, the detective chided him for returning to pimping. "Yeah, man, I'm back in The Game—but not here," the player corrected him. "I'm living out west now. Things are too tough around here with JTF all over my ass all the time." The pimp who made that comment was not part of the apparently fearless—and undoubtedly frightening—group of Maritimers who were muscling old-timers like this transplanted local off their turf. Still, his attitude encouraged Perry: if the task force could gain enough knowledge about the Scotians and their activities in the endless Toronto-Montreal-Halifax loop they traveled, with dozens of brutalized teenage girls in tow, they could make the transition from surveillance to arrest. The arrest had not yet come for several reasons; chief among them was a lack of luck. Perry knew Manning Greer was a criminal and knew he ran girls in Toronto. Greer did not live in Toronto though, and Perry often learned of his presence after he had come and gone. Without finding a girl to make a statement against him,

Perry had to catch Greer in the act and that was not going to happen. Street sources were pivotal to a police investigation, but a statement made by an informant will not stand up in court. Dave Perry had nothing more than second-hand information and rumor. Had Manning Greer made Toronto his base of operations Perry believed he would have been in jail by now. Perry also blamed senior police officers in Halifax. Until they accepted Brad Sullivan's proposal and began a crack-down there, young pimps would continue to learn the trade on Hollis Street and then ply it in his city. Perry resented that but knew he was powerless to change it.

Month by month, Perry tracked Manning Greer and his cohorts, staying in close touch with Halifax's Brad Sullivan. That information was valuable, but it too was piecemeal. It was important to know how often the Scotians moved from city to city and to get a sense of how big their operation was, but it was not enough to make an arrest. Perry had derived a little satisfaction from a story he picked up early in the summer when he asked a girl about the activities of the Scotians. The girl told him Manning Greer had been beaten outside a Montreal club and was now in a turf war with some Jamaican pimps. Maybe the Jamaicans could do what the police could not, get Greer out of The Game. As summer gripped Toronto in a muggy haze, the street trade reached fever pitch; more girls from the east coast appeared on the steamy Church Street stroll—and Dave Perry watched and waited for his chance to tackle the Big Man, and waited for that thing all police officers long for—a little luck.

That luck came on September 15 when Perry got a call from Sullivan. The Halifax police officer had received a call from a woman named Debbie Howard—a frantic call, he said; there was a seventeen-year-old daughter who'd gone missing, and maybe she was in Toronto, and possibly she had become involved in prostitution. All very speculative, Sullivan said, but this woman sounded genuinely frightened. She talked about seeing marks on her daughter's neck that looked like the result of an assault, and she described the defiant girl's determination to leave for Toronto with her new friend, whom Mrs. Howard felt certain was a prostitute. The teenager had been away for just over a week.

"Do you think it's the Scotians she's gotten mixed up with?" asked Sullivan. "Anyone new on the street that you know of?"

"No, but it's very possible," Perry said.

"Well, I don't even know if she's in The Game for sure—her mom gave me a picture, and she doesn't look familiar. I'll try and circulate it on Hollis, see if any of the girls recognize her."

"Why don't you send me a copy over the wire," Perry said. "We'll try to keep an eye out for her." He paused for a moment.

"Dave?"

"Yeah, I was just thinking—"

"What?"

"Well, if it is the Scotians she's involved with, you know they're getting pretty spooked with all this turf-war stuff—the New York players comin' in here as well as Montreal, maybe—"

"Which means their girls take the brunt of it."

"Right, and they're not gentle types at the best of times," Perry said. "But maybe we can get to her—and maybe get to them, too."

"Gotta be one of these girls who just won't take it anymore, decides to open up and nail them."

"I sure hope so, for your runaway's sake. Or could be she'll lead us to them. What was her name again?"

"Stacey Jackson."

"Jackson?"

"Yeah, the parents are divorced," said Sullivan. "Tough background, though the mother seems truly concerned. She' been there—I mean, not on the street, but she said she could recognize abuse when she saw it. Her ex, I guess."

"Same old story."

I t was like old home week in Toronto that September in 1992. Stacey Jackson and Annie Mae Wilson arrived from Halifax on the sixth, and after an uneventful night on Church Street, returned to the apartment Smit and Peanut shared in the neighborhood around Maple Leaf Gardens in downtown Toronto. A few days later, the Montreal contingent arrived: Taunya Terriault and Teri MacDonald were told to change into their work clothes in the back of the rental van driven by Manning Greer. It was the middle of the afternoon and Taunya knew Greer wasn't about to take her to the stroll but she complied. She did not want to start a fight. Greer was behaving oddly, he seemed agitated and she knew that could mean trouble for her. The Big Man had obscured several of the windows with green plastic garbage bags; so no one could see who was inside, he was definitely on edge, even irritable with his cousins Eddy and Slugger. The girls knew better than to pry; instead, after they had checked into the downtown hotel, Taunya and Teri took a deck of cards and started a game. "I've got things to do," Greer said, rather mysteriously. "You be ready to go to work in a couple of hours." Taunya was ready to go anyway, he had told her to dress in the van, but she didn't bother to point that out.

What the girls didn't know was that all the intrigue—the sudden call to Toronto, the covered van windows—stemmed from the Big Man's continuing preoccupation with the Jamaican pimps from New York and their encroachment on Scotian territory. Greer was certain that High T., Sweet Lou, and the other American players who had been giving him trouble in Montreal had plans to make a move on his Toronto turf as well. That was why he, Eddy, and Slugger had made the trip to Ontario—they could check on their stroll and let their aggressive, intimidating presence be felt. At the same time, the Big Man wanted to keep a close watch on the family's main girls (and the new acquisition), so he wouldn't be humiliated again as he had when Taunya took up with Sweet Low, or, more recently, when Lynn Buchanan disappeared—into the arms of one of the Jamaicans, Greer was certain. While Taunya and Teri played cards Manning Greer cruised around Toronto considering his options. He went to the apartment where Peanut and Smit were staying and told them to

Three friends work the Scotian stroll in Toronto.
[Print from ATV video tape]

keep an eye out for any sign of Lynn or any sign of Sweet Lou and his crowd.

Slugger, with Gizelle in tow, arrived at the hotel in the early evening to pick up Teri and Taunya. Teri's pimp dropped the three girls off on Church Street. Teri immediately began waving to an attractive young woman who was just returning from a fast-food joint with a couple of cups of pop: "Look, it's Annie Mae!" she exclaimed. "She's from Halifax too; let's check out how she's doing." They soon met Stacey, who had just returned to the stroll from a date and gratefully accepted the cold drink, chatting happily with her compatriots.

From then on, the four Nova Scotia girls and the shy young Quebecois were inseparable—at least, while on the stroll, since their opportunities to socialize were severely limited. A day off was almost unheard of, and the girls weren't encouraged to visit each other at their pimps' apartments or hotels. By the weekend of the fourteenth, three more Halifax girls joined the east coast clique—two of them, Amber Borowski and Sheri Fagan, had served the Scotians for three years, the last two of those spent working together. Although the eighteen-year-olds functioned as a team, the two young women differed in many ways. Amber, the single mother of a daughter six months old, had a hefty, muscular physique; while her partner was so thin and frail looking that she seemed no more than a child. Amber and Sheri had been on the street long enough and earned enough for the family that they were allowed to work unsupervised, traveling between Halifax, Montreal, Ottawa and Toronto; they had been on their way to Niagara Falls to catch the last of the tourist season when the Big Man told them to come to Toronto for a day or two to make some fast cash for him. The girls' busy traveling schedule required special arrangements—their earnings were deposited in the Big Man's bank account through automated teller machines; and then there was child care to consider, not a problem because the family provided baby-sitting for their teenage mothers, usually using bubble-gummers, for the "service." If Amber had been able to consider the kind of life her child was embarking upon, she might have noted a sad parallel with her own. At thirteen, after being shunted from group home to group home, she briefly found stability with devoted foster parents, Frank and Gloria Richardson, but by fifteen the quiet life in Dartmouth had become tedious for Amber. She fell in with a crowd connected to The Game and quickly joined in, opting for the streets when the Richardsons gave her a choice between their home and life as a prostitute.

Though Amber stayed in touch with her foster parents, she didn't return home.

The decision to become a full-time prostitute and leave her foster parents behind was the first major mistake Amber made in her life; the second was on that first night back in Toronto. Amber was chatting with Annie Mae when a large white car slowed at the curb. She walked over and leaned into the window to see what the driver was shopping for. At first her street sense told her to back away, there were

Headed for work in Toronto. [Print from ATV video tape]

two men, not one, in the big car. She relaxed when the man on the passenger side announced, "We're looking for a couple of girls who know how to party." Two guys, two girls, that wasn't unusual, so Amber motioned for Sheri to join her at the curb. The two men sized them up and appeared to be pleased with the contrast offered by the heavy set Amber and her delicately thin companion. "Jump in." Before opening the rear door of the car Amber wanted to make sure the men knew what they were buying. "Two of us means two hundred dollars an hour." She looked at the passenger who smiled, "No problem, get in."

The two men drove to a strip mall just north of the city and on the way announced they were real estate agents who had just closed a major deal. It took almost thirty minutes to get to the mall and Amber smiled in the back seat as she calculated the drive to and from this party would cost these men two hundred dollars and so far nothing had happened. The "party" the men talked about was no party at all, at least there was no crowd celebrating the "big deal" the men bragged about. Inside the office the realtors let the girls know what they wanted and it wasn't sex. They opened a brown paper bag and spilled its contents on a desk. It was a cluster of tiny white rocks of crack cocaine. The girls watched as one of the men took the ink refill from a pen and placed the hollowed out tip over the flame of a disposable lighter. He inserted the heated pen into the side of a small plastic shampoo bottle and placed some tin foil over the top. The foil had small holes in it and the gerry rigged crack pipe was ready. Amber looked at Sheri and shrugged, why not? The girls would never have smoked crack if another girl was present but they trusted each other and had even developed the habit of skimming a little money from the Big man when they were on the road. A party tax they called it. The four spent a night smoking crack and drinking tequila, the drug giving them a high like neither had ever experienced. In the morning the men paid them for the time spent partying and gave them cab fare to return to their hotel.

Back at the hotel they began to worry about becoming addicted. They knew girls who had become dependent on crack after trying it only once. "We better get out of town for a while," Amber told her partner. "Yeah, should be easy pickings in Niagara Falls," Sheri said. The Big Man was more than pleased with the money they'd earned in that one night in Toronto and agreed they could move on. If he had known about the party, they would have been in big trouble; Clara Ferguson's episode with her enforcer, Bullet, was just a sample.

For Taunya, Stacey, and the other Scotian girls who stayed behind in Toronto, the atmosphere surrounding their pimps was more than a little stressful, as the Scotians continued to indulge in their paranoia about their Jamaican rivals' supposed intention of scooping their girls right off the stroll, turning them out in New York, then returning to Canada to parade them on territory that was once Manning Greer's domain. There was nothing to indicate that the Jamaicans had any plan to raid the Scotians, but the more Manning Greer thought about it the more he was convinced the trouble with that New York crew was just beginning. One night, while all the Nova Scotia girls except for Taunya and Teri were with clients, Eddy and Slugger pulled up to the curb on Church Street; as the girls watched in shock, Eddy jumped out of the van with a gun in his hand. He looked up and down the sidewalk, gestured for the girls to get in, then told Slugger to "drive, man!" Twice, as they careened around downtown streets for a half-hour or so, he had his brother stop the vehicle, then stepped out and stood by the side of the road, brandishing his gun. Finally the girls were taken back to the stroll. It was almost as if the pimps were warning their rivals that the Scotians had not forgotten the Halifax turf war of 1989 and were perfectly willing to heat things up again, if they had to.

Indeed, many Scotian players, minor and major, nostalgically recalled the rout of the Jamaicans and looked forward either to having another crack at them—or getting in on the act, if they'd been unlucky enough to miss out on the première. Comers like Stacey's man Smit and bigger players such as Eddy all wanted to prove their loyalty and usefulness to Greer; as well, they were feeling the pressure of the Big Man's anxiety—and that made them as jumpy as he. As usual, it was the girls who bore the brunt of their nerves. The maltreatment began that first week in Toronto, and none of the teenagers under Scotian dominance would be neglected by the pimps' paranoia-driven violence. The only question: would any of them survive?

Stacey's pimp, eager to increase his profit margin and his level of respect, decided to add a new girl to his stable of one. Glenna Lombardy had chosen Smit and he took her to the apartment. It was an indication of a startling change in Stacey's attitude towards prostitution that she rejected Smit's request for her to show Glenna the ropes that night—she wasn't about to share her man with some newcomer. From tearful recruit who only wanted to go home to a square life, to hard-eyed hooker with a baleful glance at new talent: the transformation startled even Annie Mae, who tried to explain that it was a compliment for Stacey to be asked to look after Glenna. As for Smit, he was singularly unimpressed by his main girl's attitude; when Stacey retorted that it wasn't her job to baby-sit Glenna, he struck her across the face so hard she almost toppled, then backed her into a corner: "You are disrespecting me in front of these girls," he said. "Do you want me to beat you? Is that what you want, Stacey? I don't want to beat you, girl, but I told you before, you can't dis' me. I won't let you. Now you know I love you, girl, but I gotta be a man—do you understand that? Now, you are leaving and you are leaving now. Isn't that right, Stacey?" Nodding stiffly, the girl walked out of the apartment and stood in the hall to wait for Smit and Glenna. Her whole body was trembling, but if the reaction might once have signalled terror, it was now an expression of anger and frustration. Smit must have realized this, and evidently valued his main girl's income potential (and its implication for his status in The Game) enough to figure out a way to keep Glenna while placating Stacey. Hearing of Amber and

Sheri's sojourn in Niagara Falls, he sent the newcomer to join those experienced girls and get her training with them. Stacey had Smit all to herself again—but she was already starting to wonder whether she should choose another pimp, since all Smit seemed to do was lash out at her every time she spoke a word of protest.

While Stacey was considering her options in The Game her mother was fighting to get her back home and out of it for good. Stacey had been gone for a week but had only called once to check on her son, and Debbie Howard was certain her daughter had been drawn into the world of prostitution. Debbie assumed Kenny had her daughter in Toronto and she set out to find a way to reach him. Rachel, who was still living in Stacey's Highfield park apartment reluctantly gave her the phone number of Kenny's parents. She called but the man who answered would not help; he didn't know where Kenny was, or with whom, or when he would be home. The anxiety-filled mother could not, would not, sit at home and worry; she needed to do something. She jumped to her feet, grabbed her purse and car keys, and headed downtown to Hollis Street. The girls on the stroll were polite—one of the teenagers wistfully admitted wishing her own mother would come and get her. Some of them knew who Stacey was with, but they feared telling her anything that might get them in trouble with Smit or the other players in Toronto. As they spoke, a fiftyish businessman drove up to the curb and gestured to the girls; the frustrated mother saw a target for her anger and fear, and went after it with all her might: "You're nothing but a child molester!" she screamed at the would-be client. "Look at you with your briefcase and your nice suit—you've probably got a daughter at home yourself! How would you feel if you knew some pervert like you was dragging her onto the street? Go on, get out of here, you creep!" As his car pulled away briskly, Debbie Howard burst into tears and ran back to her own vehicle. She sat crying in the dark for a few minutes, then looked up to see a shiny sports car with tinted windows pull over in front of her. One of the girls came over and passed something to the driver; Mrs. Howard, convinced the man was a pimp, decided to follow him. At a fast-food restaurant on Kempt Road, across town in Halifax's industrial north end, she saw her chance to confront him; terrified but determined, she pulled in front of him and walked over to the car. The bored-looking young man rolled down his window and, looking straight ahead, told her in a monotone to move her car.

"Please, just give me a minute," Mrs. Howard said, introducing herself and explaining that she only wanted to get in touch with her daughter, to make sure she was all right. "I think she's with a pimp—er, I mean, a man named Kenny Sims, and I just thought you might—"

"I don't know what you're talking about." The voice was flat, implacable. "So just get that car our of the way now, lady. I gotta go." There was no point in arguing; Mrs. Howard moved her car and tried to figure out what to do next. After sitting in the restaurant parking lot for more than an hour, she drove home, phoned the Halifax police department, and asked to speak with an officer who specialized in prostitution. Redirected to the local RCMP detachment, she was told that the officer she should contact would be available next morning, and after a sleepless night—her husband was away at sea, so there wasn't even anyone to talk to— Mrs. Howard finally reached Constable Brad Sullivan. Reassured by his concern, and his promise to send Stacey's photo to the Toronto policeman he knew, she returned home feeling better than she had in days.

Dave Perry did take prompt action when Stacey's photograph landed on his desk at the Juvenile Task Force office in Toronto, circulating the image to his contacts on the downtown strolls. None of the girls recognized Stacey—or weren't saying if they did—but promised to keep an eye out for the pretty blonde teenager.

Unfortunately, Debbie Howard's actions to help her daughter would have met with a wall of resistance from an utterly transformed Stacey Jackson. If Dave Perry or Brad Sullivan had approached Stacey and offered to take her home, she would have refused. Everybody she knew, from her best friend, Annie Mae, to newer acquaintances like Amber, to the players and clients of The Game, was certain that police officers abused and robbed working girls and deliberately targeted black men as the likeliest suspect in any crime. The more deeply Stacey became involved in The Game, the more readily she believed even the vaguest stories of police brutality—no dates, names or places, but if her friends were telling it, well, it had to be true. The capper came when Annie Mae told her she'd been forced to give a cop a blow job in a police cruiser—again, no specifics, but that was enough to convince Stacey that all cops were scum.

She might have been better to question the increasingly nasty behavior of the pimps. Stacey and Annie Mae heard from several girls on the stroll that they had received severe beatings for minor infractions, and they were beginning to get nervous. Maybe a bit of a break would help, Annie Mae suggested to Stacey; here it was September fifteenth; they had been working every night for two weeks; and they deserved to have some fun. Each of them had made more than five hundred dollars that night, and there wouldn't be a problem if they went for a quick drink before returning home. The girls walked north on Yonge Street until they found an alternative music club—their clothes wouldn't raise too many eyebrows in a place that catered to the body-piercing crowd. Two drinks each and an hour of wild music; it was only one in the morning when Stacey and Annie Mae grabbed a taxi back to the apartment. Their men were in front of the TV, and barely looked up when the girls walked in—until Annie Mae tried joking with Peanut when he asked why she hadn't called him for a ride home instead of spending money on a cab. Annoyed at her light remark about his aggressive driving, he got up and walked over to her, his expression showing he was not amused. When he smelled liquor on her breath, Peanut grabbed her in a fury and threw her into the bedroom by the hair. Tears sprang to Stacey's eyes as she heard the enraged pimp slapping and kicking her friend, bellowing at her for wasting *his* money drinking.

"I think you get the point, Stacey," Smit said, calmly looking away from the TV set. "You should never do something like that. We need to know where you are; she knows better than that. I was going to give you a night off and maybe take you out on the town, and now you've ruined it." Stacey stood up without a word, went into the room she shared with Smit, and crawled into bed; a few moments later, he joined her, and, to Stacey's disgust, forced himself on her while Annie Mae could be clearly heard in the bathroom, crying as she tried to bathe her wounds. The incident strengthened Stacey's resolve to find a new man.

Leaving was also on the mind of Taunya Terriault and her young friends from Halifax and Montreal; they too were noticing the growing violence of Eddy, Slugger, and especially the Big Man, increasingly annoyed that he could not track down his former main girl. He knew Lynn once worked as an exotic dancer and favored a particular club in Toronto; so he took Taunya there to look for her—seeing him might scare Lynn away. On the way inside, Greer saw another Nova Scotia player; the young man, a seventeen-year-old who went by the street name Joystick. He had been in the bar watching the strippers but had not seen Lynn, so Taunya checked things out. She too found out nothing; back outside, her man was gone and she decided to wait for him in Joystick's car. They'd met at Teri's apartment in Halifax and could chat about home. When Greer got back, he demanded to know if she'd found anything about Lynn and, obviously suspicious, what she and Joystick had been talking about:

"Did he ask you how business was up here?"

"Yes."

"And what did you tell him?"

"I said it's great here, busier than Montreal, but the dates aren't as nice."

"Stupid fucking bitch. You never tell another man how my business is goin'. How the fuck do you know I don't owe him some money? Maybe I been tellin' him things are pretty slow and he's gotta wait for his money. Goddamn it, girl, you never talk about my business with anyone but me." He reached over and slid open the compartment beneath Taunya's seat, revealing the gun she had seen Eddy brandishing on the stroll; beside it lay Greer's latest toy, which looked like an electric razor but was a stun gun, designed to deliver electric shocks that could disable an attacker. Police forces in some American cities use them, and Greer had gotten hold of one on a recent visit to Buffalo. He ordered Taunya to hold out her arm. "You're not going to use that on me, are you?"

"Yes, I am—and if you move away, I'll do it again and again until you learn to keep your arm there for five seconds. You understand? Now keep your arm there." The fiery pain across her forearm was excruciating, and Taunya almost instantly pulled away; but she must have passed the test because Greer just glanced at the device and tossed it back in the drawer. "Now you get back in that car with him and tell him to drive you to the hotel," he said curtly. "And you don't say one word to him, you understand? I'm gonna follow and watch, so you let him know who's woman you are. Now go!"

Taunya did as she was told, and it didn't take long for the young pimp to realize she was ignoring him. "What's up? Why aren't you answering me?" he asked. "Taunya, what's going on?" Taunya felt ridiculous, but she didn't want to look behind them and see if Greer was watching, nor could she turn towards Joystick, so she hissed quietly: "He says I can't talk to you." Joystick was shocked. He wasn't in the Scotian inner circle, and he knew he was a minor player who spent as much time in the video arcades as on the stroll, but Joystick figured he was at least a nominal part of the family. He and the Big Man had even worked together on occasion and he figured Greer should know better that to think he would try to steal his main girl right out from under his nose.

"You've got to be kidding," he finally said. "What the fuck is his game? Man, this is stupid—forget it, Taunya. I'm sorry if I got you in trouble." She said nothing more for the rest of the drive. That night on the stroll, Taunya talked with Teri and Gizelle about running away, maybe to New York, where they could connect with Sweet Lou's family or maybe to Buffalo; they could freelance there. Around mid-night, they returned to the hotel—only chumps kept their girls work-ing all night, Greer had always insisted—and as Taunya and Teri took their regular nightly bath, they raised the issue again. They were too afraid of being overheard to flesh out a plan; like Stacey, they decided to play a waiting game—just try to avoid their pimps' unaccountable anger and see what ideas arose. Neither they nor Stacey once even entertained the notion of going home.

Approaching a date on the Scotian stroll. [Print from ATV video tape]

The night of September 14 was a particularly profitable one for Taunya, Teri, and Gizelle—twenty-five hundred dollars in total, in-cluding the three hundred Gizelle had charged for a "golden show-er"—a bizarre procedure in which a client masturbates while the prostitute urinates on him. Taunya's theory was that men who want-ed this and other services involving verbal or physical humiliation were managers, business owners, or other powerful people who need-ed to be abused to feel a sense of reality in their lives; she recalled one corporate executive in Montreal who paid her one hundred and fifty dollars an hour to scold him, then comfort him by holding him in her arms afterwards. As the three girls arrived at the hotel, still gig-gling over Taunya's story, they saw that Bullet was in the room—not a good sign—and their playful mood evaporated. Their pimps were grouped around one of the beds, and when Taunya peered past the Big Man's massive bulk she recognized Star Franklin, a prostitute of about fourteen who worked for a Toronto-based Jamaican pimp and thus was off-limits for even a conversation with one of the Scotian girls.

Eddy, seated in front of Star, was demanding that she answer him when he told her she had to choose him—or stop working. Infuriated at her stubborn silence, he barked: "You wanna call your man? Here, call the motherfucker! I'll deal with him!" With that, he snatched his cell phone from the bedside table and tossed it into Star's face, smashing her front teeth. Blood streamed from between her lips, and Eddy laughed hysterically as he wrenched the weeping girl's hands away from her mouth, then hauled her into the bathroom. The girls could hear him taunting his young victim, ordering her to look in the mirror and guess how much she'd be worth on the street now. Gizelle shook uncontrollably as she listened to the man who had flattered her into joining his "family business"; Taunya, patting the nervous girl's hand, warned her to keep quiet.

The next move was to take Star into the bedroom of the hotel suite, where Eddy, the Big Man, Slugger, and Bullet briefly conferred about how best to send a message to their rival that the Church Street stroll belonged to their family. Since she refused to join them, she would simply disappear: the sobbing teenager was thrown onto the bed, and Eddy shoved two large pillows against her head as she struggled wildly, terrified of being smothered. That was not the plan. Bullet drew his gun and slid it between the pillows to reduce the report, then prepared to fire. "Not here," Slugger suddenly intervened. "Too many people around, man—that guy in the lobby saw her come in with us. This is not a good place." The Big Man agreed. Star might have been destined to become a victim of his private turf war, but this would not be her night.

With Bullet back in town, the quarters were cramped and the Big Man had taken to sleeping with Taunya on a mattress on the floor— and, tonight, Star as well! One on the left, one on the right; within moments he was sound asleep. Not Taunya, though: appalled at the brutality, disgusted by Slugger's forced attentions on the loudly protesting Teri; frightened by the blank stare of the girl on the opposite side of the mattress, she waited until everyone else in the room was clearly asleep. Then she tilted her head towards the door to let Star know it was safe for her to slip away; at least, if she and her friends couldn't get away that night, she could help this girl escape— otherwise, Taunya was certain the teenager would lose her life come morning. Star seemed frozen on the other side of the mattress. Finally, she realized Star would not move because she was afraid Taunya was watching her. The young Nova Scotian pretended to fall asleep and listened as the rustling sounds proved her theory. Star quietly left the room when she believed Taunya was sleeping.

In the morning, the Big Man strode around the room, raging like a caged beast and accusing Taunya of letting Star escape; Taunya retorted that she'd simply slept right through the night, "just like you did." Greer apparently didn't care for her tone, because he lashed out with a backhand to her head, then glared at her while he got dressed, as if daring her to say anything more. Taunya stayed silent until he left with his three sidekicks; when they were gone, she heaved a sigh of relief and expressed the fervent hope that all four of them would be killed in a car accident or a gun battle. She and Teri then sat down to a game of cards and listened to their portable tape player, while Gizelle brooded in a corner, contemplating the nightmare her life had become. Eddy never hit her hard and only yelled at her occasionally, but after last night's terrorization of Star, she realized what he was capable of. She had to get away, somehow; and as they dealt each other hand after hand, Taunya and Teri were silently telling themselves the same. Soon enough, Teri articulated what they had all suspected from the scraps of conversation they'd overheard the night before: the four men had been planning to kill Star—Slugger had bragged about it to her while they were having sex; that's why she had objected so strenuously. Escape was no longer a late-night fantasy, they knew; it was a matter of life and death. Each of the girls realized, too, that they needed each other to flee these monsters who called themselves men.

On the morning after she had spoken to the RCMP's Brad Sullivan, the one parent of the Scotian girls who had become involved in the nightmare herself was determined to take further action. She'd heard nothing from the police, and her frustration level was mounting. Debbie decided to go to North Preston where Gordon had told her many of the pimps lived.

Once she had reached the small community on the outskirts of Dartmouth, Mrs. Howard parked her car and began going door-to-door, asking anyone and everyone who would talk to her if they knew anything about Stacey. Debbie Howard believed that just about every young man from North Preston was a parasite preying on teenage girls like her Stacey: had she known how small that minority was, she might have been initially relieved, but her worst fears—and more— would have been realized if she learned how very dangerous, and brutal, the Scotian minority was. As it turned out, the visit to North Preston was an eye-opener, not that Mrs. Howard found out anything about Stacey, but because she discovered that the community, like any other, contained more solid families leading average lives than it did gangs of monstrous pimps—that, indeed, the pimps themselves often came from good, hard-working families who had an equally negative view of her and other parents of young prostitutes as she did of them. As one woman bluntly and revealingly told her, "If more of you mothers would come out here and get your daughters, they wouldn't be getting the boys from here into all this foolishness," she said.

Debbie Howard was no further ahead in her search for Stacey, however, and she had no option but to go home and wait for word from the police. She couldn't sit still for long; again and again she tried to get a name—just a name—of one of the people her daughter might be with. Finally she returned to Rachel who told her Stacey was not with Kenny but with Peanut and Smit. With this new information, Debbie Howard formally filed a missing persons report at the Cole Harbour detachment of the RCMP; there, the constable who opened a file on Stacey decided to talk to one of the detachment's investigators—none other than John Elliott, the officer who had worked with Brad Sullivan on the 1990 fact-finding study of pimping in Halifax.

Elliott quickly contacted some of his informants on the Hollis Street stroll and began gathering some data on the two Scotian players; and he called his friend Sullivan, who had asked Debbie Howard on the night before to find out, if she could, who Stacey was with. Sullivan called Dave Perry again, passing on the valuable new information. The net was beginning to close around the Scotians: Perry did not know who Peanut and Smit were but he passed the information on to other members of his task force. For his part, Dave Perry was busy working with another worried mother of a teen who had disappeared in Halifax. Meanwhile, officers at the Cole Harbour RCMP promised Debbie Howard they would call when they had any news for her, and urged her to phone them if she heard from her daughter.

If Debbie Howard had seen her daughter through the afternoon of September 16, she would have had to agree that Stacey seemed as taken with the life as she was trapped in it—or perhaps it was that the excitement and occasional pleasures kept her trapped in it. That afternoon, Peanut and Smit decided to give their girls the carrot instead of the stick: two hundred dollars each for "some nice new 'ho clothes and maybe something to eat." As they browsed in clothing and record shops on Yonge Street south of College, Stacey and Annie Mae, in jeans and T-shirts with just a touch of make-up, looked more like kids from the suburbs than street-hardened prostitutes, but the image vanished when they headed for the seedier sex shops just off Yonge. There, they expertly picked through flashy fishnet stockings, body-hugging bustiers, and thigh-high vinyl boots; and if Stacey laughed a little too loudly or flaunted her tawdry finery a little too obviously while checking it out in the mirror, she certainly looked the part. "Can't wait to show these off for Smit," she confided to Annie Mae, who smiled knowingly in agreement. "Yeah, Stace, they really like the look of this kind of outfit—and a man that's turned on is a happy man, so flaunt it, girl!"

Flaunt it Stacey did when she and Annie Mae got back to the apartment; she teased and taunted Smit, trying on all her new finery and asking him suggestively which outfit he'd rather see her strip off. Smit usually enjoyed her flirtation, but tonight he was preoccupied with his new girl, Glenna, who'd just phoned from Niagara Falls in a rather befuddled state—Amber and Sheri kept disappearing, she said, and they'd be gone sometimes overnight without telling her what she should do.

Smit hung up shaking his head and remarking that he wasn't looking forward to a drive to the Fall just now, but that "stupid 'ho" would have to learn from someone reliable. He told Stacey she was the only person he could trust to do the job. Even this direct flattery wasn't enough for the still-defiant teenager, who immediately started to complain. Smit, true to form, seized Stacey and pushed her violently against the living room wall, then slapped her across the face and told her to shut up and get ready for work. Stacey obeyed, but inside she was fuming.

Across town in their hotel room, Taunya, Teri, and Gizelle were also dressing for work. It was Slugger who returned with the van to drive them to the stroll, and no sooner had he dropped them off than the usually quiet Gizelle brought up the idea of getting away; she confessed her fear of Eddy and her certainty, shared for some time by Teri and Taunya, that their pimps could well kill them. They settled on Taunya's plan to travel to Buffalo and try to contact Sweet Lou from there; they would ask him to take them to New York and never bring them back to Canada.

"But when can we go?" the nervous Gizelle asked; she didn't want to spend one more night with Eddy.

"Just as soon as we get some bucks together," Taunya answered. "So let's do it, girls."

The three young prostitutes hustled as never before, and within ninety minutes they had more than five hundred dollars—plenty to get them to Buffalo, where they could work the streets to collect enough for the rest of the trip. Taunya phoned a taxi company and asked for a driver to take them to Buffalo, or at least to the U.S. border if drivers weren't allowed to cross. Buffalo would not be a problem according to the dispatcher. Taunya ordered the cab, which arrived shortly; their bid for freedom was under way.

They didn't make it as far as Buffalo. In Niagara Falls, the girls discovered they had left their identification at the hotel, and they were pretty sure that in their provocative clothing, without I.D., they would never be able to get by the immigration officers. Instead of trying, they headed downtown to the busy prostitution stroll; first they'd recoup the cost of the cab ride, and then they'd figure out a way to get into the States next morning. What they didn't count on was running into someone they knew; as the girls stepped out of the cab, there were Amber and Sheri, waving at them with delight. Taunya's quick mind started concocting an explanation almost instantly, and as they approached the two other girls, she whispered to Teri and Gizelle, "just go along with whatever I say." She was already spinning her yarn before Amber and Sheri were within earshot, talking about the white guy in the van who picked them up on the stroll, saying he wanted their services for a party. "So we get inside, right? And that's when we see the two black guys in the back, and, like, we're goin' faster and faster, and Teri's, like, 'Where are you taking us?'" Teri just nodded, astonished by her friend's inventiveness and understanding perfectly that Taunya's tale would perfectly dovetail with Greer's belief that Jamaican pimps were continually trying to steal Scotian girls. "So these guys are trying to take us to Buffalo, right? But we haven't got any I.D. so they kick us out of the van, and I go, 'Well, what are we suppose to do now?' And they're, like, 'That's your problem, bitch.' Can you imagine those assholes?"

Taunya was wasting her breath; Amber and Sheri were too high to care about the compelling story. The two girls had been smoking crack every night since arriving in Niagara Falls—they'd been avoiding Glenna in the hopes that word of their habit wouldn't get back to the Big Man through Smit. If Taunya, Teri, and Gizelle had stuck to their plan—hustled for a few hours, then found a way either across the border or to another southwestern Ontario town—they would have been safe. The two older prostitutes probably wouldn't have remembered seeing them, and wouldn't have said anything about it anyway, since they were trying to stay clear of Greer. Now Amber felt compelled to help; doing nothing might get her and Sheri in even more trouble, in this situation. The five girls went to Amber and

Sheri's hotel where Amber called Greer's cell-phone number and told him the girls were with her. "Let me speak to Taunya," he said flatly, and Taunya repeated her tall tale. The Big Man had no comment on the story, just said she and the others should wait for one of the Scotians in the Niagara Falls area to pick them up and drive them back to Toronto that night. "Well, let's hope he believes us," Teri said as they waited in the lobby. "He's go to," Taunya said. "We've got to have another chance to get the fuck away from him."

Back in Toronto, Stacey was taking her chance with Joystick, who had just driven onto the stroll with his partner to check out the action. As every other girl on the street watched her bold move, the teenager calmly stepped out to the curb, motioned him over, and smiling alluringly, asked if she could get in the car. "You know what you're doing, girl?" Joystick looked as if he couldn't believe his luck. "Yeah, can I get in?" Stacey just didn't care what Smit thought; she just couldn't take his unpredictable behavior any longer. "Sure, get in—" They pulled away from the curb and negotiations began immediately—Stacey offered youth and beauty—but she only had $175 as a down payment towards the leaving fee. Joystick and his partner would have to provide the rest to Smit. Joystick would have accepted the money, but his colleague wanted more; they agreed that the eight hundred Stacey was confident of earning by the end of the night would be more than adequate—she would be coming home with him, Joystick assured her. Stacey returned to the stroll and, as Taunya, Teri, and Gizelle had done earlier, she began to hustle hard to buy her freedom from Smit. Annie Mae warned her friend that she was taking a big risk openly approaching the man that way, but Stacey wasn't worried. Smit had gone to Niagara Falls to find Glenna, and by the time he returned, she would be safely at Joystick's apartment; once he'd paid the leaving fee, Stacey would belong to him, and Smit would never dare to make a move on another man's property, no matter how angry he was. Besides, Joystick would protect her if Smit did try anything.

She was wrong on all counts. Neither she nor Annie Mae had noticed the older Nova Scotia prostitute watching with keen interest as Stacey got into Joystick's car. The twenty-three-year-old woman had been trying to persuade Smit to take her on, but he was balking; she didn't have many good years left, he figured, and as the young star of the Scotians, he wasn't about to make a move that detracted from his image as an up-and-comer. Well, here was her chance to earn some points with the elusive Smit; she reached his cell-phone number while he and Peanut were en route to Niagara Falls. "We gotta go back, man," Smit said, slamming his fist into the window so hard it rattled. "Stacey's giving play to another man." His partner immediately wheeled the car around and, tires squealing, they raced towards the city. It was a long enough drive for Smit to build up a real good head of steam over the betrayal—not only choosing another pimp, but that chump Joystick! The Big Man dis'd Joystick big time; he'd said so—only used him as an errand boy once in a while. How would it look for this video junkie to grab his main girl. It just wasn't going to happen. He'd get Stacey back, and teach her a lesson she would never forget.

Shortly before midnight, Peanut's car pulled up to the curb in front of a stunned and terrified Stacey, who looked around wildly for Joystick. He was nowhere to be seen, and she thought of running—but Smit was too fast for her. The enraged young pimp threw Stacey into the back seat of the car, and Peanut ordered Annie Mae into the front. She stared straight ahead as Smit demanded: "Who were you talking to?" This was Stacey's chance to confess, but she was too frightened. "no one," she replied. "I wasn't talking to anyone." Smit flew into a rage, swiveling in the seat and grasping her entire face in his huge, muscular hand. She could barely breathe as he pressed against her nose and mouth, lifting her up, then slamming her head into the window as if trying to break the glass. "You think I'm a chump!" he bellowed. "You think you gonna dis' me in front of everyone! You want the players to think Smit is some pussy they can whip and steal from! Not this man—no, woman—not this man!" On and on it went—the pounding, the ranting—until Smit suddenly stopped, and shoved the unresisting teenager towards the other side of the car; then he looked away from her and stared out the window, brooding. Everyone was silent; Stacey didn't even dare raise her hand to her head and find out if she was bleeding. She felt numb, and nauseated, and thought she would vomit, but as they neared the apartment building, a faint sense of hope began to set in: at least she had survived, and now she could go to sleep, maybe figure out what to do in the morning. If Stacey thought the beating was over, she was very wrong. It hadn't even started. Not for Stacey, and not for Taunya and her friends. As Peanut wheeled his car through the quiet streets of Toronto, the three thwarted young fugitives were being whisked eastward from Niagara Falls, back to face the wrath of the Big Man.

From the Brink of Death

No sooner had Smit and Stacey walked into the apartment when the enraged pimp let loose with a vicious blow to the teenager's face. In a low angry voice, he ordered her to get into the bedroom; then, without another word, he strode to a closet, took out a wire coathanger, and began unwinding it, working slowly and with great determination until all the kinks had been straightened out. He bent the length of wire in the middle, pulling the ends together to fashion a loop about a half-metre long. Annie Mae sat silently on the sofa and watched, digging her nails into her palm. She'd seen other pimps use the wire whip on girls before—and she couldn't believe this was going to happen to Stacey, at the hands of the guy who used to enjoy looking after the prostitutes' babies. There was nothing she could do to help, if she said anything, Peanut would go after her, too.

The angry pimp walked into the bedroom and ordered Stacey to stand; she did not notice the weapon until Smit raised it above his head.

The first blow struck Stacey across the front of her legs just above the knee. The seventeen year old screamed in agony and fell to the floor. Smit raised the whip and struck Stacey a second time on the side of her now folded legs. She screamed again and told him to stop it.

Smit began to preach and lecture as he raised and lowered the coat hanger turned whip. He kept repeating he was not a chump that Stacey could not disrespect him that she owed him an apology. Smit swung the wire whip so hard it whistled in the air as it moved toward Stacey. In an effort to stop the pain in her legs Stacey raised her arms but the whip struck them with the same violent force until she no longer had the strength to keep them raised. Stacey began to separate from what was happening. Smit had struck her more than twenty times. He was still swinging the whip but Stacey could no longer feel the blows. A dangerous numbness had set in all over her body. She could see that the wire was hitting but it felt as though her body was falling to sleep and the impact just moved her. It didn't hurt any more. Stacey could see Annie Mae on the couch and wondered if she had phoned to warn Smit. Stacey could still hear Smit preaching but she stopped listening to his words. Her mind was filled with a wild laughter and she couldn't understand where it was coming from. Stacey struggled to focus her thoughts on the laughter and to ignore the torturous abuse. Suddenly she realized she was not losing her mind; there was real laughter in the room. Stacey could see Peanut lying on the bedroom floor laughing, she could hear his laughs above everything in her mind and she could not understand why he was laughing. Stacey did not understand that Peanut was laughing at what was happening to her, the possibility of that kind of cruel sickness did not even enter her mind.

As he laughed, Peanut kept encouraging Smit and telling him to show her who the man was.

"Be the man, yea you be the man."

Smit continued the beating much longer than he should have or would have had Peanut not reacted in that way. Smit wanted to be sure Peanut repeated the story of how he beat the whore who disrespected him. Smit was certain the story would reach Manning Greer and he kept whipping Stacey in the hope of impressing Greer. Long after Stacey's arms and legs had grown numb and she turned her back into the blows, Smit grew tired and stopped swinging his whip. He picked Stacey up from her position on the floor and carried her into the washroom. Stacey was not responding to anything Smit said so he decided to bring her out of shock. Smit reached in and turned on the shower and then he dumped Stacey into the tub beneath the pounding hot water.

Smit walked out of the bathroom and into the kitchen area of the apartment. The workout had apparently given him an appetite.

Stacey had remained silent as Smit carried her across the bedroom she simply stared over at Annie Mae, a distant look in her eyes. The pain had yet to return and her body felt like it belonged to someone else. She could feel the movement as he lifted her and guided her toward the tub but is was as though her body was not hers at all.

When Smit lowered Stacey beneath the flowing water that sensation changed in an instant. All of the pain and more raced through Stacey's legs as soon as they hit the water. Her sudden scream caused Annie Mae to run to her friend's aid. Annie Mae quickly turned off the shower and helped Stacey sit on the edge of the tub. Stacey looked at her arms and legs; the pressure building beneath the skin and the pain it caused was unbearable. She was certain her legs were going to explode. Stacey began to bawl hysterically. She could not catch her breath, she could not free herself from the agony and she could not begin to tell Annie Mae how the water had hurt her more than the whipping.

Annie Mae began to cry as she looked at Stacey's legs. They were a mass of bluish red mush with bleeding welts sticking out through tears in her fish net stockings.

She ran to the kitchen and grabbed a pair of scissors, she wanted to cut the stockings from Stacey's legs, she was afraid pulling them off would add to her friend's agony.

When Annie Mae cut the stockings off, what she saw made her think she was cutting open an over-stuffed sausage. The welts began to expand and Stacey's legs were a grotesque mass of bloodied flesh.

"Smit you bastard, get in here and see what you did to this girl. Goddamn it Smit we gotta take her to a hospital."

Annie Mae had forgotten herself in her anger and cursed the pimp for his abusive behavior. Smit was too tired to care and appeared not even to notice her anger as he walked into the bathroom and looked at Stacey's bloodied legs. Smit said she wouldn't need a hospital; the open whip didn't cut that deeply. It was one of the reasons the pimps liked that weapon. It caused a great deal of pain but no permanent damage to the girl. Pimps like to teach a girl a lesson. They do not like to decrease her value in the street by filling her with scars. Smit hadn't realized he used the whip with far too much force. He should have made it a point to hit Stacey where she was protected by clothing; her stocking covered legs might as well have been naked.

When Smit looked at Stacey's face his defiant indifference appeared to melt away. The violent pimp began to weep, as though what he had done finally began to sink in. He knelt in front of Stacey crying and begging her for forgiveness. Annie Mae was sickened by the sight and walked away from the couple. Stacey began to feel anger along with all of that pain and she cursed him, swearing she would never forgive him.

Smit picked Stacey up and carried her to the bed telling her he would make love to her to prove how he felt. Stacey cried at the thought and told him to leave her alone that she was in too much pain. Again there was a change in Smit's behavior. In an instant he was again the angry pimp.

"I'm getting mine tonight girl and don't you tell me different."

"You're not getting anything, I can't move, look what you did to me."

Smit stood beside the bed and looked at the bloody cuts on Stacey's body and realized there was no way to touch her that wouldn't hurt. The pimp walked up to the head of the bed near Stacey's face where he forced her to perform oral sex on him. When it was over Stacey was physically and mentally defeated; she sobbed and begged Smit to let her die. She cried herself to sleep, repeating her plea to die over and over until it was an unintelligible mumble and she was asleep.

Stacey Jackson spent a painful night of fitful sleep after being whipped by Smit. Across the city at the hotel, Taunya, Teri and Gizelle were subjected to a different level of abuse at the hands of The Big Man. It was almost three in the morning when the three young girls returned from their aborted escape attempt. When they stepped into the room Manning Greer ordered Taunya to go with him to the washroom. Greer closed the door behind her and then half sat, half stood with most of his weight resting on the vanity sink. Greer looked at himself in the mirror; he then turned to Taunya.

"I don't see no fool in that mirror, do you?"

Taunya knew she was in trouble. Greer stretched his arm out toward the mirror, his long arms and large body filled the room making it impossible for Taunya to escape his reach. Greer pulled Taunya close to him; he pushed her shoulders against the wall opposite the sink.

"Now tell me what happened and don't lie."

Taunya started her story and Greer reached up and placed his palm on her forehead and then with a sudden fury pushed her head into the wall.

"Let's start again, now what happened."

Taunya tried her best to be convincing and again started her lie. Greer repeated his reaction, knocking her head against the wall with an even more powerful shove.

After three more blows to the head Taunya confessed and told Greer the truth.

Greer opened the door and called Teri into the bathroom. He would not violate the rule that prevented him from beating another man's woman. He could have asked Slugger to help but he had other plans.

"Teri I want the truth, what were you doing in Niagara Falls?"

Teri looked at Taunya and began to repeat the lie the girls had agreed upon. Greer reached over and smashed Taunya's head against the wall again, this time with a force that caused her knees to weaken but Greer would not let her fall. Teri tried the lie again but after watching Taunya's head strike the wall she could lie no more; she confessed. Greer told her to get Gizelle and to shut her mouth while he talked with the third girl.

Gizelle had her right index finger wrapped tightly in her blonde curls; her other hand was nervously jamming her hair into her mouth, and her eyes were wild with fear. She did not know what was happening but she did not like being summoned by the Big Man.

Greer stared at the nervous young blonde and told her he wanted the truth and once again asked his question. Gizelle did not have the same loyalty to Taunya and she had a much more intense fear of Manning Greer. Gizelle confessed the whole plan the first time she was asked. Greer's reaction surprised both Taunya and Teri. He grabbed Taunya and began pounding her head off the wall repeatedly as he berated Gizelle. Greer ranted and raved about the value of family and the loyalty everyone in the family was supposed to show for one another. He kept asking Gizelle if she thought so little of Taunya that she wasn't even worth lying for. Greer was more upset at the blonde for telling the truth than he had been at Taunya or Teri for lying.

Gizelle could not stand the strain. She watched as the entire scene began to blend and blur before here eyes. She could hear Greer but the voice was distant and it was quickly replaced by a strange ringing in her ears.

When Gizelle fainted, Greer stopped pounding Taunya's head and ordered her and Teri to do something about their fallen friend.

Greer talked with Eddy and Slugger and they agreed on the best way to punish the girls for their attempt to run away. He pulled the stun gun from a kit bag and having cleared the punishment with Slugger he first called Teri over. Greer explained it was important for the girls to know what the zapper could do. His plan was to give them a sample and a warning that any attempt to run away again would lead to a very liberal dose. Greer again promised longer exposure to the weapon, if the girl pulled her arm away too soon. Teri had heard from Taunya about how the stun gun felt and she wanted no part of it but she also knew Greer was not bluffing. Teri put her arm out and closed her eyes, the shock sent her to her knees and she cried as she rubbed the burning flesh of her arm.

Gizelle again became weak and had to sit down. Greer gave her a disgusted look and called Taunya over. She protested saying she knew exactly how the stun gun felt and she didn't need to be reminded. Greer agreed not to use the weapon on his girl and thought zapping Gizelle might just kill her, he decided that if he couldn't punish the girl he'd punish her man. Greer turned to Eddy who was laughing on the couch looking at Teri rubbing her arm. Greer reached over and released the charge from the gun into Eddy's thigh. The big pimp squealed louder than Teri had and he stopped laughing. He did not curse The Big Man but he did tell him the demonstration wasn't needed.

Greer had had enough fun and decided it was time for everyone to go to sleep. The girls went into the washroom to freshen up and

Greer relaxed on the mattress on the floor, Eddy took the only remaining bed; Slugger was already sleeping in the other.

When the girls stepped out of the washroom Greer decided he wanted to play one more game.

"Taunya you get behind me and Gizelle you're sleeping here in front of me tonight, I wanna be warm."

Gizelle began to walk toward The Big Man when Eddy spoke up.

"Girl don't you even think it. You get the fuck over here where you belong."

Gizelle froze in the middle of the room. Greer started to laugh and kept taunting her telling her she had to come stay with him for the night. Eddy issued a stern warning insisting she would pay if she did. The two men were struggling with each other in a head game that neither could lose and Gizelle could not win.

Taunya climbed onto the mattress and asked Greer to stop it but he was having too much fun. Taunya was afraid to tell Gizelle what to do so she started to glare at the skinny blonde hoping she would get the message and go where she belonged. Taunya knew Greer wanted no part of Gizelle because she was too fragile for his taste. The Big Man just wanted to prove to Eddy that this girl had more respect for him than she did her own man. Eddy knew what it was about and could see in Gizelle's face that he was going to lose this power play.

Gizelle's eyes filled with tears as she inched her way toward the mattress and climbed in next to the Big Man. Greer began laughing at her and at Eddy. Taunya leaned over and through clenched teeth told Gizelle to get the hell out of the bed. Tears poured down the young girls' cheeks as she stood and walked over to the bed to join Eddy. Eddy was sitting on the edge of the bed and watched her approach. When she was in front of him he leaned back and lifted his leg driving a kick into the centre of her stomach with all of his force.

"Don't you come over to me now you stupid 'ho. You're not gonna dis' me and then expect to climb in my bed, get the fuck away from me."

The force of the sudden kick threw Gizelle across the room. She climbed onto an arm chair and cried herself to sleep alone in the corner.

The next morning the three pimps headed out early as usual. The girls were never sure where they were going but were always relieved to see them go. Gizelle offered to go to the fast food restaurant a block or so down the road from the hotel to get burgers and fries for the girls. The pimps had left enough money for each of the girls to buy cigarettes and fast food for the day so Gizelle took a twenty dollar bill and headed out the door. She looked back at Taunya and Teri as she closed the door behind her. The two girls were sitting at the small writing table near the hotel room window. They were busy playing cards, smoking and listening to music the same way they did every day as they waited to return to the street. Gizelle knew she would not be coming back to the room. She hoped her actions would not cause the Big Man to lose control and hurt or even kill one or both of her friends. Gizelle worried about that as she walked toward the elevator but she had made up her mind, the others would have to look after themselves. Gizelle was going back to Montreal and leaving this life behind for ever.

As Gizelle made her final bid for freedom Stacey Jackson woke to find she could barely move. The badly beaten teen was unable to get out of bed and walk to the bathroom so she called out to Annie Mae to come and help her. The two girls cleaned the blood from Stacey's arms, legs and back and looked more closely at the damage. There were several groups of large welts that looked like open sores. Annie Mae was sure her friend needed medical attention but she was more worried about Stacey's attitude. Stacey spoke very softly and didn't seem to care about the wounds that made Annie Mae cry just to look at.

Annie Mae convinced Smit that she had to take Stacey to the hospital to get a prescription for the pain. Surprisingly the pimp agreed but he told Stacey she would have to tell the doctor she fell down a flight of stairs and the welts were from the treads impacting with her as she rolled down. Stacey said she could not go to the hospital because she had no health insurance card. She asked Smit if she could phone her aunt in Halifax and get her mother's Blue Cross number so she would be able to get the prescription. Smit agreed but said he would listen to her end of the conversation and she had better not say anything unusual.

Stacey made the call and her mother's sister picked up the phone on the second ring. Shirley screeched when she realized it was Stacey on the phone.

"Stacey, where are you? We've been worried sick. Your mother is frantic."

"Shirley, can you call Mom at work and get her Blue Cross number. I had an accident and I need the number."

Shirley questioned Stacey about the accident and noticed the lack of animation in her niece's voice. Shirley knew something was seriously wrong and did not accept the explanation that Stacey had fallen down a flight of stairs.

"Stacey, what's wrong is someone there?"

"Yes, can you please call my mother and I'll call you back later for the number."

Stacey hung up the phone before her aunt could question her further. Shirley called Debbie when the connection was broken. Mrs. Howard was not at work but instead was at home waiting for any word about her missing daughter. Her heart sank when she heard that Stacey was looking for her medical insurance information and she did not believe Stacey had fallen down a flight of stairs. That story was a lie she had told many years ago to explain marks left by the physical abuse she suffered at the hands of her ex-husband.

Desperately worried, she sped over to her sister's home to await Stacey's second phone call; when she arrived, she contacted the constable at the Cole Harbour RCMP. The news of Stacey's call to her aunt made its way to Brad Sullivan, who immediately tried to contact Dave Perry in Toronto. If Stacey called again, and her relatives could find out where she was, the Toronto police would have to move quickly to find her; that she was talking about needing medical attention meant she'd probably been abused by her pimp—at this point, all evidence indicated she was over her head in The Game—and the officer was deeply concerned that the girl could still be in grave danger from a Scotian player.

Sullivan couldn't reach Perry right away; the Toronto policeman had his hands full, to say the least. To begin with, he was in the middle of planning a news conference with the mother of a missing British Columbia teenager Andrea King, who had disappeared after getting off an airplane in Halifax in January. For six months, her mother had traveled from city to city, asking for public assistance in locating her daughter. One police theory was that Andrea had been abducted by one of more of the Nova Scotia pimps, who might have approached the pretty girl because she was obviously alone and perhaps seemed a bit disoriented. As Perry considered the case yet again, a station sergeant called to say that a teenage girl had just walked into the office, claiming she had been forced by several violent Nova Scotia pimps to leave her home in Montreal and travel to Toronto. It was Gizelle Vachon.

Perry, who had been working at home, raced out to his car and sped over to the office. This might be the break he'd been waiting for; Manning Greer's days of flouting the law could well be numbered, and Dave Perry hoped he would be there to see the Big Man take the fall. When he got to the station, shortly after noon, Perry found the message from Brad Sullivan and decided to call him before he interviewed Gizelle. His Halifax contact told him about the call from Stacey, and Perry agreed the teenager had probably been abused and could well be in further danger if she was still in the hands of pimps like the Scotians. "We've got a possible witness to some kind of assault, Brad, and I'm just going in to talk to her," he said. "We'll see what we can find out about your girl, and you let me know if she calls again with a location, OK?" Sullivan agreed, and wrote down Perry's cell-phone number.

Gizelle was already sitting in the interview room when Perry walked in and introduced himself. The girl's body language spoke volumes to the experienced policeman: her knees pulled up to her chest; her left arm wrapped tightly around her legs; her right hand clutching at a tangle of blonde curls; her eyes filled with fear. Perry offered her a Coke, and while he was out of the room, the officer quickly assessed the situation. These Nova Scotia pimps were experts at intimidation, and they knew enough about the law to continually warn their young prostitutes never to sign a complaint implicating them in a crime—a sworn statement, and they could well be prison bound. This girl looked utterly intimidated, but then she had made the decision to seek out the police, so maybe, just maybe, she'd give them enough to make a move on Greer and perhaps find Stacey Jackson as well.

As it turned out, Perry hardly even had to emphasize that if Gizelle cooperated, the police could lock up the men who had tried to kill her and her friends. She launched into a statement that provided much more than Perry had expected; not only did she tell him where the pimps were staying—even the room number—and how many girls they were running on the stroll, but Gizelle also named Manning Greer. For the first time, police had evidence they could use to arrest and prosecute the Big Man. When Gizelle had finished describing how she had been taken to Toronto, she unhesitatingly signed her complaint. As for Stacey, Gizelle said she believed she'd seen her on the stroll, but added that Stacey wasn't staying at the same hotel; nor did she know who the missing teenager's pimp was. With her statement signed, Gizelle waited as the police began to make arrangements for her return to Montreal.

"If it was me, I'd be at the police station," Taunya said with daring aplomb, and she barely looked up from her card game with Teri to answer the Big Man's question about Gizelle's whereabouts. Manning Greer must have been more than a bit preoccupied as he and Eddy returned to the hotel, moments after the source of his concern had signed a statement against him. Of course he couldn't have known the young Montrealer had gone to the cops—and he wouldn't have believed she'd sign on him anyway, let alone get up on a witness stand—but something was on his mind, and Eddy's as well. Otherwise, he would probably have lashed out at her for such audacity. As usual, the Jamaican pimps were occupying the Big Man's attention, and Gizelle's disappearance simply underscored his usual obsession with the American players. For the past few days, he, Eddy, and Bullet hadn't traveled anywhere without at least one gun—always kept in plain view on the dashboard of the van, for the benefit of any rival pimps who might be lurking nearby. Any of the other Nova Scotia players who had observed Greer's terrifyingly aggressive ways with his girls would have found some amusement in his fear-driven single-mindedness about what was, frankly, an imaginary threat; and they would have advised him, if they thought Manning Greer could ever take advice from anyone, to heed the warning of Taunya Terriault and get his mind off the Jamaicans. That was not to be.

The Big Man could well imagine those chumps trying to take revenge on his family by stealing Gizelle in retaliation for his move on their girl, Star. Still, he thought, maybe it wouldn't hurt to be cautious and switch hotels; Greer told the girls to pack—they'd be moving somewhere closer to the stroll that night—and he and Eddy also threw their things into their kit bags. "Take that gun with you now, man," he told Eddy, who retrieved his weapon from Taunya's suitcase. The Big man wasn't taking any chances on anyone; not with all the running around these girls were doing—Taunya and Teri, and that woman of young Smit's, Stacey. Now Gizelle. Nor had Greer yet managed to locate his former main girl, Lynn Buchanan. Greer and Eddy left for a favorite pool hall, where they were meeting Slugger—and, later on, Smit and Peanut. Before Stacey's pimp left the apartment he wanted her to make that second call to her aunt. No way was he letting her keep the cell phone to talk to a relative when he wasn't there to monitor every word.

The call was brief but, as it turned out, crucial. Debbie Howard, on the advice of her doctor, had taken a sedative and was asleep when her daughter called, but Stacey got the insurance number from her aunt, who asked—expecting her niece to say no—if there was a number where her mother could reach her later. To Shirley Townsend's surprise, Stacey gave her a number—the one to Smit's cellular phone—evidently unconcerned whether or not her pimp overheard her. He did not; Smit had been talking to Peanut during Stacey's conversation, believing his presence alone was enough to keep her in line. After she'd said good bye, her tormentor of the night before solicitously offered to take the wounded girl to the hospital later in the day; maybe she'd like to come along to the pool hall, since Annie Mae was going with Peanut. Stacey declined, saying she would rather lie down for the afternoon; the burning pain in her legs had become so intense that she could barely walk without crying out. Smit shrugged, and headed out the door after Peanut. Stacey fell into a stupor that was only half-sleep, and her dreams were full of fever images of shooting flames.

In Halifax, Stacey's mother and aunt tried to figure out what to do next. They had what they thought was the phone number of the apartment where Stacey was staying, so Debbie Howard sensibly decided the call the Cole Harbour RCMP and share the information with that nice constable. Then the whole family got into the act as Stacey's mother tried to decide if there was anything more she could do to help her daughter—her sister, brother and other relatives who had gathered at the Townsend home, all had a view to express, and after two hours of talk, a consensus emerged: Debbie Howard should call the number, and if one of the pimps answered, she should tell him she knew his identity, as did the police. If any of them had told one of the officers about this plan, there might have been a differing opinion, but the family was simply doing what they thought best.

Smit was sitting at a table in the pool hall in the early afternoon with Annie Mae when his cellular phone rang. He had just heard, with considerable satisfaction, his partner Peanut's animated narration of the session with Stacey, described in intimate detail for the benefit of Eddy and Slugger as they stood at a nearby pool table. He had seen the pleased expression of the Big Man's face as he leaned against a wall beside the table, taking it all in. Manning Greer knew Smit was a real man, a player to be reckoned with. His smile vanished within moments of answering the call. Annie Mae could hear Smit telling someone they were crazy, that he didn't know anyone named Stacey. Annie Mae looked away, pretending she wasn't listening. At the other end of the line, Debbie Howard was pretending too—she was pretending not to be terrified, and she was pretending to sound aggressive: "Goddamn you, listen to me!" she shouted. "I know who you are, I know where you are, and I know you have my daughter—and you'd better make sure there's nothing wrong with her, because the police are coming to get her."

By then the conversation was drawing attention, and Smit's buddies quickly figured out that Stacey's family had somehow managed to get the cell number. There was silence on the line for a moment, and then Mrs. Howard heard a new voice: "Look, lady, you better not call the cops. If you do, your daughter is dead." The anger in her voice vanished as her heart filled with a mother's worst fear. "Please don't hurt her," she begged. "We just want Stacey home; we don't want any trouble."

"You'll get your fuckin' daughter home all right, lady," the man replied. "We'll mail her to you one piece at a time."

The line went dead and Mrs. Howard's knees shook as she realized they had made a dreadful mistake; the pimps on the phone didn't care about the police. They were going to kill her little girl! She frantically called Brad Sullivan and begged him to put her in touch with a Toronto police officer; he gave her Dave Perry's cell-phone number.

The call to the pool hall marked the second time in only a few hours that Manning Greer had heard the police mentioned as a possible threat to his family business. Still, he wasn't overly concerned, although a few precautions would have to be taken—he would move Taunya and Teri to another hotel before they started to work. Smit said he would get rid of Stacey.

Annie Mae's heart sank as she heard the men talk. This was her terrifying theory about the Scotians' secret club—you had to kill a girl to become a member—and it seemed to be coming true. These men were going to waste her friend and bury her body so it would never be found. Annie Mae walked out into the bright afternoon sunshine and found a pay phone about a block from the pool hall, then dialed the apartment. "Get out of there right away, Stace!" she pleaded for the third time; yet again her friend offered an almost inaudible "Okay." What more could she say? "Stacey, honey, listen to what I'm telling you! Don't take anything—just go. I think they want to kill you—do you hear what I'm saying?" There was still a strange distance in Stacey's voice as she answered yes, but Annie Mae couldn't stay away any longer, or someone might notice her absence. She could only hope her warning was enough to save Stacey. Annie Mae ducked into a convenience store and picked up a chocolate bar and a bag of chips to help explain her absence from the pool hall. That those things were available there as well did not occur to her.

Although the injured girl's reactions were much slower than usual, she did understand what her friend had told her. As soon as she hung up the phone, Stacey walked out of the apartment and stood in front of the building, looking up and down the street. She couldn't get far on foot, it hurt too much to walk. Stacey headed to the small convenience store, just down the block. As she hobbled along the sidewalk, a distant memory flashed vividly before her eyes. A sense of *déjà vu* could have set in but Stacey's pain was too great and she was not thinking of her childhood. Just as it had been when she was three years old, and her mom had rushed her out of the house and away from her abusive father Stacey was headed to a corner store for refuge. In the store she asked to use the telephone and fumbled in her purse and came up with a cell-phone number for Joystick. The clerk allowed the obviously stricken teenager to use the store's phone—"Local call, right?" she nodded—and she reached the pimp in his car. "I'll be right there," he said, and Stacey felt tears of relief spring to her eyes. Joystick arrived moments after Smit and Peanut pulled up at their apartment to find Stacey gone; by the time they came back downstairs to Peanut's car and had a quick look up and down the block, she had been whisked away to safety. A questionable safety, perhaps—Joystick was no philanthropist, and planned to make some money from this girl—but at least she would have a little time to relax. The hashish and vodka he offered her provided relief from the persistent pain in her bruised and battered limbs, and Stacey almost didn't care what happened next.

Stacey settled in at Joystick's apartment, the thwarted Smit and Peanut drove back to the pool hall to tell Greer and the others what had happened; once again, the Big Man decided to move ahead with his plan to get Teri and Taunya out of the hotel—this time, he would send them straight to work, along with Annie Mae, while he and Eddy checked into a new hotel. Smit and Peanut thought about looking for a new place, too—maybe Stacey's mother hadn't been bluffing about the police coming to get her daughter.

They were all still pondering their next move but taking no action when Dave Perry and seven members of the Juvenile Task Force made their way to the hotel. The JTF raid was in the planning stages when Debbie Howard called Dave Perry's cellular phone and as he raced to the hotel in search of the Nova Scotia pimps he hoped he would capture before they carried out their threat to send Stacey home in pieces. Gizelle had told Perry about the 9-mm handgun Eddy had been waving around, so the team members were taking no chances: all the officers wore bullet-proof vests, and just before two o'clock, they took up position against the wall on either side of the door to Greer's suite. Their guns were drawn as Perry knocked, then stepped to the side.

Teri turned down the stereo and Taunya went to see who was knocking; she had barely opened the door a crack when what looked like an army came bursting inside. The first guy pushed Taunya to the floor, rolling her over on her stomach and ordering her to stay still; meanwhile, another officer was doing the same to Teri. The two girls were confused and frightened, but they managed to remember the Big

Man's warning never to answer a police officer's questions, and both refused to speak to Perry when he asked where Manning Greer was. No one else was in the suite, but there were all kinds of kit bags and other items lying around; clearly the pimps were coming back. While the other officers set up a stakeout inside and outside the hotel, Perry returned to the station with Taunya and Teri, who continued to ignore his questions. Well, they could just cool their heels until he had time to find their families and send them home. First he had to take care of a few other priorities.

At about four o'clock, the mother of the missing British Columbia teenager spoke with the large group of reporters at the station; after her news conference, several journalists lingered, asking pointed questions not about the girl's possible abduction but about an even bigger story they had heard rumors about all day. After the third or fourth demand for information on a pending arrest of several dangerous Nova Scotia pimps supposedly operating on the streets of Toronto, Perry decided to cut a deal with the reporters: he would tell them where the arrest was going down, and they would keep far enough away from the scene not to alert the suspects returning to the hotel; after police had the pimps in custody, the cameras could move in for some good shots.

Dave Perry wasn't just being a nice guy for the benefit of the media; he and his superiors at the metro police department knew the value of the publicity these arrests could create. Perry had spent nearly a decade wrestling with the thorny problem of juvenile prostitution—and, most recently, the dangerous Scotians' role. This was an opportunity to let tens of thousand of people know about a major national pimping ring—and one that hopefully would be broken, here in Toronto, within hours. The publicity could also convince officials in Nova Scotia that they should take on the issue with a full-scale task force, as Perry knew his Halifax colleague Brad Sullivan had been urging for two years.

Just as Dave Perry was preparing to return to the hotel at about four thirty, his cellular phone rang—it was Debbie Howard, calling from Halifax. Here was his chance to attract even more public attention to the issue: after assuring the anxious mother that police were tracking Stacey even as they spoke, and could have news for her within a few hours, he asked whether she had spoken to the media. "Not yet," Mrs. Howard said, "but my sister's husband works for ATV here—" the widely watched Atlantic Television System. "I think you should talk to them—it could help Stacey and many other young girls like her," Perry advised. "You can tell them that your daughter has been abducted by a ring of pimps from Nova Scotia and that she's been forced to work—and by the time you go on the air, we'll be that much closer to making sure she gets home to you safe and sound. Oh, and don't forget to let them have a photo of Stacey."

There wasn't much time—the ATV evening news airs at 6 P.M.—but the emotionally charged story of Stacey Jackson's disappearance did make it onto that broadcast. Henry Peterson, Stacey's uncle, was the family's representative in front of the camera—her mother felt too emotionally exhausted to make a statement—and his comments were brief but moving: they just wanted Stacey home, and were reaching out to the community to call police if they had even a scrap of information that could help.

While Maritimers listened in shock to the account of a dangerous group of pimps operating from Halifax, police and reporters in Toronto waited patiently for Manning Greer and his family to show up. Unbelievably, they were still hanging out at the pool hall, still obviously unconvinced they had anything serious to worry about. At about seven, Peanut told Annie Mae to get back to the apartment and pack; she'd be joining Taunya and Teri on the stroll later. Then, the five pimps had a bite of dinner.

It was close to nine o'clock when they finally arrived at the hotel. Officers watched from their concealed positions as the gray van with the garbage-bag-covered windows pulled into the parking lot. They became concerned as they watched not one but five men step out. Annie Mae was back at the apartment where Stacey had been beaten. Peanut had told her to pack her things and get ready to go to work.

The information was radioed to the officers upstairs in the hotel room and the others in rooms on that same floor. Inside the hotel room the officers had their guns drawn as they sat in silence listening for the sound of footsteps in the hall. They heard the voices first as the pimps walked toward the door where they expected to find Taunya and Teri waiting to go to work. Only four of the pimps made it to the hotel room door as Eddy reached for his key to open it. Manning Greer had been walking with his colleagues when his cellular phone rang. Amber was calling from Niagara Falls and Greer slowed his pace as he talked with her.

When Eddy opened the hotel room door all hell broke loose. Two men pointed what Eddy saw as a couple of very big guns at his face. They ordered him to drop to the floor and at the same moment doors from the surrounding rooms opened. Other police officers jumped into the hallway and began to scream orders at the three remaining pimps. Officers grabbed Slugger, Peanut, and Smit and threw them to the floor outside the room. The pimps squirmed, cursed and struggled as men knelt on their backs and pulled their outstretched arms back behind them to be cuffed.

Manning Greer swore as he saw what was happening only a few metres in front of him, in the initial confusion the officers did not see Greer as he turned and raced for the stairs. By the time the task force members realized Greer was not there he was already bursting through the hotel doors and running for his van. The police officers outside saw the Big Man running and screamed for him to stop. No one had yet moved to the van and Greer had a clear line of flight.

Officers raced back to their patrol cars to give chase as Greer floored the accelerator in the gray van cursing its slow response and wishing he had his 'Vette. He raced over the sidewalk and onto the road. The chase began and the sirens blared and the reporters waiting a block or so away joined in. Manning Greer raced dangerously through the streets of downtown Toronto with several police cars and news vehicles not far behind. The police knew they had a dangerous man in front of them as Greer pulled his van off the busy road way and raced down the sidewalk forcing pedestrians to jump out of the way or be killed. Greer turned onto a side street and raced toward the next block. He looked ahead and saw a chain link fence and gate blocking the way. He had made the mistake of turning into a delivery lane and not a side street. Greer pressed the accelerator and held onto the wheel as the big van crashed through the gate and entered the loading area parking lot. The police were not far behind and Greer soon realized he had led them into a box canyon. The only way out of the parking lot was the same way Greer had just come in. As he looked back at the police cars spilling in through the only available exit, Greer raced the van to the outer edge of the parking lot and slammed on the breaks. The van had not finished sliding to a stop as the driver's side door flew open and the Big Man leapt to the pavement. Police officers had no time to get out of their own vehicles and train their guns on Greer. They watched him bound over a small fence and into a bush-filled lot behind a row of houses.

Greer swore as he looked between two of the houses at the next street and saw police cars. Two of the cars giving chase had circled the block when Greer headed down the delivery lane and they were already on the street in front of him. Greer crawled beneath a sprawling evergreen bush and tried to figure out a route of escape.

He could hear the officers behind him. They had already scaled the fence but were moving very slowly with their flashlights trained ahead of them. Adrenaline flowed through the officers leading the search. They had all been briefed on the violent nature of the man they were hunting and while they all wanted to make the arrest, no one wanted to find the cornered suspect alone.

The fugitive began to consider what was happening; he had a violent temper and he was angry but he was not stupid. There was no way to escape and he wasn't about to start a fight with a bunch of armed men in a darkened back yard. Greer was pretty sure someone would just shoot him. Some of his cockiness began to return as Greer considered what it would take to convict him. None of the Big Man's girls would dare to sign on him. He might do a little time for the attempted escape but nothing serious. As the officers approached, Manning Greer knelt with his hands behind his head welcoming them. There would be no struggle from the Big Man. He was too smart.

The police pushed Greer face down into the grass and cuffed his hands behind his back. Greer could smell the freshly cut lawn clippings as they patted him down, carefully looking for the weapon he was supposed to be carrying. It was not there. Greer had left the gun in the van. His favorite 9-mm was for the war with the other pimps and Greer hadn't even considered grabbing it as he ran from the police. He knew he could use the system in his war with the police and a gun would just complicate his problems. Many of the older pimps had told Greer how easy it was to beat a charge—as long as your girls don't sign you're safe they'd told him. Greer also knew he could beat a wrap even if a girl did sign. He had to make sure she did not testify at his trial. Manning Greer was startled as he was led out of the field to the next street and the waiting police cruisers. He was suddenly blinded by the lights from television cameras and the quick burst from flash cameras used by the newspaper photographers. Greer hung his head and leaned forward to shield himself from the cameras. His big upper torso leaned so far forward the officers leading him to the car had a difficult time preventing Greer from falling in front of them.

Back at the station, the task force officers began to sort out the suspects and charges. Eddy and the Big Man could face counts of exercising control and living on the avails of prostitution arising from Gizelle's statement; but Perry realized he would need cooperation from Taunya and Teri to prosecute Slugger and extend the charges against Greer. While Perry did the paperwork, other officers interrogated Smit and Peanut about Stacey's whereabouts, and were met with a wall of silent contempt. It didn't phase the investigators; they'd seen it in almost every pimp they arrested. The Scotians, like the others before them, had confidently defied the law for so long that even under arrest, they were confident the police were just spinning their wheels. Soon enough, they were certain it would be back to business as usual.

At Joystick's apartment, Stacey's respite was coming to an end; her new pimp made it clear he expected her to repay his kindness, starting that very night. She had no choice but to return to the stroll. As she stood silently on Church Street, Stacey began to wonder where the other Nova Scotia girls were. Taunya and Teri were at the station, and by now, so was Annie Mae. Smit and Peanut had given the Toronto address of the apartment when they were booked, and police found her there waiting for her ride downtown. Meanwhile, one of the task force's informants spotted Stacey on the stroll, and only an hour after she arrived for work, two unmarked cars and a cruiser pulled up the curb. Mesmerized by the flashing lights glinting off their badges, the confused, exhausted teenager allowed herself to be led to a car and whisked off to the station.

Taunya, Teri, and Annie Mae had been taken to a waiting room while members of the task force waded through the paperwork and made arrangements for Taunya and Teri to be flown back to Nova Scotia. Both fourteen, they could be held by police and returned to their families, unlike Annie Mae, who at nineteen was considered an adult—and a very noisy, angry adult who had been demonstrating her feelings for the police ever since they'd brought her in. Why had she been arrested? When was she going to be released? Where was her friend Stacey? The answer to at least one of those questions was right around the corner. Annie Mae suddenly screamed as she looked through a window out into the busy squad room—Stacey was being led in by two officers. The three girls tried to get to their friend, but police stopped them at the door and soon afterward, the still-befuddled Stacey was led to an interrogation room for questioning, while Dave Perry made the call he'd been looking forward to all evening—"Mrs. Howard?" he asked, and his cheerful voice was all she had to hear to know that Stacey was safe.

The interrogating officers immediately noticed Stacey's horribly mangled legs, and asked her what had happened. No more stories about accidents on the stairs—Stacey was ready to tell the truth. In the same flat, off-handed manner she'd been using all day, she told them how Smit had whipped her. Well, any further questioning would have to wait; much as they and Perry wanted to hear more, they wanted most of all, to get a signed statement against the pimp. This girl needed medical attention, fast; the emotionless tone of her description indicated a state of shock. The police officers accompanied Stacey to a hospital where they photographed the marks left by Smit and his wire whip; she would heal before the trial and they wanted a jury to see what they were seeing.

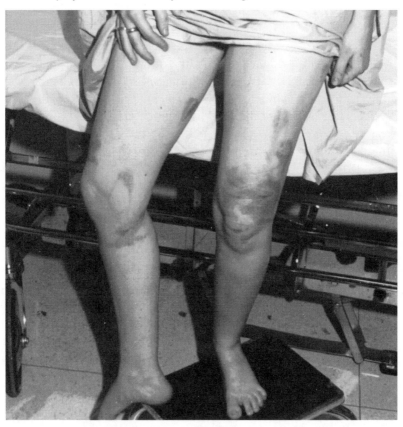

Stacey's legs had almost healed when this photo was taken, but still show bruises from the awful beating.

While Stacey was being treated at a nearby hospital, Taunya, who had been guzzling can after can of pop from the squad-room machine, found herself in dire need of a bathroom. As a female officer escorted her down a narrow hallway, she noticed the open door to a small room; peering inside, she saw Manning Greer, shirtless, his feet bare. Glancing up, Greer saw his main girl and flashed her a bright smile, completely unrestrained by the presence of the officers in the room with him, or the policewoman at Taunya's side. She walked on, surprised by her own reaction. Taunya hadn't felt in the least frightened at the sight of Greer; she was deeply relieved that he was in custody, and she decided then and there to give police the statement they wanted—and advise Teri to do the same. The police hadn't been able to help her in Montreal, but maybe that was because she hadn't signed on her pimp. Well, she wouldn't make that mistake again: Taunya was tired, and she wanted to go home, and she wanted to live like a normal human being again.

Taunya and Teri gave their statements and Dave Perry had what he wanted, solid evidence to go with the information he had been gathering on the Scotians. By the time all of the statements were analyzed Manning Greer faced a total of twenty charges ranging from kidnapping and living on the avails of prostitution to possession of a weapon. Slugger, Eddy, Peanut and Smit faced twenty-six charges among them.

Meanwhile, the treatment Stacey received at the hospital was clearly restoring her usual mood—which is to say, the arrogant, angry and defiant attitude task force officers often observed in prostitutes first dealing with the police. Oddly, though, the teenager also answered every question the investigators asked. It was a strange interview for the investigators who listened as Stacey alternately cursed them, then responded to every query in great detail, without hesitation, from her recruitment into The Game to her experiences in Toronto. They had their signed statement, but what were the police going to do with Stacey now? Perry pondered the question as he read through the account of her nightmare. Understandably, her mother desperately wanted Stacey home in Halifax, but it wasn't quite as easy as that. She was seventeen, and hadn't been declared a ward of the court, so he had no authority to hold her or send her home.

Perry would have to play it by ear: he started by telling Stacey who he was and that he'd been speaking with her mother. The girl promptly turned on him, cursing and shouting and demanding to be released; familiar with this reaction, the officer gently explained that everyone around her, including her mom, knew she was a victim and had no intention of pointing fingers at her. Perry understood that Stacey was judging herself, that she believed everyone would think she was nothing but a "whore," and that her sense of guilt could be very dangerous; it was a feeling that could drive a girl back to prostitution as much as a year after she'd left the streets. A girl misjudged or ostracized by former friends in the "square" world often began to feel cut off from mainstream society, and understandably inclined to seek questionable comfort even in the welcoming arms of a pimp.

Dave Perry knew he had to keep this from happening if he possibly could, and his first step was to make sure Stacey stayed away from the lawyers arriving at the station to see to the needs of Manning Greer and the other Scotian players. These lawyers, who had previously represented Annie Mae and a few other incarcerated prostitutes, also wanted to talk with Stacey and her friends, to ensure their rights were respected.

As the police tried to find a way to convince Stacey to return home they took her back to the waiting room where Annie Mae was sitting alone. Incredibly, Annie Mae who had no intention of leaving The Game had given the police a signed statement. She did it, she told Stacey, because she was angry at Smit and Peanut for their behavior the night before and she wanted to scare them a little. Annie Mae told Stacey she would not testify and would not cooperate any further when the cases came to trial. She kept her word and avoided the police after that night. She also gave Stacey a bit of advice. "Our lawyers are coming now honey, you talk to them and they'll get you outta here. If you want to testify against Smit that's your choice, but first you need some cool down time and they'll get you away from the police."

Stacey thought she would testify but she still wasn't considering leaving The Game, even as she glimpsed the horrible results of its down side each time she looked at her injured legs. It was only sheer circumstance—or luck—that got the seventeen-year-old Haligonian away from the pimps and their high-priced legal help, and out to the Toronto airport. Mrs. Howard had told Perry that her brother was on the next flight to Toronto, so the constable asked two task force officers to drive with Stacey, treat her to some coffee or a snack, then get her to the airport to meet that flight. Her uncle could take it from there. When the two men in suits came to the interrogation room and told her to follow them, she thought she was being freed by those lawyers Annie Mae had told her about. Annie Mae waited, and when the real lawyers arrived she left the police station with them. Annie Mae was free but her pimp was not. She returned to the stroll and told the few Nova Scotia girls left there what had happened. Ever the "Choosy Suzy" Annie Mae picked one of their pimps and, agreeing with his assessment that Toronto was too dangerous, returned to Halifax and continued to play her part in The Game.

As Annie Mae linked up with another player, Stacey drove around with the two police officers, convinced the pimps were making sure she was safe. Even when they got to the airport, she did not realize something unusual was going on: Stacey sat numbly, watching as a throng of journalists, some wielding huge cameras, begin to gather around a man walking towards her and the officers. Suddenly he was beside her, smiling. It was her Uncle Henry.

Now completely confused, she stared uncomprehendingly at Henry Peterson. How had he known where to find her? Why were those reporters bothering him? And what would these lawyers do if she tried to talk with someone from home? Stacey's uncle embraced her in a big hug, but he could feel her whole body recoil, partly because the physical contact renewed the discomfort in her arms and legs, partly because she did not want affection. His concern mounted as he glanced at her bruises and her street clothes. The two officers guided them outside to escape the suddenly converging reporters who wanted a word with the Maritime teenager who'd been at the centre of the police raid, and as they sat in the officers' car near the entrance to the terminal, Peterson started chatting encouragingly about how happy the family was that she was coming home. "I'm not going back to Halifax," Stacey retorted defiantly, looking at the "lawyers" for confirmation. Instead, they started talking to her uncle about severe trauma, and recovery period, and support mechanisms— what did that have to do with the family? Heartbreakingly, Stacey was still thinking of the Scotians as her family—not her devoted uncle, or her mom waiting anxiously at home. Stacey's uncle described every-thing he felt she had to look forward to at home—her old friends, her plans to go back to school—and finally he hit on an effective approach. "Stacey, if you don't come home now you can forget about ever seeing your son again," Henry Peterson said, bluntly. "They'll take Michael away forever."

"They can't do that, can they?" He nodded, gravely. In the weeks since coming to Toronto, Stacey had banished all conscious thoughts of her child, telling herself he'd be better off with any of his other rel-atives, hers or Roger's, than growing up with a prostitute for a mother and pimps for baby-sitters. Suddenly she desperately wanted to see her baby again. "Do you think it'd be okay if I went home for a little while?" she asked the two men, who glanced at each other, confused; didn't she understand that home was exactly where they wanted her to be? They didn't understand that Stacey still thought they were lawyers for the Scotians—lucky thing, too, for the officers. "Of course you should go home" would have met with utter opposition, coming as it did from the police. Well, she would go home for a bit, but as Stacey sat next to her uncle on the plane, her mood grew aggressive again; she answered all Peterson's questions with contempt and defiance. Her whole family was so square it hurt! Then she saw

Taunya and Teri sitting a few rows away, and Stacey felt a bit better just knowing the girls were there. She couldn't have known that her two friends were experiencing an entirely different range of emotion—guilt at having turned to prostitution when all they had wanted out of their trip to Montreal was a bit of adventure; anxiety that their families would hate them for making that decision; and fear that they would be unable to fulfill their goal of leaving The Game.

At the Halifax airport, Constable Brad Sullivan was sitting with Debbie Howard, waiting for the arrival of Stacey and the other girls. Sullivan had made sure there was a private room for the families, so they could have a reunion untroubled by a barrage of journalists' questions about what it was like to be a juvenile prostitute. Debbie Howard appreciated media efforts to focus public attention on the serious issue, but she too wanted to avoid a mob scene. As she sat waiting with the other families, a woman walked over and asked who she was.

Mrs. Howard smiled and introduced herself but the answer was not what the woman was looking for.

"No I mean who are you, you must be someone important the way everybody is talking about your girl. It was on TV and the radio and everything."

Debbie was puzzled by the question and explained that she wasn't anyone special, just a mother who wanted her girl back. That answer didn't wash; Teri's mother, Lorraine MacDonald, also wanted her daughter back, but she explained, no one had seemed to care.

"Did you call any reporters and tell them about her?"

"No."

Teri's mom had been trying to hide what had happened to her daughter from others in her family. She had considered it a very private matter to be dealt with discretely, she had contacted police and filled out a missing persons report but had not gone further. Debbie explained it was a police officer from Toronto who told her to contact the media and she was glad she followed the advice. Mrs. Howard had a very different view of what had happened to her daughter. Mrs. MacDonald believed Teri had chosen to run away and be with the pimps and she was ashamed of her young daughter's decision. Debbie knew Stacey had gone with the pimps but she knew first-hand how an abusive man could force a young woman into almost any decision. Debbie wasn't much older than Stacey when she married her first husband and she knew when she walked down the aisle that he had a drinking problem and that he was prone to beating her but she still went through with the marriage. Debbie had gone through a great deal of self analysis in the years since she walked away from Stacey's father. Her understanding of her own guilt and confusion would be a valuable asset as she tried to help Stacey cope with the decisions the teen had made.

When the flight arrived and the girls were re-united with their families Brad Sullivan introduced himself to Stacey and told her he would like to have the opportunity to talk with her about the people in the Halifax area that had been involved in her recruitment. Stacey became defiant very quickly; she still believed it was the lawyers for her pimp who had freed her and allowed her to return to Halifax. She had no intention of talking to some cop and getting herself into trouble with the family. For weeks Smit had been lecturing Stacey about how she was now a part of the family and that only the family would look after her if there was ever trouble. At the time Stacey thought he was being foolish but the moment she was free of Smit and her life in the street she began to use the expression "my family" whenever she talked about Annie Mae or the others she had left behind. The phrase would lead to some heated arguments between Stacey and her mother.

Brad Sullivan decided he would give Stacey some time before he tried to get any real cooperation from her. Sullivan left to allow the family time to deal with the emotions of the moment. For Debbie the emotion was more than she could handle, she had promised herself she would be strong for Stacey but that resolve had melted away the second she set eyes on her daughter.

There had been no effort made to get Stacey any new clothing in all the confusion at the Juvenile Task Force office. Stacey arrived in Halifax dressed like a hooker in a tight-fitting miniskirt, a T-shirt and her usual choice: fish net stockings. It was not the clothing that had reduced Debbie to a mass of tears, it was what she saw beneath those stockings. By now Stacey's legs were a horrid mass of red, black, yellow and blue as the welts from the coat hanger began to heal. Debbie's heart was broken; she had been unable to protect her little girl from abuse at the hands of a man, and it was more than she could handle. Her only relief was that she could see Stacey, she could touch her; her little girl was alive.

Part Five:
Operation Hectic Heats Up

The core of downtown Halifax offers an irony to the law makers and law breakers who people it. Hollis Street is home to the historic stone home of all Nova Scotia law makers, Province House. A block away sits the tall office building that is home to many of the top prosecutors whose job it is to make sure those laws are upheld. Much of the work done by the prosecutors takes place a block further down toward Halifax Harbour in the Province's supreme court building, the Law Courts. All of that surrounds a stretch of Hollis Street pavement, several blocks long, known as the downtown stroll. Long after all but the most dedicated government officials and Crown attorneys have packed it in for the night, the prostitutes are starting work. The girls of Hollis Street can be found just after dark lounging against buildings or power poles, waiting for a client to drive by; a quick discussion of service sought and price expected, and the date begins, usually concluding no more than a half-hour later. This scene is still played out on the sidewalks of Hollis today with one crucial difference. There are fewer girls now than there once were, and although their pimps call them girls they are no longer the thirteen- and fourteen-year-olds who made Hollis Street the centre of prostitution in Halifax.

A single police operation launched in the fall of 1992 is credited with the remarkable achievement of strangling the life out one of the city's most disturbing problems: juvenile prostitution. A joint-force task force whose twelve members included municipal, regional, and federal police officers, as well as a provincial Crown prosecutor, Operation Hectic was established as a direct result of the pressure politicians felt after media revelations of the abduction, abuse, and torture in Montreal and Toronto of four Nova Scotia teenagers—Stacey Jackson, Annie Mae Wilson, Taunya Terriault, and Teri MacDonald.

Action was demanded, and action was taken. The operation was announced by area police chiefs one week after Toronto juvenile task force officers moved in to arrest the man they called the pimping kingpin, Manning Greer. A little over a week later the Nova Scotia government handed one hundred thousand dollars to the task force to help it begin the job of tackling the pimping problem. The move was exactly what longtime Toronto task force member Dave Perry had been hoping to see; and he was certain that his main Halifax contact RCMP Constable Brad Sullivan, would be delighted at the decision. Indeed, Sullivan, who with fellow Mountie John Elliott had conducted a 1990 study of pimping in Halifax was more than happy with the announcement. It was his and Elliott's detailed proposal for a massive attack on pimps who preyed on juveniles, that formed the basis for the new task force's objectives. The two RCMP officers were also asked to help select their teammates for what would come to be known as Operation Hectic. Among those who became key members, along with Sullivan and Elliott, were three men whose backgrounds made them clear choices.

The members of Operation Hectic, including clerical staff.

Mitch Ginn, age forty, a senior constable with Halifax police with twenty years experience, was responsible for a sting operation between April and August 1992. That operation shut down the Hollis Street nightclub that was the front for six girls working for a Halifax pimp. He had been involved with surveillance activities for sixteen weeks before the perpetrator was apprehended on August 29. The arrest was made through evidence gathered with electronic surveillance monitored by Ginn, which saw the pimp charged with living on the avails of prostitution and conspiracy to commit an indictable offense. Ginn was keenly aware of the extent of the problem on Hollis involving juveniles.

Operation Hectic task force member Darrell Gaudet.

Darrell Gaudet, age thirty, was a junior constable with the Dartmouth police who was currently gathering information on his own time about escort services in Dartmouth. His interest in prostitution dated back to a job as a counselor in a facility for young offenders. His clients included two juvenile males convicted of rape who had insisted it was their right to have sex with the girl any time they wanted because she was a prostitute working for them. He never forgot their arrogance, and promised himself he would do something about it someday. The young officer's concern and determination more than compensate for his inexperience.

Craig Botterill, age thirty-one, was a Crown attorney in the provincial justice department. He had volunteered for the operation as the lead prosecutor and consultant on points of law. He recalled his frustration of a lost case in 1983 involving a pimp charged with assault and living on the avails of prostitution after the victim, age seventeen, was allegedly kept against her will in North Preston home, beaten with a wire whip, and punched through the padding of a pillow to avoid bruises. The pimp was acquitted on basis of believability of the witness. The prosecutor intended to accompany officers on interviews with juvenile girls in the hopes of establishing credibility of potential witnesses. He was hard working and committed to the issue of prostitution.

Craig Botterill was appointed to Operation Hectic before most of the investigators. His job would be to guide the officers in their investigations, examine the statements obtained, and determine what charges would be brought against the pimps. In the early days of the investigation into the Nova Scotia pimping problem the task force members realized Botterill was not your average persecuting attorney. He was more than willing to become involved in the investigations at the street level.

When the justice department decided to appoint one of its attorneys to work with the Joint Force Operation, Craig Botterill was in the right place (or wrong place) at the right time. In early fall of 1992, he was chatting with a number of other Crown Attorneys who had gathered around his work area in the Halifax office. The lead prosecutor approached the group, saying he was looking for a volunteer to be assigned, for six months, to a special police operation. Botterill asked his boss what the operation was—an attack on the pimping problem in Halifax. The other attorneys gradually returned to their desks, leaving Botterill and his boss alone. Botterill knew it would mean a heavy work load but decided a break from the regular office routine would be refreshing, so he offered to take the job. The six-month projection was a very optimistic one.

Crown prosecutor Craig Botterill.
[Print from ATV video tape]

When he learned some of the task force officers had been driving down to Hollis Street at night just to introduce themselves to the girls and hand out business cards, Botterill asked if he could go along. For the task force officers to have a prosecutor willing to become involved in the investigation at the street level had a number of unexpected benefits.

The task force members had developed a straightforward routine. They approached the girls to explain what the task force was all about and to ask if they wanted to help. For the most part the girls refused, but the officers left their business cards and asked the young prostitutes to call if they ever needed help. The officers were surprised by the lawyer's more aggressive approach. When Botterill accompanied a team of investigators, they would park the unmarked police car just off Hollis Street and walk up to one of the girls to introduce themselves. The officers would tell the girl the prosecutor in charge of the case wanted to speak with her. The girls often agreed to go meet with Botterill who then made his pitch. A career lawyer and a gifted debater since childhood, Botterill used his powerful persuasive skills to good advantage.

Botterill is a small man, about five foot six and weighs one hundred and fifty pounds on a good day. His close-cropped curly dark hair, wire-rimmed glasses, soft voice and tendency to maintain eye contact put the girls at ease. The street-toughened girls took to Botterill fairly quickly. The prosecutor sold the girls on what he knew would be the most attractive thing the task force had to offer. His pitch always began with a sympathetic acknowledgement of how hard they worked every night and his conclusion that they must be making lots of money. He told them how unfair it was for them to have to hand all of their money over to a man who did none of the work, and who beat them savagely if they stepped out of line. Botterill told the young girls he was building a team that would help stop that abuse and that they would be a valuable asset to the team. Once he had their attention, he explained to the teens that they were the most important ingredient in the operation designed to protect them. Many of the girls had never heard anyone tell them they were important, let alone someone as powerful as the police officers had said this man was. Although Botterill won a good deal of support from the girls on the stroll, very few would go so far as to give him a statement against a pimp. The prosecutor's approach was not that different from the one used by pimps recruiting the same girls. The difference was that Botterill was not lying when he told them they were very important to him. Many girls offered information the investigators accompanying Botterill found valuable, but in the early stages of Operation Hectic that was as far as the girls were willing to go.

As committed as he was to Operation Hectic, Botterill was worried that the team might end up thwarted, as he had been during his 1983 case involving the supposedly violent North Preston pimp who'd been set free. When he read through the statements that Stacey, Taunya, and Teri had made in Toronto, Botterill was overcome by the same feeling of unease he'd experienced about his young witness' assertions—the accounts of brutality were so extreme, so protracted, as to strain even his credibility, let alone that of a judge. The team would need to amass a great deal of corroborative evidence—and persuade a convincing number of girls both to sign statements and testify against their pimps—if this operation was to be a success.

Brad Sullivan and John Elliott knew the operation would be a success—it had to be. The two RCMP constables attacked their work load with the voracity of a cat deprived of food for a long time. They had waited, watched and wondered; now they were ready to act. Initially the two worked as a unit but that was changed when it became clear the other task force members were starting from scratch and Sullivan and Elliott were not. They were teamed with different partners to spread the advantage around. Both officers had already emphasized many times in team meetings how important it was for everyone involved to fully recognize that the young prostitutes they were dealing with were victims—potential witnesses—who deserved support; the pimps, not the girls, were the criminals. This viewpoint had been adopted by every juvenile task force in the country, from the Metro Toronto operation, to the equally successful "Pimp Program" developed in Vancouver in 1988. As their contacts on these task forces had warned them, it was not necessarily a viewpoint police officers would instantly embrace; many members of Operation Hectic, including its most senior policeman, twenty-five-year veteran Sergeant Gary Mumford, started out with the belief that anyone working as a prostitute is, quite simply, a criminal. "Whores are whores," was the attitude Mumford had before his new assignment. Sullivan and Elliott were certain the officers would quickly change their minds when they met teenage girls who had been whipped and kicked into criminal activity by powerful, intimidating armed men who took advantage of the vulnerability produced by their frequently troubled backgrounds. They were right.

The two officers were especially charged when Dave Perry suggested they go to Toronto to interview Manning Greer and his legendary Uncle Popeye. Sullivan and Elliott hoped the two pimps might be able to shed some light on the August 1989 disappearance of Kimberly McAndrew, the Halifax teenager whose case was the reason for the investigation of Halifax area pimps, a case they continued to work on. If anyone would know if McAndrew had been abducted by a pimp, it would be one of these major Scotian players; but the Greers were typically uncooperative with men who carried a badge. The older pimp, the worse for wear, simply quoted the Bible in response to every question the officers asked; and the Big Man, towering over the two officers, arrogantly folded his arms across his chest and refused to talk to them. Kimberly McAndrew? Never heard of her. No, don't know anyone who might have. The Halifax policemen were forced to leave the Don Jail with no more information than when they'd arrived. Sullivan and Elliott returned home with a deeper-than-ever commitment to protect the girls who'd been hurt by the likes of this man—and to bring their abusers to justice.

The scope of the problem they had undertaken to solve was daunting. Police estimated that at least one hundred pimps were operating in the Halifax Metro area in the fall of 1992, double the number observed by Sullivan and Elliott only two years before, while they were conducting their fact-finding project. The new, much higher figure, came from the persistent young officers who continued to gather information on Halifax pimps long after Operation Heart ended. They still had no clear sense of how many prostitutes worked for those men, the trade was too fluid and the people seemed to be in constant motion. They did know that most of the girls were under age eighteen, and had learned of at least one who entered The Game at the tender age of eleven.

Slowly, but surely, fired up by the determination of Sullivan and Elliott, the team began to gain the trust of the girls on Hollis Street. The first statements, scrutinized by the increasingly confident Craig Botterill, were put on file in the task force's Dartmouth office. Finally, one sunny afternoon in early winter, the task force mobilized for its first takedown. The target, a thirty-three-year-old pimp whom prostitutes had identified as an active player in Halifax, was based in Montreal but had come home for what turned out to be an untimely visit. The pimp did not know that a girl he had beaten and abandoned when he last visited Halifax had given a statement to a task force officer. He'd been signed on. A minor player, the girl's statement indicating he ran one or two girls at a time and had little or no contact with the Big Man, he was suddenly the most important pimp in the eyes of Nova Scotia's new task force. He was important because he would be the first. One moment he was driving down a busy street in downtown Dartmouth, the next, he was forced over to the curb by an unmarked task force vehicle and ordered to step out of his car and extend his hands for the cuffs. Within moments, several other team members who had heard the radio message alerting them to the bust—John Elliott was among them—had converged on the scene to witness what they considered history in the making.

The team's media relations officer badly wanted this piece of history recorded for posterity, most importantly because he knew what a positive impact extensive coverage could have on Operation Hectic's early efforts. Sergeant Bill Price, the RCMP media liaison officer for Nova Scotia, contacted local reporters, triumphantly reporting that the task force, only in its infancy, was already making a difference in the battle against juvenile prostitution. Reaction to reports of the arrest was overwhelmingly positive: an outpouring of support from the public, congratulating police for tackling a problem that had been too long ignored. Interestingly, a number of calls from parents requested that task force team members speak with their daughters—who they were concerned were hanging out with the wrong crowd—about the dangers of prostitution. This preventative action became a regular activity of Operation Hectic, and one the officers welcomed: keeping a girl away from The Game was a lot easier than rescuing her from it after she had chosen to play. Even more significantly, there was a noticeable increase of calls from girls who had been approached on the stroll by Botterill and the others; apparently, they were beginning to believe that police truly meant to crack down on violent pimps, and not on the young prostitutes themselves. The officers began to hear stories of brutal torture that at first seemed too horrendous to be plausible—like the statements of Stacey, Taunya, and Teri. As they heard similar accounts from girl after girl, police realized the pimps' abusive behavior was both widespread and extreme.

Most of the girls told their stories in the interview room at the Dartmouth police station, which had been pressed into service as the task force's office. The rooms, with their cinder-block walls and sparse furnishings—a table and three chairs at most—provided starkly dramatic backdrops to the graphic stories. One of the first accounts the task force heard was the experience of Linda Devoe, a seventeen-year-old prostitute who at eleven had run away from an abusive family in rural Nova Scotia and headed for the big city. In Halifax, she met a man of thirty-three who quickly persuaded her to move in with him: in rapid succession, he had sex with her, talked her into working the Hollis Street stroll—proof that she really loved him, as he put it— and subjected her to a taste of what she could expect if she ever opposed his wishes. Overcome with guilt after her first night as a working girl, Linda told her pimp she was leaving; the price of his love was too high. His reaction was swift and violent—and a chilling reminder to task force officers of Stacey's brutal treatment. Unwinding a wire coat hanger, he beat Linda repeatedly as she begged for mercy. That was not enough for him. He took a small steel bar from the pile of weights he used to keep his impressive physique well toned, and kneeling beside the terrified child, he ripped off her clothes, and raped her with the bar. Linda went back to the stroll the next night; she never argued with her pimp again.

It wouldn't be the last time the task force members heard of the Nova Scotia players' use of the wire whip that the girls described as a "pimp stick." They also learned submersion was a common form of abuse. An errant prostitute was forced into a full bathtub and her head held underwater until her tormentor felt she was certain she would suffocate. The punishments often seemed completely unprovoked—some pimps would whip a girl because they thought she might be talking to another pimp, or because they didn't like the way she answered when she was called. The beatings often took place in front of other girls—just as Manning Greer had alternately terrorized Taunya, Teri, and Gizelle—leaving them all feeling brutalized, demoralized, and completely powerless. Such subservience was the purpose of the torture: a passive girl tends not to struggle against her servitude in The Game. As they listened in shock, and with growing determination to put an end to such practices, the officers began to believe that many of these men had adopted the practice of beating prostitutes for fun, or to have something to tell their cohorts.

One teenager told investigators about an experience that seemed to support that theory. Her pimp had taken her to a card game, along with several other prostitutes enjoying a rare night off; the girls were drinking and joking, and the pimps were having a good time too. "I had a bit too much to drink, so he told me I couldn't have any more; well, I just laughed at him and said he was making me 'blue mad'— that's something I said all the time, not an insult or anything." She drew a deep breath and sipped at the Coke one of the officers had brought her. "But I could see he didn't like it, because he said we were leaving." Before returning to his apartment, the pimp stopped to pick something up at a pharmacy; when they got home, she found out what it was. "So he fills the tub and adds what he bought at the store—a bottle of blue dye. Then he tells me to get in, right up to my neck so I'm all covered with this tuff, from head to toe. After that I have to get into a bathing suit, and put my coat over it because we're

Blue jeans on the stroll. [Print from ATV video tape]

going back to the party." There, he ordered her to remove her coat and model for the other pimps: "She's real 'blue mad' now!" His buddies hooted and hollered, but the other prostitutes weren't impressed, not only because he'd punished her for no reason, but also because he'd totally outsmarted himself. That girl would have to wear slacks on the stroll, instead of a miniskirt—and she'd be in long sleeves, too, until the dye faded—which meant she'd be pulling in a lot less cash for her pimp. "That made it a little easier to take," she told the officers—but they surmised, with growing awareness of the methods of these players, that when the girl did come home with less money than usual, her pimp put the blame on her and probably came up with another gruesome punishment.

A critical aspect of the task force's approach involved befriending the girls whose trust the investigators earned, and providing support to them whenever they called. Some of them simply wanted a quick chat to break up the day or relieve an unpleasant night, while others were seeking a serious discussion of the reasons for staying away from The Game. It wasn't just phone calls, either. A number of team members were driving out to the Truro Training School for girls on an almost daily basis. This facility had quickly become a holding area for the youngest prostitutes caught up in Operation Hectic, and a safe haven for two of the teenagers whose rescue in Toronto had launched Operation Hectic—Taunya and Teri. Stacey, at seventeen, was too old for the facility and was still living with her family when the task force got its start.

It was on one of Craig Botterill's regular visits to Truro, this time to talk to Taunya, Teri, and another girl, that the prosecutor's last lingering doubts about the veracity of his young witnesses' horror stories faded away entirely. Botterill picked the girls up at the training centre and took them to a local steakhouse for lunch; during the meal, face to face for the first time with the heartbreaking youth of the individuals behind the graphic words of their sworn statements, he realized with a rush of sorrow and outrage that the task force was truly dealing with children. The girls acted silly and giddy in the restaurant, three energetic and slightly unruly daughters with an indulgent dad. He began to wonder if he should be considering child abuse charges instead of pimping. That night he talked with his wife about the issue, and both felt a surge of anger at the renewed awareness that fully grown men were preying on youngsters because other fully grown men were willing to pay a lot of money to have sex with them. Craig Botterill felt a new resolve to make the justice system work for girls who had been ignored by society for so long.

Operation Hectic Heats Up

What Botterill and the other investigators didn't know was that a serious problem was beginning to develop at the school they were visiting in Truro. Taunya, Teri, and some of the other girls held fast to their decision to stay away from The Game. For them, the institution, with its rules and mandatory training programs, provided a positive experience that also allowed them leisure time in the evenings and on weekends. Others used the freedom to return to Hollis Street for a couple of nights' work and some ready cash; they'd return to Truro fairly bursting with tales of pimps and dates that fascinated some of their schoolmates—like Keri Sherwood, a sixteen-year-old who had never been involved in prostitution. Keri was at the Truro school because of emotional problems: a foster child, she had been sexually abused by a youth at her foster home. Although she hadn't shared the experience with her counselors, she had described it extensively in her diary. Keri was impressed with the apparent independence of the young prostitutes, and on Sunday nights she would eagerly await their return—with new stories of money, sexual aberrations, and the adrenaline rush of life on the street. She soon decided to give prostitution a try. Taunya got wise to what was going on and tried to talk Keri out of her plan, but she could see the girl's quiet demeanor—and a confidence problem that bordered on self-hatred—made her a prime target for the pimps.

A few weeks after her first foray onto the Hollis stroll, Keri failed to return to Truro; she had been taken to Montreal by her pimp, Eric Conrad, who had spotted her freelancing downtown with some of her school friends, and claimed her as "his" girl. Actually, he had accosted her while she was making a phone call, ordering her into his shiny red sports car and informing her sternly that she owned him money for working on a corner he considered his exclusive property. The painfully introverted teenager just sat there silently, unresisting. A perfect situation for Eric, who much preferred the sound of his own voice. This was just the right girl to take on the road: Eric Conrad didn't like to stay in one place longer than a couple of weeks, and the prostitute he was running tended to be a chatterbox, anyway. Before leaving he handed his current girl over to another pimp. He decided to waive the usual leaving fee, not as a favor to the pimp but because he simply wanted to be rid of her. Just as she'd obeyed his command to get in the car, Keri quietly accepted Eric's announcement that they were going to Montreal. Inside, as recorded in the secret pages of her journal, Keri Sherwood was filled with excitement at Eric's descriptions of the places and people they would see, in Montreal and other cities. The budding writer within her thrilled to the opportunity for new material, but the naive adolescent could not know that life-as-work only goes so far; the journey on which Keri was embarking would take her way over the line, into an inexpressible nightmare.

Keri and Eric spent the night at his cousin's apartment in Dartmouth, and by noon the following day, she was on an airplane for the first time in her life. In Montreal, Eric rented a large car—the nicest Keri had ever been in—and checked them into a big, sparkling-clean hotel room. While she sat at a small writing table near the window, gazing out past the parking lot into the hot blue sky, her man phoned room service and ordered lunch. That night, her work began—and it was the beginning of the end of the daydream. The other girls working the Scotian stroll saw quickly that Keri wouldn't offer serious competition; she was young and pretty, but terribly passive, waiting for clients to approach her rather than accost them with the boldness she would need to develop if she was going to make enough money to satisfy her man. "You're not gonna get a date sittin' in Harvey's with your head down," one of the other girls succinctly put it.

At first, Eric didn't seem perturbed by his new girl's measly take. It was party time—2:00 A.M., and back at the hotel, a few other pimps and their girls were waiting for them. Eric and the other guys shared a few lines of pure coke, ostentatiously using a rolled fifty dollar bill for the purpose. The girls, as usual, were not invited to participate, and had to content themselves with pizza and beer. The routine continued for several nights before Eric began to get suspicious about the amount of money Keri was making; pretty and slim as she was, she ought to have been pulling in double the $400 she was averaging. First he accused her of withholding "his" money, and then he berated her for laziness. How was he supposed to pay for all these goodies if she was dragging her sorry ass around like an old nag put out to pasture? She'd just have to work longer hours. Eric's decision meant Keri had to go to the stroll in the middle of the afternoon. The move did nothing to improve her technique, if anything it made her even more reluctant to hustle. At night she assumed every man coming to the restaurant or the curb was looking for sex. In the daylight there were too many people around and she didn't know who to approach. She resorted to her night time habit of waiting for someone to approach her. After spending ten hours on the stroll, Keri only managed to bring in $600. The infuriated pimp turned on her, whacking her repeatedly in the head, then ordered her to spend the rest of the night on the bathroom floor. A few more nights of this, and Keri began forcing herself to hustle more actively; she hated what she was doing, but fear of Eric triumphed over her reluctance. Besides, the loathing she felt about herself was familiar territory.

Within two weeks, the "couple" was on the road again—Toronto, Winnipeg, Calgary, and finally Vancouver—another city, another stroll, another predawn party; Keri was amazed at the number of people Eric knew across the country, and it never occurred to her that anyone offering free coke and lots of drinks would find instant friends without too much trouble. It also didn't occur to her that she was paying the freight on this cross-Canada party. She even started to enjoy the late-night "fun," although in the morning, a profound depression would overcome the confused teenager; the only relief was her writing, and luckily Eric found all the poetry stuff more of a joke than a possible threat to him. He let her continue to keep her journal.

Before long, Eric's restlessness struck again, and Keri soon found herself back on the Hollis stroll, where her shy, immature appearance caught the attention of the task force's Mitch Ginn. The constable called her over and introduced himself, then asked her to get in the car so they could talk; as usual, she obeyed without hesitation. When Ginn asked who her man was, she refused to answer—Eric had told her countless times never, ever, to identify him to police. Ginn backed off, but he did wonder aloud whether she might be willing to go with him to Dartmouth to take part in a program the task force had set up for prostitutes; to this Keri agreed. Task force officers had started to keep a photo log of girls working on Hollis, as a way of monitoring their numbers and identifying new arrivals—and to initiate a before-and-after record, essential for Botterill's eventual court corroboration, of any abuse their pimps might subject them to. After the photo was taken, Ginn asked Keri if she would be willing to spend the night at a new, safe place that had been opened to house some of the participants in the program. Then they could talk. That was Ginn's plan when he dropped her off for a night at the safe house. Unfortunately, Keri was long gone by the time Ginn arrived the following morning. She had called Eric, and although she assured him she had told the police nothing, he decided to get her out of Halifax in case they tried again. He came to pick her up shortly after 9:00 A.M., and by early afternoon they were on a flight to Montreal. It would be more than two years before anyone in Halifax heard news of Keri Sherwood again.

The safe house that Keri never had a chance to truly take advantage of was the task force's response to a growing awareness that its increasing number of potential witnesses were in urgent need of support services. Officers had spent weeks observing pimps and gathering evidence to lay charges against them, but by late fall, the team was spending much of its time cultivating ongoing relationships—with the girls who could eventually testify against them. As more and more teenagers expressed an interest in breaking free of violent pimps, investigators found these girls had nowhere to go where they could avoid the street life and find the kind of counseling and support they needed.

The lack of support services was clear to Brad Sullivan and John Elliott as they continued to try to work with Stacey Jackson, who continued the aggressive stance to which she'd grown accustomed on the street. She was angry about being in Halifax, she was angry that Michael wasn't coming back to live with her right away, she was angry about almost everything. When Debbie Howard decided to move her daughter to a relative's home in another part of the province, she began refusing to sleep at night, preferring to sit up until dawn and sleep all day. She threatened to return to Toronto and the street life whenever she felt she wasn't getting what she wanted. Her deeply concerned relatives worked in shifts to make sure someone was around to talk to her at any time, but Stacey, far from appreciating this solicitude, felt trapped, and judged, by her "square" family. Not to mention that cop, the same one who'd been bugging her at the airport. Now here he was again in the kitchen, yapping on about his task force, how it was there to help girls like her—and there was her mom and Uncle Henry and everybody taking it all in...."Fuck off!" she shouted at Sullivan. "If I want help, I've got a family to help me!" She ignored her mother's pain, knowing Debbie Howard was well aware that "family," in this case, meant the Scotians.

Before he left, Brad Sullivan promised to seek some support for Stacey, and some relief for her mother and other relatives. Indeed, before the day was out, the officer contacted the province's community services department for advice, and was able to find space for her and another seventeen-year-old former prostitute at an Annapolis Valley shelter for battered women; department counselors had to bend the rules to get them in, but agreed with Sullivan that the teenagers' treatment at the hands of their pimps certainly constituted physical abuse. Surprisingly, Stacey accepted the move and agreed to give high school another try—deep within her remained the seeds of ambition for higher education—but after only two days in a classroom with "little kids" who knew nothing of the "real world," she and the other girl took off for the city. They were found on the outskirts of Dartmouth by a Cole Harbour RCMP officer; both of them had been drinking and were detained at the detachment overnight. The next day, the other girl agreed to return to the shelter, but Stacey insisted she would never return.

Stacey's family was exhausted and out of answers, so Sullivan continued to try to find help through the Department of Community Services. Stacey was sent to the Princess Alexandra unit of the Nova Scotia hospital, a ward for young people who need both counseling and educational facilities. At first, Stacey exploded in another burst of rage so extreme that she had to be sedated—the hospital is a psychiatric facility, and Stacey felt the police were treating her like "a crazy person." Within a few days, however, the unit's experienced counselors had enabled her to realize she was there to be helped, not judged. Still, Sullivan and the other task force members needed to find a long-term solution to accommodating their potential witnesses once they were off the streets.

Finally the decision was made to establish a safe house in the Halifax area: there would be no age restrictions, and investigators would no longer have to travel to Truro to talk to the girls, although some of them, like Taunya and Teri, opted to stay at the girls' school, a decision applauded by their parents who were beginning to believe the girls really did want help. The new safe house was located in an unused wing of the Nova Scotia Hospital, at the bottom of a hill just below the task force office in the Dartmouth Police Station. For the police the location was perfect. While the girls were in Truro, it took an hour to drive down and meet with them and the police were never

Dave Perry, left at table, briefs Halifax reporters October 1992.
[Print from ATV video tape]

sure what the girls were doing when they were not there. The new unit was a two minute drive from the task force office and they could see it as the drove to and from work every day.

The task force officers could thank their Toronto counterparts as much as anyone else for helping to get a safe house up and running. In the weeks and months following the Toronto raids Dave Perry became a regular visitor to Nova Scotia where he continued to interview his witnesses, guide the members of the new task force, and meet with the media. Perry had become a favorite of local reporters. He knew prostitution better than most people and he knew how to speak in the sound bytes that were the lifeblood of modern journalism. Perry condemned the "monsters" he said were behind the "highly organized and far reaching" Nova Scotia pimping family. He claimed his raid had "just barely reached below the tip of the iceberg." On October seventh, Perry described the success of Moberly House, the JTF safe house in Toronto, to reporters. He told them a safe house was "essential" if the fight against the "vicious men who prey on these children" was to succeed. Perry well knew the local Task Force needed and wanted a safe house and he told the reporters as much, saying if the resources were not available "I can only humbly say that I think they should be given them. If the dollars aren't there it can't be done." The following morning, the provincial justice minister announced the formation of a committee whose first priority would be to look into setting up a safe house. Hardly a firm commitment, but that came two months later when Roland Thornhill, Minister of Community Services, announced a half million dollar a year budget for the operation of the safe house.

The new residence was named Sullivan House, much to the delight of task force officers who teased Brad Sullivan by claiming he had insisted the house be named for him. The name actually originated from the name of small pond in Halifax. When community service workers met in Halifax to discuss the establishment of the safe house they met in another youth facility across from Sullivan's Pond. At the end of the meeting when someone asked what the new house would be called they all agreed Sullivan House would be appropriate enough. After that meeting Shane Kirk, a twenty-four-year-old child services counselor, began preparing Sullivan House for its new role. Kirk and other workers did everything they could to remove the institutional appearance of the old hospital building and give it a more relaxed home like feel. Stacey Jackson was the first resident, and she was met at the door by a smiling Shane Kirk. Stacey thought Kirk was another task force officer; his muscular build and short hair were

Sullivan House.

enough to identify him as a policeman for her. Kirk quickly informed Stacey that he was not a policeman but that he was there to help her make the transition to a normal lifestyle. Within days, other girls began arriving, and Stacey found herself among friends who shared her problems and frustrations, and understood where she had come from. The girls lost no time redecorating their small rooms, putting up posters from their favorite magazines and setting out their jewelry and scarves to brighten up the usual institutional beiges and yellows that Kirk had unthinkingly used in his efforts to make the place more homey. The girls also did some redecorating in the large common room they shared when they were not in their own bedrooms. The common area gave the girls a lovely view of the tree-filled lawn of the hospital—and, unfortunately for girls wavering on the brink of a return to The Game, an unobstructed view of the lower end of Hollis Street, just across the Harbour.

Access to Sullivan House was closely restricted, and even relatives had to observe visiting hours. Kirk and the others running the facility heeded warnings from task force officers concerned that pimps would try to kill one of the girls as a means of getting a strong message to the others. Sullivan House followed a double lock down routine. The girls were housed on the second floor behind a large wooden locked door. On the main floor even task force officers were required to show their badges through a hole in the main entrance before they were granted access to the lobby. Visitors would walk through the large lobby, then up a flight of stairs that looked like it had been taken from a 1950s

Hollywood musical. At the top was a foyer with a door that opened onto the residence itself—and no one without clearance from counselors and the task force was permitted beyond either the main entrance or the one at the top of those stairs. Along with Sullivan House's location, on the second story of a building minutes from a police station, investigators had imposed the stringent visiting rules to protect the girls.

In its early days, Sullivan House was also a locked unit, but some of the girls became so outraged—they had come from Truro, where no such restriction existed—that they lowered themselves on bed sheets from the common-room window and took off, some never to return while others came back reluctantly after being found by task force officers. A system of supervised releases took care of the problem. At first, the supervised releases were a challenge for the counselors required to provide the supervision. Shane Kirk recalls one trip to a Dartmouth bowling alley that proved disastrous. "There were five girls, and the minute we arrived at the bowling alley they all ran. We had task force officers, regular Dartmouth police force officers and every spare body from Sullivan House out looking." The girls were not intent on escaping and had just run off to give their young counselor a tough time. They all returned after a few hectic hours of searching on the part of Kirk and the police.

The task force officers saw Sullivan House as a safe refuge for the girls but those working inside the safe house saw it as much more. To counselors like Kirk, Sullivan House was the first step toward the beginning of a new life for the girls. The Sullivan House staff consisted of trained child care professionals who had no trouble seeing the girls as victims, and they set out to help them. The most common problem faced by the counselors was developing a sense of self-worth in the former prostitutes. "A lack of self-esteem was evident in all of the girls and we set out to use a system of rewards to help them feel good about themselves." Kirk recalls, "It was very important that we set goals the girls could easily achieve, if they failed they would return to the negative self image that had led to so much trouble for them in the first place." The system devised in Sullivan house served two purposes: it gave the girls a sense of accomplishment and taught them basic life skills they were lacking. Simple hygiene became the first lesson and the first reward based incentive program at Sullivan House. Many of the girls had come from families where they had endured years of neglect and had not been taught the most basic skills. The Sullivan House rules were simple, when residents got out of bed they were required to make the bed and then head to the washroom to wash and brush their hair and teeth. "It was really easy for the girls to develop those habits but we made a big deal when they did" says Kirk. "We used every opportunity to tell them what a fine job they were doing or how good they looked."

Sullivan House was the answer to many problems but presented several of its own. Many of the problems came about because of an apparently innocent piece of technology in a short corridor linking the common room to the dormitory's main hallway—a pay phone. Several girls had taken to calling their pimps, sometimes complaining about being kept in the "loony bin." A few of the girls had jotted down the cell-phone numbers for their men on the wall by the phone, while others had written their initials and their pimps' inside penciled hearts.

That same telephone also created a great deal of trouble for Stacey Jackson, just at a time when she was beginning to settle down and start to seriously plan her future. It started when a girl arrived at Sullivan House from the Truro school and immediately began to taunt Stacey, who had no idea why. She confronted the girl, who said she was in love with Smit and would be joining him the moment he was set free. It was all Stacey's fault that he was behind bars, and she'd better not make matters worse during his trial in Toronto. The girl had signed on her own pimp but that did not alter her judgment of Stacey. One day, the girl was talking on the pay phone when Stacey walked by.

"Here, Stacey—someone wants to talk to you," she said, and Stacey took the phone. "Hello, who is it?"

"Never mind that, girl. I got a message for you and the rest of those bitches planning to go to Toronto." Stacey recognized the voice; it was a seventeen-year-old nephew of Manning Greer's. She called him by name and asked what the message was, trying to stay calm. "No one is gonna testify at those trials," he said threateningly. "Anyone who tries is gonna be shot on the courthouse steps."

"Fuck off," Stacey offered in response, then handed back the phone and walked away. She heard the other girl express surprise that she'd recognized him, but that was just plain stupid. The pimp had a bad lisp and always sounded hoarse; anyone who heard him once would know his voice forever.

Later in the evening, Stacey called John Elliott and told him she wanted to talk to him. In the weeks after moving into the safe house, she'd developed a strong bond with the officer, whom she trusted in a way that was not possible for her with Brad Sullivan. For his part, Sullivan considered the relationship between girls and their case officers much more important than trying to prove anything with

Stacey, and he willingly passed her file to Elliott. The initial animosity between Sullivan and Stacey could have been worked through but her fondness for Elliott made that pointless, as long as she trusted a police officer they were happy. The constable was at the task force office when Stacey called, he said he'd be right over. They went to their usual spot to talk—a nearby Tim Horton's coffee shop—and a badly shaken Stacey described the pimp's threat. Maybe she shouldn't testify after all; maybe the family really would gun her down on the courthouse steps. No way, Elliott assured her; he would take care of that pimp, and she would have nothing to worry about. Stacey cracked a smile, but Elliott knew he would have to make good on his promise. Her confidence, like her emotional stability, was newly won and could be so easily tipped in the wrong direction.

The next morning, as Elliott grimly prepared the paperwork for his planned arrest of Greer's nephew, two visitors arrived at the task force office who were in town to interview Taunya about their case against the Big Man, Eddy, and Slugger. When he heard what had happened, Dave Perry was relieved that Elliott planned to move against the young pimp, and following his trip to Truro, was delighted to hear the Mountie was only just setting out for the high school his suspect attended; the Toronto officer looked forward to

Another suspect is arrested in Toronto as the pimping investigations continue.
[Print from ATV video tape]

being there for the takedown. Perry, his partner, and their escorting officer arranged to meet Elliott in the school parking lot just before classes let out; the Mountie had informed the principal of the pending arrest and confirmed that his suspect was there that day. Like most bubble-gummers, he only played The Game after school.

Elliott arrived first—but he was too late; the young man had just pulled out of the schoolyard with a group of friends. Elliott got a description of the car, raced out of the parking lot, and spotted the vehicle after only a few minutes. Slapping his portable flashing light on the dashboard of his unmarked cruiser, he gave chase; the pimp's car pulled over on the highway leading out of Cole Harbour and towards North Preston. Perry and his companion officers were on the same highway having linked up with it on their way back from Truro; they arrived just in time to see John Elliott approach the passenger-side window of the pimp's car. Elliott identified himself, asked the suspect to get into the cruiser, and told him why he was being arrested. A short time later, the seventeen-year-old was in the task force office, charged with obstruction.

The growing number of arrests, albeit still mostly in Toronto and Montreal, and the increased cooperation from girls involved in prostitution led investigators to expect a change in the behavior of the pimps. It didn't happen. The Scotian players' arrogance was unwavering: they continued to blatantly run girls on the Hollis stroll and to recruit new victims; even the incarceration of Greer and his cohorts hadn't crimped the style of their Halifax-based "relatives," who gave the impression that the Big Man and company would soon be back on the street. While many young prostitutes were giving up The Game, many more were still trying to survive their dangerous profession. Amber Borowski was one of them.

Amber was still in The Game; although her long time partner Sheri Fagan was out, for good she claimed. Sheri was more afraid of her crack cocaine addiction then she had been of her pimp. When the Big Man went to jail, Sheri went to a social services counselor for help. She was placed in a detox program and managed to beat the crack and The Game. After the arrests, Amber left Niagara Falls and Sheri and returned to Toronto where she was reunited with her daughter and moved in with a businessman, a client who'd taken a liking to the prostitute over the year or so they had known each other. She continued to work the Scotian stroll—but as a freelancer—and, unencumbered by a greedy pimp, was able to take in a great deal of money. Unfortunately, one jealous master only substituted for another: crack cocaine, to which she was so seriously addicted that she ended up

A Nova Scotian girl tells her story to the author, just off the Scotian stroll in Toronto. [Print from ATV video tape]

with about the same pittance she'd been given as a member of the family. Most times, there was only enough to pay a baby-sitter and buy a few necessities for her daughter. One night, she spent an unbelievable eight hundred dollars on the deadly drug, and when she returned home, she found a note from her lover. He was tired of her new routine and told her to make a decision, was it going to be The Game and crack cocaine or a life with him for her and the baby. Amber thought she wanted to make the right choice—not only could crack kill her, she realized, but if she landed in jail, her child would certainly be taken away. She wanted to make a clean break but she couldn't stop hustling, and she couldn't stop smoking crack.

Ironically, the Nova Scotian pimps ultimately made the decision for Amber: she was told by one of the pimps that she could no longer work for herself, and rather than try to find a man again, Amber decided to phone her foster parents, Amy and Steve Nicholson, and ask them if she could come home for Christmas. "It'll be the best present you could give us," her relieved and delighted foster dad told her. The reunion in Halifax began with joy, but Amber's mood swung into suspicion when the Nicholsons introduced her to a friend of theirs, the task force's Darrell Gaudet; like most street-hardened prostitutes, she deeply mistrusted the police.

As for Gaudet, he was seriously worried about Amber, not just because of her hostility, but because her appearance clearly showed she was a crack addict. Indeed, the teenager who used to laugh about her bulky body was now almost anorexic. Her skin was a pasty, ghostly white behind the sunken, black-rimmed eyes. Gaudet gave Amber one of his cards and offered to help if she was pressured to return to The Game, or if she was having trouble re-entering the square world. Only a few days later, she had left that world behind—at least at night—and taken up prostitution again, this time on the north-end Halifax block, known as the crack stroll, because its girls serviced clients only to pay the price of admission to a dingy neighborhood crack house for another little rock. For two-weeks the eighteen-year-old spent nights on the stroll and days lying to her foster parents about what she was doing. But the pressure and guilt became unbearable, and Amber found a place to stay temporarily; the apartment of a girl she had previously worked with. Amy Nicholson agreed to watch the baby for a few days, and Amber went back to work, on Hollis Street this time.

It didn't take long for the unattached teenager to come to the attention of a pimp, Jeremy ("Jay") MacDonald, who played The Game as a sideline to his main activities—robbery and assault. A three-time loser who had spent most of the 1980s in federal prisons, Jay always ran a couple of girls just to make ends meet when his primary professions weren't yielding either enough income or enough satisfaction, but he never considered himself a potential as a major player—until his employee of the moment, Deena Jacobs, told him about Amber, whom she'd befriended on the stroll. Amber had worked for Manning Greer, Deena pointed out, and Jay became keenly interested. Here was his chance to make it big at something: robbing innocent citizens wasn't paying nearly as well as it used to, and there seemed to be no chance of reviving his dormant career as an entertainer. Oh sure, he'd played with a band in Ontario and Quebec in the early days, and there was that time he worked as an exotic dancer—Ottawa or someplace; the ladies really took to his tall, lean, wild look, he reminisced egotistically—but he was too old for the nightclub biz. He had to admit he was not the only one showing signs of age. His gal Deena was getting a little long in the tooth. Twenty-seven, wasn't she? Another good reason for checking out the new talent. As he was fond of pointing out, "Jay ain't nobody's fool." Recruiting this girl should be a piece of cake, he told himself; she didn't have her own place, Deena had told him, and she desperately wanted to make a home for her baby daughter. Those were facts he could use.

Indeed, when Jay promised Amber he could find her an apartment, her interest was immediately piqued—and he could already see himself paying off that whopping five-thousand-dollar fine that prevented him from renewing his driver's license and getting a set of wheels again. The fine had long been forgotten by the irresponsible pimp; it was an insurance company judgment issued against him in 1972 when he had been at fault in an accident and did not have coverage. He had forgotten about it but the registry of motor vehicles had not. He had been informed of the problem when a Nova Scotia police officer ordered him to get a valid drivers license after he was stopped for running a stop sign. His license had long since expired and when Jay went to get a new one he was told the price would be five thousand and ten dollars. Five thousand would cover the insurance judgment and ten would take care of the renewal fee. Jay was using Amber to get what he wanted, but she was also using him to find a place for her and the baby to live, and an incentive to kick her crack habit. Pimps, she knew well, did not tolerate their girls using drugs, and she hoped the fear of violent retaliation on his part would be enough to keep her clean.

Unlike Manning Greer, who could take in more money in a month than Jay often made in a year, Amber's new man couldn't afford to rent an apartment for her—but he did know how to work the system. After the teenager picked up her daughter, telling her foster parents she'd found a job and an apartment, Jay took her to the local welfare office, and—presto!—a bit of cash and a place to live. Her objective, unfortunately, dissolved in the fumes from her first crack pipe as Jay's girl. Only a few days after going to work for the pimp, Amber found a way to work both the north-end and Hollis strolls— one early in the evening, the downtown area later at night—thus earning enough to satisfy both her habit and her new man.

It was perfect; at least, for awhile. The Game's information pipeline eventually led Jay to the truth; he caught Amber in the apartment one night passing around a pipe with another prostitute and a taxi driver she'd befriended on the crack stroll. The cabby took up Jay's invitation for him to leave—"You, get the fuck out *now!*"—and the pimp turned on Amber in a wild rage, kicking her violently in the stomach and legs, cursing her as a useless crack-head who was wasting his money, and finally, exhausted by his workout, adopting his familiar line of asking his girl if she somehow *needed* such punishment because she only felt loved when beaten. "Most 'hos" come from broken homes and they see a beating as sign of affection: that was Jay's rationalization for whatever viciousness he felt provoked to express. His bizarre "therapy" out of the way, Jay brought in Amber's daughter: how would *she* feel to have a crack addict as a mom?

He raved on, as the other prostitute sat numbly in a corner and Amber, her dizziness still making the room spin around her, wishing Jay would shut up. Finally he ordered her to dress for work; Amber obeyed sullenly, but her attitude soon changed when he casually informed her, en route downtown, that her daughter would not be coming back to the apartment that night; the child needed protection from such a drug-infested environment. Amber's frantic tears and pleas were all Jay needed to hear; he knew he had a powerful weapon against her, and fully intended to use it. He took Amber's baby to his apartment and found a bubble-gummer to do the baby-sitting.

For three days, obedient and terrified, Amber stayed away from the crack stroll and the addictive drug; but still Jay refused to return her child. One late December night, as the emaciated, miserable teenager stood shivering on the stroll in her spandex pants and a jacket, Darrell Gaudet and his partner cruised by. The officer invited Amber to get warm in the car for awhile—and maybe she just wanted someone to chat with—and she gratefully complied. The young woman desperately wanted to ask Gaudet for help, but she didn't dare risk Jay's wrath; he had her baby, and the child was really all that kept her going. When Gaudet saw he wasn't going to get anywhere, he dropped Amber off on the stroll, once again reminding her that he would be there to help any time she needed him.

At the end of the night, Jay met Amber and Deena on Hollis and took them to his place, telling the younger girl he wanted to talk to her. Amber had fallen off the wagon and was still a little high. She had managed to sneak a hit before the end of the night—and she slumped gratefully into the sofa at Jay's invitation, looking around with disgust at her man's slovenly housekeeping. Like that of most pimps, his sparsely furnished apartment was a disaster area, strewn with dirty dishes, bags, cans, and fast-food wrappers. Amber and Deena settled down to watch a late-night TV talk show, and Jay joined them. He seemed affable at first, but suddenly he whipped around on the sofa and slapped Amber, then hauled her into the bathroom, where the tub was brimming.

"Jay, what's wrong? Why are you doing this?" She knew what was coming.

"Gonna sign on Jay, bitch? Jay ain't nobody's fool, woman. Jay knows who you been talkin' to, you stupid 'ho." Deena had spotted her getting into the cruiser with Gaudet and had called Jay. Amber was terrified as Jay pushed her into the tub and forced her head under the water. She'd fallen in backwards and managed to drape her right arm over the side, so she pulled with all her might to stay on the surface.

"Jay, please! I'm not signing on anyone!" she insisted. "He's a friend of my father, and he just wanted me to leave and go home, Jay, stop pushing me—I didn't tell him about you." By now the pimp was too angry to placate. "Jay knows you still takin' crack, too. That's my fuckin' money you been wastin', slut. *My* fuckin' money, not yours. You ain't gonna waste no more of Jay's money, you hear me?"

Amber did hear him—and so did the upstairs tenant, who sat up in bed, unsure what to do next. They were arguing about money, he could hear; and you didn't necessarily want to intervene in an argument between a couple over financial matters. He decided to wait and listen. Downstairs, Jay was still trying to get Amber's head underwater; his hands too slippery to hold her, he tried standing and kicking her over and over in the chest, then the face. There was a terrible crash as the shower curtain and rod came down—he'd been yanking on it to stand up—but Jay just kept slamming his foot into Amber's body. Closing her eyes, Amber tried to resist the downward slide into the water, but the arm holding her up was growing numb, and the blows to her head were weakening her resolve. Suddenly, Jay stepped away from the tub, and Amber opened her eyes to see her baby crawling towards the bathroom, gurgling happily. She wanted to call out to the child but she didn't have the strength, and Jay had already carried the little girl back into the bedroom, where she'd been sleeping on the floor with the sitter. Amber later recalled the incident, "It was a miracle, she had never crawled before and if she didn't do it at that moment I know I'd be dead." Weakly, Amber hauled herself out of the tub and staggered into the living room, where she sat stiffly on the sofa, her sopping body trembling with shock and cold, her helpless tears coursing down her ravaged face. All was deathly quiet; the man upstairs drifted back to sleep and the now calm Jay who'd lost his resolve at the site of the baby was rummaging through the linen closet for a bath towel. Returning to the living room, he wrapped the towel around Amber and calmly began to reprove her for "forcing" him to punish her that way—another familiar approach pimps take to avoid responsibility for their brutality, as Stacey Jackson had discovered after Smit beat her with the wire whip.

When he got tired of talking—and that took quite some time—Jay scooped up a few blankets from the filthy floor and tossed them over Amber, who, ignoring her wet clothes, curled up and fell asleep. When she awoke, Jay and Deena were gone, and so was her daughter. She didn't bother to look for something to change into, just staggered out into the cold, grey morning, found a pay phone, and called a friend, who agreed to let Amber come to her place for a few days.

Darrell Gaudet had spent a sleepless night worrying about finding a way to help the badly addicted and obviously frightened Amber, but he had to put her out of his mind for the moment; the officer was about to move on a nineteen-year-old pimp who had savagely beaten a prostitute of sixteen. The girl, who had come to the task force looking for help, warned police that the man had a gun and had boasted of a black belt in Karate. "He'd rather die than get arrested," as she put it to Gaudet. It was bullet-proof vests all round as several unmarked task-force vehicles started their pursuit early in the evening. The detectives waited for the best opportunity to make their move. It came when the pimp cruised down a quiet tree lined street. There were no pedestrians, and that reduced the risk of someone getting hurt if the pimp started shooting. Gaudet slipped the portable flashing light onto the dash of the unmarked car and watched as the pimp pulled over to the curb. As his partner covered him, Gaudet approached the car; the teenager stepped out quickly, his hands behind his head. By the time he was in the back of the cruiser, listening as Gaudet read him his rights, the dangerous martial artist with the death wish was weeping like a toddler. Gaudet and his partner exchanged disgusted glances as they headed back to Dartmouth. It was a scene that would be played out again and again, as investigators discovered many of the pimps, so fearless about brutalizing a slight teenage girl, turned to jelly when confronted with aggression. Like schoolyard bullies, or wolves, they culled the weak from the herd and only struck when they knew they had the upper hand.

Gaudet would soon have another opportunity to test his budding theory on the psychology of bullies. In the first week of January 1993, Amber finally decided to talk to the task force investigator who had patiently held out his promise of help for almost two months. She had been working the crack stroll and getting high ever since New Year's Eve, when Jay, once again using her child as leverage, spent what was supposed to be a celebration dinner with his family, trying to persuade Amber to return to Hollis Street as his girl. She refused, and he told her to forget about ever seeing her daughter again. He had visited the social worker at the welfare office and told her all about Amber's crack habit, and soon she would be declared an unfit mother and her baby placed in care. That wasn't quite true: Jay had seen Amber's worker—and done nothing to correct the woman's inference that he was the child's father—but no mention was made of action against Amber. The social worker simply told Jay that Amber would have to decide that she wanted help to break her habit. Amber knew nothing of this; when Jay left the party briefly, she met her friend the crack-addicted cabbie and made for the north-end stroll—and some all-too-temporary relief for her anguish. Four days later Amber finally made her move. She went to visit the welfare case officer.

Amber told the understandably confused social worker that Jay had abducted her daughter in an attempt to force her to return to prostitution; the woman took in Amber's black eye—a legacy of Jay's submersion attempt—and gaunt, agitated appearance, then told the teenager her pimp's version of events. Jay, who had come into the office the day before, claimed she had abandoned her child to work the streets and take drugs. With him on the visit was Amber's daughter, who was now in care. She couldn't promise anything, the social worker said, as gently as possible, but perhaps Amber would be willing to talk to someone from the task force on prostitution. "Darrell Gaudet—" the teenager said. "He said he would help me." And she burst into tears.

Later that day, Amber finally told Gaudet all about Jay, and her daughter, and the beatings. He immediately made arrangements for her to go to Sullivan House, and obtained a warrant for the pimp's arrest. Taking Jay into custody was even easier than nailing the nineteen-year-old bully. Still obsessed with that unpaid fine but unable to come up with the cash, Jay decided to fight it out in court; an official at the provincial courthouse in downtown Halifax called Gaudet shortly after the warrant was issued, telling him the suspect was there to argue his case. When Jay finished testifying, Gaudet simply walked up to him and placed him under arrest for assault, attempted murder, and living on the avails of prostitution.

Stacey and Amber bonded quickly at Sullivan House—hardly surprising, since they were among the oldest girls at the safe house and had already met in Toronto. They were both single mothers of very young children they faced losing to the courts. The Nova Scotia Department of Social Services sought custody of Amber's daughter, arguing that the child deserved more stability than her mother could provide, and the family of Stacey's former boyfriend had asked for full custody of her son. Both teenagers already sensed the inevitable— their children would be taken from them— and soon began to reconsider their decisions to leave The Game.

Stacey openly discussed her doubts with John Elliott: Why should she leave the street for a "shit job" paying minimum wage, and live in the square world with people who could never understand what she'd been through? And yeah, she was talking to a pimp on the phone these days; why shouldn't she? It was a free country, wasn't it? Besides, he had promised her that he would never, ever treat her the way Smit did. And speaking of Smit, maybe she wouldn't testify against him after all. Maybe the task force was all just about using her and the other girls—as her would-be man had told her—just to get their statement and their testimony, then the officers would move onto the next case and forget all about them. Elliott argued passionately with Stacey, who had, he told her, the talent and energy to be anything she wanted in life. She only had to be patient with herself, learn to believe in herself again. It was the pimps who were playing the manipulation game, who were using the girls—not to mention beating them within an inch of their lives, as she well knew. Sure, they were polite and gentle on the phone, but what evidence did she have that they wouldn't turn vicious when she joined them? Hadn't they done that in the past, to her, to her friend Amber, to her friend Annie Mae? Didn't they deserve to be put away where they could never hurt another girl again?

Throughout Halifax-Dartmouth, in coffees shops and parents' homes, at Sullivan House and at the residential school in Truro, over the phone and in police cars and at the task-force office, conversations very similar to this were playing themselves out, again and again, as investigators and counselors fought to get their points across to deeply troubled young people like Stacey. The stakes were immeasurably high. Those struggling to save the girls knew there would be some lost—but Stacey Jackson would not be one of them.

She did come precariously close to returning to The Game; John Elliott's mention of her dear friend Annie Mae prompted a renewed bout of nostalgia for the good times and laughs they'd shared. All the terror, pain, and confusion of her experiences in Halifax and Toronto began to recede into the rosy haze of a daydream—she and Annie Mae together again, sharing a little apartment, maybe even working for themselves. Or maybe not; all pimps weren't as screwed up as Smit, and they came and protected you when you lucked out and got stuck with a bad date. Stacey had pretty much decided to give it another go.

On January 28 she changed her mind. It took a tragedy—a heartbreakingly ironic tragedy—to finally set Stacey free. Annie Mae was dead, slain in an apartment only a few kilometres from Sullivan House. Slain by a pimp whose anger against her decision to choose another man got out of control. She knew about that one; still had bruises on her thighs to remind her of what had happened when she tried to leave Smit for Joystick, way back in the summer. It seemed so long ago, but it was only four months. So much had happened, and so much still faced her—the custody battle, the trial, school.... But Stacey Jackson, perhaps for the first time in her life, felt a deep certainty she knew could never be destroyed: she would keep two very important promises. One she made to John Elliott, earlier in the evening, when he'd come to tell her about Annie Mae—she would testify against Smit. The other she was making to herself, now, alone in the common room at Sullivan House; never again would she work as a prostitute. Raising her glass of Coke, Stacey offered up a toast: "Here's to you, Annie Mae."

Within a few days of her friend's death, police had decided to move Stacey to Toronto pending the trial of Michael Sears—Smit. Investigators were concerned about her facing any more pressure from pimps like the one she'd been talking to (although they needn't have worried about her yielding to the persuasion), and although Smit's trial was still more than a month away, it was decided Stacey should be sent to the safe house Dave Perry had described to local reporters months earlier. It was in a part of the city far from the downtown stroll.

Back in Halifax, the teenagers at the safe house and the residential school in Truro continued to develop closer bonds with the investigators handling their files. There was still the daily struggle to keep girls from returning to the street but there was also reason for the task force officers to feel a sense of accomplishment. Teri MacDonald had left the Truro training school but not for a return to The Game. Teri promised her case officer she would testify in Toronto when the time came but told him that until then she did not want to hear from him. She was not upset with the officer, she explained, she was just making a clean break from everyone and everything associated with the part of her life. Teri was returning home to live with her mother and restart her life and to do it she wanted to erase that sordid chapter completely. Teri's mother promised to call the officer at the first sign of trouble; she never had to. Taunya was another success story; she remained at the Truro school but had shown the counselors there she was committed to remaining free of The Game.

With new witnesses coming forward all the time, and existing ones often seeking conversations with the officers every day, task force members had their hands full. It was in the winter of 1993 that

The arrests continue in Halifax. [Print from ATV video tape]

the representatives of Operation Hectic began to realize how appropriate the name was. The number of files grew steadily. Between January and March of 1993 the task force officers arrested twenty-five pimps who had not been picked up, or even identified in the statements obtained, during the Toronto bust. More importantly in the eyes of Brad Sullivan they had managed to convince thirty young girls to leave the streets and take up residence in the safe house or the Truro Residential Centre. Each new case brought revelations of cruelty and violence that stunned and angered investigators all over again, strengthening the officers' resolve to see the project through.

In early 1993, despite the growing number of pimps in custody at the Halifax County Correctional Centre, most of the remaining players carried on their business as freely as usual. Investigators learned that a few minor players had left The Game for other professions, but the others continued to take their chances. Other than Manning Greer's family of players, most Nova Scotian pimps worked in small independent groups. They knew the value of the blowfish approach. Many had helped Greer when he needed it and now they joined ranks to take on this new, police threat. Ironically in their twisted logic it was not the threat of imprisonment they feared. They believed they were losing the respect of their girls and that they would not tolerate. They did not want over confident prostitutes who knew a simple call to the task force would take a player out of The Game. They needed to return fear to the streets. The newly formed cooperative of pimps decided to make an example of one of the prostitutes; fifteen-year-old Clara Ferguson was in trouble again.

Clara, who had been forced to chose the bullet that would kill her during the incident Manning Greer's enforcer had so readily bragged about, had returned and had managed to stay away from crack cocaine. She found a new pimp, but by January, with his demands for countless attentions and services becoming an increasing burden, she made the mistake of threatening him. She would call the task force and sign on him—then he would stop being so pushy. Her rash action was more the result of outrage than thoughtless defiance: her elder sister, who, like Clara, had run away from home in her early teens to escape sexual abuse by a family friend, had been badly beaten by the Scotian pimps as a supposed cure for her cocaine addiction. From the day she chose to become a prostitute, Clara had been following her older sister's lead, first into the Scotian family and later into crack addiction. By January of 1993, Clara's sister was working as a freelancer in Toronto; long after being beaten and turned loose by the family. She worked now to pay the pusher not the pimp.

Clara's pimp and a group of other players talked over the young prostitute's threat; if she was hanging out on Hollis bragging about that threat then they were all in trouble. The girls would start losing respect for their men—that is, stop fearing them. Something had to be done. Clara's pimp, Miguel Joseph, picked her up on the stroll one night in January and drove her to a house in North Preston. It was the beginning of three days of hell for the teenager, who was repeatedly gang-raped, beaten, and threatened with worse reprisals if she ever stepped out of line again. The message worked, to a degree. Clara was demoralized and defeated, she would never again threaten or disrespect Miguel, at least that was how she felt upon leaving the house where she had been so savagely tortured. What the pimps had not counted on was Clara's friends on the street. Clara was well liked by the other girls on Hollis Street, and they were infuriated when a couple of the pimps involved in her brutalization started bragging about what they'd done. By then, the information pipeline was moving, and task force investigators found out what had happened—the torture, and the message it was supposed to send to officers about the esteem in which Operation Hectic was held by the Halifax pimping community.

The girl they found on Hollis Street was angry, bruised, and more than a little confused. Clara had worked the streets for two years, and her mistrust of the police was even stronger than Stacey Jackson's; the cops had busted her and booked her—and, worst of all, sent her home when her age was discovered. She was not inclined to cooperate with them now, but she could see these men were different. They weren't arresting her; they were offering her a place in a safe house where she'd find other girls trying to break free of The Game, and they were giving her plenty of time to make up her mind whether she wanted to sign on the men who had assaulted her. She decided to take them up on the offer. The girls at Sullivan House welcomed Clara and urged her to allow the task force to move on that pimp and his buddies.

This advice, sound as it was, also signaled a new motivation for some of the young women at Sullivan House who began to view the task force as a weapon of revenge against pimps, not necessarily a way to stop working the streets. The attack on Clara had fostered the very attitude it was designed to eliminate. By the time Clara arrived, house rules permitted the young witnesses to sign themselves out on passes for several hours at a time. The new procedure facilitated Amber's new routine: during the day, she talked to the counselors about her ostensible plans for the future; at night she worked the north-end stroll and partied with her cabbie friend at the crack houses.

Clara, too, started playing it both ways, giving investigators their statement and agreeing that she would testify in court against her tormentors, while at the same time shopping around for a new pimp. Like many of the other girls, Clara also fell into the habit of bartering with investigators for the treats she wanted—lunch at KFC in exchange for information about life on the street; cigarettes and conversation for the background on a certain pimp; coffee and pop for a week to tell the officers about how girls were taken from Nova Scotia to other provinces. Crass, perhaps, but the system was what the girls had grown accustomed to in their dealings with pimps; and the officers knew what they were doing, and understood why—they could only hope it sank in that task force investigators were a whole lot different than pimps in their demands and behaviors.

By the spring of 1993, the task force had discovered that the Nova Scotia pimping operation was much broader than they had thought. Greer and his family regularly ran girls from Halifax through Montreal, Ottawa, Toronto, and Niagara Falls, like Clara and Amber had informed them, but now their police contacts were describing Scotian pimping activity in Calgary and Vancouver, and, most recently, they were starting to hear about pimps from Nova Scotia operating in the United States. This realization was prompted by a call from a New York City transit police officer in April. He had noticed a man in his mid- to late thirties leading an apparently injured teenage girl through one of the turnstiles in a subway station. He didn't like the looks of the situation, so he approached the two of them and discovered the source of her difficulty—an untreated stab wound. While he was comforting her, the man—her pimp—vanished into the usual throng of commuters; the officer took the fourteen-year-old to the hospital and found out what had happened. To task force officers, it started as a familiar story: a Nova Scotia teenager lured into prostitution by a pimp posing as ardent suitor, she was taken first to Montreal, where she worked the Scotian stroll for only a few weeks before he told her they were going to New York. This was the new part, at least to the investigators: the Nova Scotia pimp sold the teenager to a New York pimp for about a thousand dollars. Two task force officers went to New York to take her home. Luckily, she was able to turn away from prostitution, but unluckily for investigators, she refused to give police a statement against the pimp who'd recruited her, saying she wanted to forget all about her ordeal. However, officers now had an untravelled path—to the United States—to explore in their efforts to combat juvenile prostitution. They questioned some of their young witnesses about other examples of international sex-trading by Maritime pimps. They discovered that the practice was sporadic. The Scotians' occasional forays south revealed a ready market. Still, the Nova Scotia pimps had no apparent connection to the huge international market in juvenile prostitutes. Their motives seemed to be consistent, the girls were a source of money and if they were on the road and someone wanted to buy a girl that was a way to make a fast buck. The pimps knew they could recruit a replacement.

Still, their brush with the international sex trade gave Sullivan and Elliott an opportunity to renew their investigation of the Kimberly McAndrew case, stonewalled yet again the previous fall during their frustrating interviews with Greer and his uncle, and still lying dormant after police departments in every major Canadian city reported no leads from the photographs of the girl that the task force had sent them. The officers now wondered if Kimberly, like the fourteen-year-old in New York, could have been taken to the United States—but such a search would be massive and extremely costly, and could not be immediately launched. The best the task force could do was forward Kimberly's picture to police forces in the United States and keep asking about her when they interviewed girls in Canada.

Sullivan and Elliott kept Kimberly's file alive while they and the other investigators explored yet another angle of the multi-faceted juvenile prostitution problem—escort services. Discussions with the young witnesses had yielded insights that mirrored the research Darrell Gaudet had been conducting on his own even before the task force was formed. His findings, now contained in a brief, "Metro Escort and Bawdy Houses," identified twenty-four advertised escort services responsible for a multi-million-dollar sex trade being carried on behind closed doors all over the Halifax area. Both Stacey Jackson and Taunya Terriault had launched their prostitution careers through escort services. According to Gaudet's calculations, based on the hourly rates reported by his contacts, each of the operations would only have to employ one prostitute in order for their combined income to exceed one million dollars; and his study had identified some services that used as many as fifteen girls at a time. The implications were financially staggering, and, like every other aspect of prostitution the task force had investigated, socially appalling. Pimps often presented escort services as an attractive first foray into The Game for girls who were initially reluctant to stand on a street corner, where someone they knew might see them. The girls soon discovered, as Stacey did, that the brothels were dirty, degrading places; or they learned that the hotel rooms contained no elegant world travelers, but drunken louts of the type Taunya encountered on her first "out call." Taunya had been lucky when she went to the escort service; she worked alone and kept her share of the money. The girls who were placed there by pimps handed it over at the end of the night as Stacey had.

The task force's probe of escort services brought Sullivan and Elliott no closer to solving the mystery of Kimberly McAndrew, but they were able to gain a wider understanding of its significance to The Game and its impact on their witnesses' experience. One of the more recent additions to the roster was Lydia Chiasson, a nineteen-year-old whose experiences left investigators stunned by both the depth of human depravity—and the resilience of the human spirit.

Lydia's childhood in rural New Brunswick was the most hideous account of early abuse that investigators had yet heard. Her father, a sometime farmer and full-time alcoholic who regularly beat his wife and daughter, also fancied himself a high priest in the Church of Satan. Lydia was only seven when he took her pet dog to one of his meetings in the big barn that dominated the gently rolling farmland. As usual, she was not invited to attend, but the child could hear the animal's terrified whining and howling as she sat on the front deck of the farmhouse; and the pool of blood she saw next morning on the barn floor told her all she needed to know. There were also the guns: Lydia's father wanted everyone in the family to know how to use one—the child got her .22 for her eight birthday—along with free lessons. Within the year, she shot him with it; he had been beating her mother on the kitchen floor for some time before she pointed the gun at him—when he ignored her please to stop, she fired twice, hitting him in the leg. It was the last time she saw her family: Lydia was placed in a foster home and later ran away to live in Nova Scotia.

Relatively mature for a recruit to The Game, Lydia was already nineteen when she met a pimp in north-end Dartmouth while she was on her way to a video store. Charlie Cochrane, a good-looking fast talker in his early thirties, easily persuaded her to get in his van and go for a spin; within two days, she was convinced that Charlie wanted to spend the rest of his life with her. His affection and attention were new experiences for the teenager, first abused, then largely ignored by the adults in her life. That she mistook his machinations for love was understandable—she had never been given anything resembling it—and her readiness to believe in the man who was providing this gift knew no bounds. When Charlie earnestly explained that Lydia could help achieve their dream of a home and family by trying out an escort service he knew about in Cape Breton, her reluctance was short-lived. She was soon on a bus bound for Sydney, and by that night she was employed, on and off the premises of a ramshackle old house in the Ashby district of the city. Money transactions for dates in the house were handled by the proprietor, a short, heavy-set, and decidedly coarse-talking woman in her late forties who had a big, hulking boyfriend with a decidedly roving eye—which Lydia studiously ignored, looking forward to her out-calls for a break from the man's uninvited attentions.

For the first three weeks, Charlie called her every other day, and made arrangements for her to give her weekly earnings to a "friend" (another prostitute) travelling to and from Halifax every Friday. He was generous enough to let her keep fifty bucks for herself for the week's cigarettes and food. The thousand dollars or more that Lydia was pulling in weekly—or at least the half of it that wasn't pocketed by the madam—began to seem like an awful lot to be simply handing over to a stranger, especially when Charlie's calls began to dwindle. When he stopped phoning entirely, she decided it was time to consider going into business for herself. There was only one problem: the proprietor's boyfriend had coerced her into having sex with him on the threat that his lady friend would have her beaten when he told her Lydia had propositioned him. Too fearful to say no to the man, or even simply jump on a bus instead of returning "home" from a date, Lydia carried on with the complicated and unpleasant situation. At least she had a few regular customers who made the experience seem less horrible.

One of them, a prominent local businessman who told Lydia that his punishing work schedule prevented him from having "regular relationships," often invited her to spend the night at his well-appointed apartment, where they would sip fine wine, munch popcorn, and watch videos; often sex was not even part of the agenda. He even took her to watch the Cape Breton Oilers of the American Hockey League trounce their opponents at a game in the Centre Two Hundred—a major event on Sydney's social calendar at that time. Lydia hatched a plan to get out of Sydney and she used her business-man friend to make it happen. She had met an actor from Montreal who was involved in the filming of a movie in Sydney and she want-ed to go live with him; all she needed was money. She began to book dates with her favorite client and not tell the Madam. Lydia pocketed the money herself until the night she was caught. To her relief, the proprietor did not have her beaten, as the offensive boyfriend had threatened. Instead, she did exactly what Lydia wanted—ordered her to leave Sydney and never return.

Unfortunately, Montreal turned out to be Lydia's worst possible choice. It would have been a clean escape if she left The Game behind when she left Nova Scotia. Instead she turned to the yellow pages, found an escort service and went to work. The service she chose had a girl working there who had a Nova Scotia pimp. When he learned a Maritime girl was freelancing at the service he threatened to beat her severely if she refused to work for him. That would have been okay too but he wanted her to work back in Dartmouth at an escort service, not in Montreal. Not long after her return Charlie was back in the pic-ture. A complicated tussle ensued over leaving fees, freelance status, and who owed what to whom; a third pimp arrived on the scene and anted up with his offer, and by the time it was over, Lydia Chiasson was the property of one Alfred ("Sizzle") Monroe, probably the portli-est crack-head—at three hundred pounds—ever to light up a pipe. Unlike other pimps, Sizzle had no objection to a girl using crack. He wasn't really a player at all—content to run only one girl so he could feed his habit, and hers, if she liked. She did, at first, but the deadly drug took its toll on the already thin young woman, whose life be-came a nightmare of hours on the stroll, and hours at home with the seriously unbalanced Sizzle, whose hobbies of choice included play-ing games with his gun when he got high.

One day, he decided it would be fun to watch his girl and a friend of hers play a little game of Russian roulette—and as Lydia willingly plunked herself into a beat-up old armchair and watched Sizzle pluck all but one bullet from the chambers of his revolver, it occurred to her for the first time that she was in serious trouble. It was an idle fleeting thought—there was a detached quality to her feelings, as if they could come and go without having a lasting effect on her. Her face blank, she took the gun, hearing in her head the voice of her father instruct-ing her on the proper grip. Then, as Sizzle urged her on, she held it to her head and pulled the trigger. Nothing. "Again!" and he giggled wildly—and she complied; by the third—or was it the fourth go-around?—Lydia found herself wishing, with that same odd detachment, that the bullet would be in the next chamber. Suddenly Sizzle called a halt; he was bored, and decided Lydia's friend—a drug addict who didn't work as a prostitute—should play the next round. As inducement he offered a free chunk of crack, and she didn't hesitate. Suddenly horrified, really horrified, and frightened, Lydia watched the deadly game unfold, her heartbeat so loud she thought it was the gun going off. Then she heard her friend laughing, and she was putting down the gun and reaching out her hand to claim her reward.

The next morning, Lydia called the task force office and made arrangements to talk to one of the officers—Darrell Gaudet. In the end, it was her friend's predicament more than her own that prompted the call, and as Gaudet listened to her spine-chilling story, he vowed to bring the pimp to justice. Tracking down Sizzle was as easy as finding Amber's pimp Jay had been; investigators simply headed out to Bedford Provincial Court, where he was answering a drug charge. After Sizzle was released, pending a sentencing date on his conviction, Gaudet identified himself to the enormous man, who meekly accompanied him to an interview room for questioning, panting and exclaiming as he hauled his huge body down the aisle: "You Tass Force guys, you're good, man. I knew you wuz gonna get me. I knew when I saw you here. 'That guy's Tass Force,' I said, 'Sizzle, the Tass Force is here to get you, man.' " So this was the Russian roulette fan who liked playing with teenagers' lives! Half-pityingly, Gaudet listened to the man's pathetic statement—the officer knew much more about The Game than Sizzle did—then placed him in custody. Charlie was not such an easy catch, hearing about Sizzle's predicament he packed up his van and headed for Montreal, a move many of the smarter pimps were making. They picked Montreal because they wanted to avoid both the Halifax and Toronto task force officers. The unlucky crack-head-cum-pimp also got to go to Montreal. Sizzle was sentenced to five years in a federal penitentiary and found himself housed just outside the city his pimping pals favored. Sizzle was telling inmates how the "tass force" had nailed him as he spent his days at the LeClaire Institute.

By the end of March, Craig Botterill was preparing for what he considered the biggest test of Operation Hectic—preliminary hearings for the pimps swept up in Operation Hectic. The Nova Scotia cases were developing much more quickly than those of Greer and his players in Toronto. The prosecutor had been given a boost by the outcome of most of the bail hearings that had wound up the month before; none of the applications presented by the pimps' attorneys had been accepted, easing Botterill's fear of being forced to tell his young witnesses in Sullivan House that their tormentors were even temporarily free. He did feel sympathy for the parents of the young men accused, who had come forward to offer the sureties required to seek bail; they were often putting their homes on the line, and always their hearts, to offer support to sons he doubted would keep their promises to stay in Halifax until their trial if they were granted bail. It was for the best all around that it inevitably was not, he concluded.

The bail hearings also changed Botterill's mind about striking back at the pimps with federal Proceeds of Crime legislation, which allows courts to seize profits of criminal activity. Although the hardest working players were bringing in a stunning ten thousand dollars per week, and more, they wouldn't have been able to make bail on their own even if it had been granted; the money was usually gone as soon as they got it—hotels, parties, full-price plane tickets, fine clothes; even a shabby apartment in Toronto or Montreal cost plenty. Then there were rental vehicles and room-service meals, and when you added it all up, the young men had little to show in the way of proceeds of crime. Botterill was shocked to find many of the pimps were in debt. It had become a tradition to take out a loan before buying a car, a tradition started years earlier by a savvy pimp. The scam was simple; the players used forged documents that showed a stable record of employment and then qualified for the loan. They even missed the odd payment, deliberately. The originator of the plan reasoned a couple of missed payments would show the police the pimps were not high rollers at all, if they were ever investigated or arrested. That part of the plan had no meaning to the newer breed of pimps who had, until the spring of 1993, no real fear of the police. They liked the idea of the loan and the missed payments though. If some bank wanted to front the money for a car then a pimp didn't have to. The pimps flashed a lot of gold but most listed no fixed address on the arrest papers and Botterill wouldn't know where to begin looking for any jewels other than those worn by the players when they were picked up. Tank, the pimp who had quickly predicted the just-turning Stacey Jackson's predilection for The Game, expressed the players' spending habits in one brief, colorful phrase: "Illegal money flows through your hands faster than a breeze through a small town."

The bail hearings were a success but the preliminary hearings Botterill faced were an even greater concern: not only would they determine whether trials would be held at all, but they would also represent a daunting challenge to his young witnesses. They wouldn't all be called to testify, but they all had to be prepared for that possibility; and they, like he, also understood the significance of the message that strong, confident testimony would send to defense counsel—and to the still thriving players of The Game who would be watching with interest as court proceedings began.

Botterill and the team had done their best to get their witnesses ready. All the girls had received extensive counseling and medical treatment, both to help them readjust to what many of them still called the "square" world, and for the more immediate prospect of extended appearances in court. The results of doctors' examinations of girls who had been injured—the bruises and cuts noted, the scar tissue recorded—would provide physical evidence to corroborate the girls' testimony. The support services would provide them with the emotional stability they needed to maintain their composure even under intense cross-examination. At least, the prosecutor hoped it would. He had noticed that some girls were responding to the pressure of the coming trials by succumbing to what some investigators dubbed "princess syndrome"—taking advantage of the spotlight being shone on them by calling their case officers, or Botterill, at any hour of the day or night, demanding to be taken our for a burger or coffee. Others were following Amber's lead and working both sides of the fence; these worried Botterill more, since their return to prostitution could undermine their credibility on the stand. Worst of all, a few were stricken with "neon fever," the call of the street was strong and they were changing their minds about testifying as the date of the first hearings approached. The prosecutor also found out from other team members, well connected to the police grapevine, that the jailed pimps had used their free time to chat about their courtroom strategy, some arguing they should smile endearingly but fixedly at their girls to elicit the "right" answers, others insisting that a threatening scowl would be much more effective. Either way, the pimps were arrogantly asserting their certainty that, face to face with "their" girls, they would somehow ensure through sheer force of will that none of them would testify. This infuriated Botterill, but it also concerned him deeply, although he hoped enough had been done to prove them wrong when the day of reckoning came.

On that sunny April morning, as his first witness took the stand, Craig Botterill knew he had his work cut our for him. He was prepared for some nervousness from the fourteen-year-old, who had been abused by her pimp for almost a year before seeking help, and who remained in such fear of the man that she constantly expressed her dread of even looking at his face across the courtroom. Botterill had tried his best to reassure her in frequent visits to the Truro school, and gently explained to her that yes, that man did have to be in court, because it was his right to face his accuser. He knew she wanted to testify—she'd said many times that the pimp had to be kept away from girls like her—but he realized that courtroom anxiety would be inevitable.

Still, he was unprepared for her reaction even to his routine questions—how old was she? Where did she go to school? The pretty young girl turned ghostly white and was barely able to raise her voice above a whisper. Hoping to reassure her, he got up from the Crown table and walked slowly across the courtroom to stand near his witness; smiling kindly and sympathetically, he asked her to tell the judge how she had become a prostitute. She visibly relaxed as she talked about her experience, but the farther along she got in her account, the more tense the prosecutor became. He knew he would soon have to ask the crucial question, and his witness, disturbingly, was still avoiding eye contact with the accused. Finally he could wait no longer; she was finished answering his question. He drew a deep breath and began: "Tell me; the man you are talking about—the man you say did all of these things to you—is he here in the courtroom today?"

"Yes." Her voice was strained and nervous.

"Can you point this man out for the court?" Craig Botterill turned away from the witness stand and walked back towards his table, every muscle in his body contracting as he willed her to respond. When she did, all the anxiety had left her voice.

"That's him, right there." Botterill didn't have to turn around to know she had raised her hand and pointed at the accused. Instead, he looked at the man who had been leaning back comfortably in his chair, his legs sprawled under the defense table, an arrogant smile on his face as he stared at his former prostitute. Now he was sitting up straight; the smile was gone, replaced by shock, then fear.

The pimp was ordered to stand trial on all the charges the task force had brought against him. When it was all over, Botterill hugged his witness: "I'm proud of you!" he said, and she beamed in delighted relief.

The scene played itself out again and again in the weeks that followed, and the Crown attorney savoured each and every hearing for that moment of truth, when a teenage girl would face down her pimp and, pointing her finger at him, transform his bully's grin to a coward's terror.

Part Six:
Crime, Punishment, and
an Uncertain Future

The courage of the teenagers who resisted their pimps' arrogant attempts to undermine their confidence during preliminary hearings had its effect on the street, as the players still in The Game talked worriedly about that "fuckin' task force" and its efforts to spoil their lucrative business. They showed no sign of cutting back on their efforts to recruit new girls to saunter down Hollis several times a night, or collect cash from prostitutes on the stroll. The number of statements from the girls was declining by the summer of 1993 simply because the task force had reached so many of the young girls on the street that there were fewer left to make statements. The girls left in The Game remained steadfastly loyal to, or frightened of, their pimps. That did not deter the officers from going after the pimps with a classic procedure: the slow, tedious, and highly effective process of surveillance. For more than a week, they set up hidden video equipment and cameras, and just sat there, night after night, watching the stroll. They soon focused in on a particular man who stopped by to pick up money from his prostitute after every date; hundreds of photographs and hours of video tape were amassed, along with meticulously detailed log-book entries on his comings and goings. Finally, Craig Botterill gave the surveillance team the go-ahead, and the pimp was arrested, charged with living on the avails of prostitution, and eventually sentenced to more than two years in prison.

The atmosphere on the Hollis stroll was transformed almost overnight, as the pimps—almost to a man—stopped collecting money during the working night. Many even avoided driving near the stroll. Their activity didn't cease entirely; however, underage girls continued to line the stroll, though fewer than ever before. And, for the first time, they had the freedom to respond to task force officers' questions without facing a punishment from their pimps. Hollis Street was still the territory of the prostitutes, but now it was also task force territory.

There was another change in the attitude of the Nova Scotia pimps by the summer of 1993. Finally, after months of task force work, the officers began to sense fear in these kings of the street. The fear was not so much exhibited on the street as it was in the courtroom. Craig Botterill who had so much enjoyed watching the change in demeanor when a cocky pimp saw his girl identify him in court would lose out on enjoying that moment again. Many, by far most, of the pimps who had gone through the preliminary hearing stage of the court process had begun to have second thoughts about their prospects before a jury. Craig Botterill's phone began ringing, the way it had in the early days of Operation Hectic. This time it was not task force officers looking for advice, or the young girls at Sullivan House looking for encouragement; it was a host of defense attorneys looking for deals. At the Halifax County Correction Centre, the arrogant self-confident manipulators were looking for a way to manipulate the system. The pimps were ready to plead guilty in the hope of receiving a shorter sentence, or in some cases to plead guilty to one charge in the hope Botterill would agree to drop another. The sentences some pimps settled for were in no way lenient; task force cases processed through the courts ran from two years to seven. Most pimps found themselves serving three to five years in a federal prison. The pimps were found guilty, or pleaded guilty, to a host of charges. The most common charges were living on the avails of prostitution, exercising control for the purpose of prostitution, living on the avails of a person under the age of eighteen years, and procuring or attempting to procure a person to become a prostitute. Those charges fall under section 212 (1) and section 121 (2) of the Criminal Code of Canada, and the basis for laying them became as familiar to every member of the task force as they were to Craig Botterill.

The almost daily procession of young men out of the courtroom and into prison cells also carried tragic consequences for the families of these North Preston residents who brought dishonor to their communities. North Preston was dubbed "the pimping capital of Canada" in one nationally published media account. The singers, the soldiers, and other North Preston residents who achieved success nationally and internationally never received the kind of attention given the few men who chose to become pimps. The negative image created by the arrests and the constant reminder that those arrested were from North Preston had a lasting impact on that community. The hard-working residents of North Preston could not help noticing the exclusively negative attention their community was receiving; the real attention it had needed for so long was still lacking. Millions of dollars had been committed to protecting young women from the violence of The Game. The money was being spent on the task force, the safe house, the courts, and the follow up support aimed at keeping the girls off the streets after they had testified. In North Preston, community-based programs had been designed to help combat the charismatic lure of the pimps and keep young men from choosing pimping over education and honest work. Those church- and school-based programs were necessary and effective; they did not, however, have the benefit of such financial largess. Even today some in the community do not trust reporters who they feel are at least partially to blame for the negative image.

North Preston is a forgiving community, and its church leaders continue to reach out to those who were arrested and jailed. In 1995, several pimps incarcerated at The Spring Hill Penitentiary formed a small chorale and were given moral as well as spiritual support from the congregation of their church back home. A prison ministry was established linking the inmates with their home. Bruce Johnson, an active member of the North Preston community, believes even the most violent and hardened pimps would be welcomed home if they decided to give up The Game after serving jail terms. "There would be those who would be angry ... for what it did to the community." Johnson says that anger would pass and the pimps would again be members of the greater North Preston community if they really did want to start over. He is certain many do, and will.

Not all of the cases were dealt with quickly or easily because not all of the pimps were willing to enter guilty pleas. The first man to try to beat the charges, and the system, was Jeremy MacDonald, "Jay," who had been Amber's pimp.

As she had feared, Amber Borowski lost her fight for custody of her daughter, who was placed in the care of the province's department of community services. Rather than drive her back onto the street, the loss reinforced Amber's determination to start a new life— and to see her former pimp incarcerated for his violence towards her. If Jay wanted a fight in court, Amber would deliver it.

His version of events was that he had arrived home to find Amber unconscious on the living-room floor; aware that she had a drug problem, he testified, it seemed logical to assume she had suffered an overdose—plunging her into a full tub was his attempt to revive her.

The upstairs tenant who had heard MacDonald shouting about money didn't quite corroborate the pimp's testimony. The neighbor had gone to police the morning after the incident, following a conversation with another tenant who'd seen Amber leave the building earlier, her eye badly bruised. His account of what he'd heard matched Amber's exactly, and this, along with the medical evidence of bruising on Amber's shoulders and side when she arrived at the task force office, and the young woman's convincing testimony, was more than enough to get MacDonald convicted. He was sentenced to seven years in prison for two counts under section 212, "the pimp section" as task force officers had taken to calling it, as well as counts of aggravated assault and assault causing bodily harm. The severity of the sentence reflected not so much the brutality of his behavior—other cases involved equally extreme violence against the girls in question—but his extensive criminal background, including three prison terms. The courts had already given him three strikes and were not ready to indulge him in a fourth.

When it was all over, the perplexed Amber asked the Crown attorney why that tenant had come forward as he did. It wasn't as if anyone was forcing him, she said; he could have just shrugged his shoulders and forgotten all about her. Craig Botterill just smiled: "That's what good people do," he said. "And there's lots of them out there—you'll see."

Craig Botterill did not always smile at the end of a case nor did he always have a kind word for his star witnesses. The passion and anger Clara Ferguson felt, after her nightmarish three days of beating and gang-rape in the North Preston house where she'd been taken, proved to be valuable allies in the trial of her pimp, Miguel Joseph. She also continued to be a strong prosecution weapon at trials for three of five other pimps she identified when she gave a detailed statement to the task force about her involvement in The Game. After that Clara's resolve faltered. Craig Botterill didn't even see it coming.

When it came time to testify against the fifth man, Botterill was stunned when Clara refused to answer any of his questions; he'd spoken with her before the session began and noticed nothing that would suggest such recalcitrance was on the horizon. The judge, frustrated with the witness, ordered her jailed for contempt of court; hoping a night behind bars would rekindle her spirit of cooperation. Clara was outraged: after all she'd done for the task force, she was the one behind bars! The angry girl used investigators own advice to other teenagers: she called a reporter she knew, and complained; when she returned to take the stand, Clara was greeted by a crowd gathered at the courthouse door to offer her support—they'd heard her story in the media—and several of her friends from Sullivan House followed reporters inside to hear her explanation to the judge.

In simple terms, Clara told the court she was finished with these cases; she'd helped put four men in jail, and that was already enough to sentence *her* to a life spent looking over her shoulder. She wouldn't do more. The pimp was discharged, the case against the sixth was dropped, and after the session Clara and the other girls held an impromptu news conference outside, complaining bitterly that the courts and the task force weren't keeping pimps behind bars long enough to make it worth their while to testify. Botterill and the investigators were pleased with sentences in the two to seven year range; the girls had been hoping for life terms. They did not want to see their pimps on the street again, ever. Luckily, most of the task force's witnesses disagreed, and continued to cooperate as the trials of other pimps proceeded. As for Clara, she left the safe house, returning to Toronto—and to prostitution. It was the first case to break Craig Botterill's heart; it would not be the last. The case that left the deepest scar on the young prosecutor was one he thought he had won; the one he thought was so easy he handed it to someone else.

The witness was one that Botterill felt broke the mould. During his interviews with the prostitutes now in the care of the task force, Botterill had recognized that all expect Stacey said they had been sexually, verbally, or physically abused as children. Members of the task force had begun to believe that there was a very simple formula at play in the streets of Canada: all you had to do was abuse a little girl and then wait ten years and you'd have a prostitute. Diane was the second exception to that theory. She was the only prostitute aside from Stacey to say she had never been abused. Unlike Stacey, Diane did not grow up in a home where there was drunkenness or violence between her parents.

Diane Dennis was eighteen when she came to the task force after being beaten by her pimp. When she came to Craig Botterill's office he realized he had met her once before. Diane had been a witness in a robbery case Botterill had tried a few years earlier. At that time she had been running with a bad crowd and happened to be in a car with two guys who decided to hold up a late night convenience store. During that case Botterill had met Diane's father who was a successful local professional who seemed genuinely concerned that his daughter was running with the wrong crowd.

When Diane walked into his office with a member of the task force, Botterill was certain she was still running with the wrong crowd. He was also pretty certain her father's heart was about to be broken. During the witness interview, Botterill got a sense of who Diane was: a wild young woman who longed for adventure. Diane was drawn to danger. She was a real thrill seeker who had finally found danger in a pimp who had beaten her until she was black and blue.

Diane was highly intelligent and had done well in school—she had no problem grasping the principles of the justice system as Botterill explained them. He was confident she would make a credible witness who would name the pimp who had abused her. When Diane's trial was about a week away, Craig Botterill realized he had a scheduling conflict so he asked another crown attorney in the office for help. The other attorney agreed to take Diane's case; the success rate for task force cases made them an easy sell to other attorneys.

Botterill wrapped up the earlier court hearing he had been committed to and decided to head to the court room where Diane was testifying against her pimp. He thought he would sit in the gallery to offer her moral support. He decided it would be a break to watch and not have to ask the questions. When Botterill stepped quietly into the courtroom he realized something was wrong. The crown attorney who had taken the case was asking the judge to declare Diane a hostile witness. Crown attorney's use that declaration when one of their own witnesses turns on them or they suspect a Crown witness is lying. The declaration gives the Crown a little more leeway during direct examination or initial questioning of the witness. The judge agreed and made the declaration. Botterill knew Diane must have been refusing to cooperate. He sat in the public gallery and watched as the Crown attorney went over the statement Diane had given first to the task force officers and then to him. Diane argued with the statement saying it was not what she meant, that she was telling the truth now. Diane had decided she would not testify against the pimp and the Crown attorney's pleas were wasted. The pimp was acquitted.

Craig Botterill left the courtroom without talking to Diane. What ever she had decided he knew it was too late to ask her to change her mind now. He worked late that night preparing a case that he would have to deliver in the morning. When he walked out of the office shortly after ten o'clock, he looked down at the traffic on Hollis Street to see if it was a busy night on the stroll. Botterill didn't notice whether it was busy; all he saw was Diane. The eighteen-year-old was standing on the sidewalk across from his office building. Botterill was certain her pimp had put her there for his benefit. Diane did not notice as Botterill walked away from Hollis Street toward his waiting van.

A few months later, Craig Botterill received a phone call from a prosecutor in Toronto asking if he knew a young girl named Diane Dennis. Botterill told the man he did and asked what had happened. That morning Diane had checked into a Toronto hospital after being severely beaten by the same pimp. The night before Diane had offended the pimp by talking back to him. In an effort to teach her respect the pimp had struck her repeatedly in the face with a metre long length of two by four lumber. When Diane woke in the morning she could not open her eyes because they were badly swollen and her eyelids were caked with dried blood. Diane heard her pimp's voice but could not see him, or believe what he was saying, when he ordered her to perform oral sex on him. Diane pried one eye open with her fingers and begged him to stop. The pimp threatened to get the board and resume the beating so Diane complied. When he left the hotel room she walked down and asked the startled desk clerk to call her a taxi so she could go to the hospital. Diane flew back to Halifax two weeks later. Botterill made sure she was met at the airport by members of the task force. When it was time for her pimp's trial in Toronto he sent two task force officers with her for moral support. At her second attempt as a crown witness Diane testified and the pimp was sent to prison.

One of Craig Botterill's toughest days in court came at the end of a trial—and the problem was neither his opponent at the defense table nor a suddenly reluctant witness. The trial had gone well and the pimp had been convicted; Botterill's trouble began when it was time for the judge to hand down his sentence.

Judge Reginald Kimball had something to say on the subject of prostitution. It was his understanding, the judge said, that "where there was a john, a whore was not far away, and where there was a whore, a pimp was usually close by." The use of the word *whore,* and Botterill's impression that Kimball saw the pimp's role as one of protective partner rather than abusive master, made it almost impossible for the prosecutor to keep his temper. The hundreds of hours task force officers had spent trying to reinforce their many young witnesses' fragile self-confidence could be undermined by such an approach, which ignored their central concept: a girl who becomes involved in prostitution need not wear the label *prostitute*—to say nothing of *whore* for the rest of her life.

What nearly finished Botterill, however, was the judge's suggestion that the Crown obtain a wider understanding of prostitution in Canada by reading a book entitled *Red Lights on the Prairie*. Craig Botterill had read the book in his social studies class at a Moose Jaw, Saskatchewan, high school, a number of years earlier. The book, a depiction of widespread criminal activity in Botterill's home town during the 1920s and '30s, extensively describes the operations of numerous well-run and flourishing brothels, whose controlled environment and adult prostitutes were a far cry from the contemporary reality of Canadian prostitution.

When he had finished delivering his oration, Judge Kimball sentenced the pimp before him to eighteen months in jail—the shortest term imposed at that point, and one of the shortest in the entire trial process. Botterill lost no time in preparing a response: immediately after the session, he prepared a motion asking that Kimball be barred from hearing any more task-force cases, on the grounds that his language might imply a bias against prostitutes.

In the spring and summer of 1993 the Nova Scotia provincial courts were kept busy with cases generated by the members of Operation Hectic, but Operation Hectic had its genesis in cases that were about to come before the courts in Toronto. Finally in July of 1993 the big players came to trial.

The month Stacey was supposed to have spent in Toronto before Sears' trial had stretched into more than half a year. The time passed quickly though; Stacey had made new friends at the Toronto safe house, a place where she found she was not judged and where the girls appeared committed to breaking free of The Game.

The first test of Stacey's resolve came in June when a preliminary hearing was held to determine if there was enough evidence to hold Smit over to trial. It was a three day hearing, half of which was taken up with Stacey on the stand. Like the girls encouraged by Craig Botterill, Stacey stood up to the pressure, and when the moment came she pointed out Smit as the man who had beaten her. Stacey also expected a lengthy stay in the witness chair during the July trial; she had been warned to expect a prolonged cross examination this time around. The warning was for not. On the first day of the trial, Michael

"Smit" Sears stood in court and changed his plea, even telling the judge he was sorry for what he had done. Stacey was thrilled but her joy was short lived. As Sears gave his apology, Stacey could hear crying. She looked over to see her former pimp's sister sitting behind the accused. The only family member able to make it to the trial—she lived and worked in Toronto—the young woman was devastated at what her brother had gotten himself into. She, like other members of his family, believed the plea change was a genuine admission of guilt. Michael Sears was ready to accept responsibility and whatever punishment the court gave him, and the family hoped that was the first step toward returning to the energetic and promising young man they loved. Smit was given six years for living on the avails and assault; he would have a long time to work at turning over that new leaf.

Peanut on the other hand was willing to fight the charge. Annie Mae had signed on him, but Peanut knew she would not have testified even if she were still alive. His only real problem was a sixteen-year-old named Norma Willis. Norma had worked for Smit on and off for two years; she was picked up by members of the Toronto juvenile task force in a routine sweep of the stroll. The officers saw her, thought she looked young, and decided to introduce themselves. They came at the perfect time; Norma was ready to leave The Game and within an hour of meeting the task force officers she accepted their offer of help and gave them a statement naming Peanut as her pimp. He plead not guilty but lost when the jury accepted her story over his. His sentence was three and a half years.

T aunya was the next girl to complete her role as star witness for the crown. Taunya traveled to Toronto in the fall of 1993 to face Manning Greer in court. The night before she was scheduled to testify turned out to be one of the longest nights in the fifteen-year-old's life. Taunya sat in a hotel room in Toronto with two police officers in an adjoining room guarding her. The presence of the tight security heightened Taunya's fears and she began to wonder if the threat delivered to Stacey in Halifax had substance to it. Taunya did not want to be the witness shot on the courthouse steps as the pimps finally sent their message to the other girls. She spent the night looking out the hotel window at the city where she and Teri and Gizelle had worked those final weeks for the Greer family. Looking at the city lights left Taunya with a strange longing. She wondered who was down on Church Street working while she sat under police guard in a hotel room. She also wondered who was safer.

Taunya was too nervous to eat breakfast in the morning and after sharing coffee with her police guards she headed to the courthouse to begin her testimony. She spent most of the morning in a small interview room in the courthouse where she paced and smoked and worried and wondered until she was finally called to testify. The court room was not what Taunya had expected; it was smaller and there were no crowds the way there had been during a hearing she had attended back in Halifax. As she walked up the centre isle toward the judge at the front of the room she finally saw the Big Man. Manning Greer was wearing crisp black jeans and an expensive blue dress shirt; his hair glistened with the oily treatment he used to pull his long curls down around his shoulders. Taunya could also see that he was smiling. She thought Greer looked more like one of the lawyers than a man who was on trial.

Greer was seated to the left of the center aisle at a table in front of the main gallery, separated from that area of the court by a small railing. Taunya walked through a small gate near the center of the railing toward the witness chair. As she walked past the railing her eyes met Greer's. Taunya was surprised to see Greer flash her a bright smile and silently mouth the words "I love you." The feeble attempt to con Taunya and regain control over her was exactly what the young witness needed to reaffirm her desire to see Greer locked up. As Taunya began her testimony she noticed a strange change in her feelings. After a night spent fearing the Big Man and wondering if he would have her killed, she felt a strange sense of relief as she looked at him from the witness chair. When Taunya was working for Greer she had always found small ways to maintain her independence. She had delayed having her tattoo changed because she knew Greer wanted it done. She had given up that bit of defiance only when he threatened to kill her. She had attempted to convince Star, the captive prostitute, to run while Greer slept, and she had been the driving force behind the plan to run away to Buffalo and make contact with Sweet Lou. In the witness chair, Taunya realized she was afraid of the memory of Greer and his reputation more than of the man himself. She relaxed as she realized she now had all of the power, and she was about to use it on the Big Man. Taunya's new-found confidence made her a very credible witness. She was not emotional and did not get angry at the defence lawyer when she was cross examined. Manning Greer was sentenced to seven years in a Federal Penitentiary bringing an end to his reign as the king of the Nova Scotia Pimps. He too fell to Section

212 of the Criminal Code, living on the avails, procurement, and exercising control.

Eddy and Slugger didn't fair any better. Their sentences were not as stiff, five and six years respectively, but Teri and Gizelle had also been strong witnesses. By the end of August all four of the main players had fallen after their teenage prostitutes had the nerve to face them in court.

Back in Halifax, with her testimony complete, Taunya's fear of the pimps returned, and as that fear grew she realized she could not return to a normal life in the Halifax area. A year later Taunya opted to join the witness protection program. Once inside the program she was given a new identity, a new background, and a new city to live in. An RCMP officer accompanied Taunya to her new home and introduced her to an officer there who knew her true identity and her background. That officer promised to help her if she ever felt threatened or if she thought a member of the pimping family had discovered her.

On the first night of her new life Taunya sat alone in a small apartment the RCMP had found for her and watched TV. The pictures and sounds coming from the television did not cut through the anxiety she was feeling. She was preoccupied as she tried to decide what to do now that she was finally free. For most of her life Taunya wanted freedom. At first she wanted to be free of school and then it was her mothers' rules she wanted to escape. Finally she wanted freedom from the pimps who had made her life so terrible. Now Taunya had her freedom and it terrified her. For several days she was afraid to leave her apartment, but gradually she began to venture beyond the small convenience store located at the base of the large building she now called home. Within three weeks the former prostitute found a roommate to share the apartment and the expenses, and with her roommates help she found a job serving customers at a coffee shop. After four months, she enrolled in a few night classes at a beauty school where she hoped to become a hairdresser.

Socially, Taunya had great difficulty adapting to her new life. Her roommate introduced her to a few young men but Taunya discovered she did not like or trust white men. Her experience as a prostitute taught her that white men paid for sex while black men did not, and she found she had more respect for black men. She finally met a young black man and started her first normal relationship. Taunya decided early on she would never tell him about her past. She believed avoiding it was the best way for her to forget it. Taunya had one problem in her new life; money or a lack of it. The witness protection program only provided financial support for a few months. That money was gone and it was up to Taunya to fend for herself. Waiting tables in a coffee shop was not giving her enough money to pay her bills. Taunya found it very hard to cash a paycheck for one week of work that was less than half of what she often made in a single night on the street. As the need for money grew, Taunya began to take chances. She made excuses to her boyfriend, and left for occasional weekend trips to a neighboring city. There she went to work as an in-service worker at an escort service. Taunya continued that delicate balancing act for more than a year. Then she finally decided to break free of prostitution for good. To force herself to stay free of the escort service Taunya took a drastic step. She quit her job at the coffee shop and convinced her boyfriend to pack and move to another part of the country far from the temptations of the Escort Service she had begun to rely on. Taunya finally made the break and stayed away from prostitution.

For Taunya's close friend, Teri MacDonald, the break was easier to make. She held true to her word and stayed away from The Game, finished school and started the normal life she promised herself she would have on that flight back from Toronto after the 1992 raid.

Whether they assumed new identities and moved away, or tried to stick it out in Nova Scotia, all of the girls who had become involved with the task force—whether as witnesses in the trial of a pimp, or as participants in programs to help them get away from The Game—faced considerable difficulty adjusting to the "square" world.

Some, like Lydia Chiasson, made the transition with surprisingly few setbacks. The nineteen-year-old, like Taunya, joined the witness protection program after her pimps' trial; she was relocated to a small town and quickly found a job. That she accepted her minimum-wage salary with a certain amount of grace was testament to her maturity; Lydia knew how to survive, and she understood that others, too, had to struggle to pay their rent and put food on the table. Lydia also had the advantage of past experience; before meeting Charlie Cochrane that day on her way to the video store she had been supporting herself with a minimum wage job. Unlike Taunya, who missed her mother and sister, Lydia had been a loner before she met Charlie; there was no one left behind to regret leaving. As for fears of being tracked down for reprisal, she had none; her new home was small enough that the arrival of a fancy car filled with men asking questions about the new girl in town would have quickly attracted attention, especially from the police chief, who knew Lydia had been a witness in a case involving a violent pimp, and who had befriended the young girl and would occasionally stop by to chat with her while she worked.

Only a few months after arriving, Lydia met a young man. They quickly fell in love and moved in together; within a year, the couple had a son. The relationship continued to flourish, and Lydia's boyfriend frequently proposed marriage, but she held back. Lydia just wanted to take life one day at a time; and he was willing to wait.

For Amber Borowski, the shift to "square" life wasn't quite so smooth. Determined to live near her elderly foster parents, with whom she had become increasingly close during Jay MacDonald's trial, she resisted task force officers' advice and decided to stay in Halifax. The job she found in a gift shop at a local shopping mall only lasted for a few weeks; a pimp she'd once worked for managed to find her. She wasn't threatened, but the man started dropping in to visit her regularly, teasing her and flirting with her in his "subtle" effort to get her back into The Game. She quit in order to escape his attentions, but it wasn't until August 1994 that she changed her mind about staying in Halifax. Amber was with some friends at the annual Buskers' Festival on the waterfront when a cousin of Jay's, drunk and obviously angry, came up to her, threatened her openly, and followed her through the crowd when she turned away.

A week later, Amber left Halifax; almost overnight, her problems ended. Like Lydia, she settled in a small town and quickly found all the necessities of life—a gentle, unhurried pace of life, a decent job, and a rewarding relationship with a well-established and hard-working young man. Indeed, her biggest challenge was learning to accept not only that her boyfriend made more money than she did, but that he insisted on turning his pay checks over to her. She was much more accustomed to financial arrangements conducted the other way around.

Of all the girls involved in the task force's war on juvenile prostitution, the one whose case launched Operation Hectic showed the most distinctive response to her experience. Not only did Stacey Jackson refuse to enter the witness protection program—despite the advice of her respected and beloved case worker, John Elliott—but she decided to offer her help in educating teenagers about the realities of prostitution. The task force had begun visiting secondary schools across Nova Scotia to promote a clearer understanding of The Game's dangers, and Elliott knew Stacey Jackson would be an asset to that program.

The very notion of speaking on-stage in front of a crowd would have been unthinkable to Stacey a year before her first "gig," in the late winter of 1994, at a school in Colchester County, north of Halifax. Her self-doubt would have made such an appearance impossible only two years ago. Yet here she was, accompanying the task force's Darrell Gaudet to face a few dozen students who, she knew from experience, would be using the presentation as an excuse to lounge in their seats and chat for an hour or so. *There they go*, she thought sourly, as several of the students in the auditorium started talking and clowning around during Gaudet's talk; others were looking bored and yawning. Then it was her turn. Ignoring the wave of stage fright she felt as she began to speak, Stacey let her anger at the students' indifference fuel her description of the life she had led as a prostitute in Halifax and Toronto. The disruptions stopped immediately, and Gaudet was afraid even to shift in his seat, lest he break the spell she had cast. At the end of Stacey's twenty-minute speech, the teenagers were hushed, almost awed; she had reached them, and Gaudet knew they would think about what she'd said.

Shane Kirk, the Sullivan House counselor who first welcomed Stacey to the safe house, was also at the school that day and he saw something Darrell Gaudet did not. "It had a dramatic affect on Stacey, it was like she was working through her own problems—really coming to grips with her experience—as she spoke to those kids. She did reach the students but I think she gained more from those school visits than anyone else."

Stacey's life changed in other ways, too. Like her friend Amber Borowski, she lost custody of her child; her son Michael was adopted by her ex-boyfriend's parents. In 1995, she had a second child with her new boyfriend and was content to spend all of her time with the baby boy. She took an apartment in north-end Halifax, and insisted on staying in touch with some of the girls she'd once worked with who had decided to stay in The Game.

In August of 1994, the task force was told of the death of Keri Sherwood, the teenager Mitch Ginn had spotted on the Hollis stroll more than a year before, but could not persuade to spend more than one night in the safe house. Her pimp Eric Conrad, true to form, had tired of the teenager, who moved on to another pimp, then another city. From Montreal she travelled to Calgary, where her prospects brightened—she was befriended by a police officer who, like Ginn, tried hard to help her break away from prostitution. She vanished again before he could reach her. She called the officer in Calgary just one more time, in August 1994, from Montreal; she wanted his help and would be returning to Calgary soon. Later that month, a businessman en route to a meeting in Laval saw an unusual looking pile of clothes in a field near the furniture store where he was headed—he went to have a look, and found the mud-encrusted body of a naked girl, bound with wire at the ankles and wrists. Keri.

It was going to be almost impossible to track down Keri's killer; her belongings weren't found near her body, so police were unable to find out where she lived and locate a clue to her pimp's whereabouts. Then there was the strong possibility that Keri had been slain by a bad date, in which case there would have been no chance of solving the murder. The Montreal police turned to the Operation Hectic officers, but all they had was the photograph taken the night Ginn met her. In short, Keri's murder would probably never be solved. Her case, like many police files on murder victims involved in prostitution, presented not even a single clue to help officers track down their murderers.

Constable Gary Martin, who had taken over as media liaison officer for the task force, contacted local reporters after hearing of Keri's death, hoping the publication of her photograph and an account of her tragic death might generate leads for investigators in Montreal. Instead, articles bearing such headlines as "Halifax Hooker Found Dead in Montreal" appeared in the papers—no mention of Keri's dream to become a writer, or of the poetry that filled her journal; she was just a dead "hooker."

For Stacey, this coverage was exceptionally frustrating. She acknowledged that the media had played a vital role in bringing the problem of juvenile prostitution to the public's attention—thus prompting the formation of the task force—but she wanted to see more articles and TV coverage about the challenges faced by young women struggling to get their lives under control—young women like herself. Stacey, like many others, adults and teenagers alike, denounced the use of words like "hooker"—like Judge Kimball's "whore"—it was completely inappropriate. Throughout 1994 the Halifax media had carried the stories of terrorized young teens who had broken free from the prostitution game but for Stacey it was not enough.

Stacey's anger turned against the police as well as the news media over the murder of Kathy Armstrong, a twenty-seven-year-old woman whose body was discovered in an alleyway in the early winter of 1995. Her throat had been cut. Armstrong had spent much of her adult life working as a prostitute in Halifax. Stacey had met her several times, and knew she was several months pregnant and was suffering from a crack addiction that not only kept her on the street, but also forced her to resort to robbery and other petty crimes. Stacey was horrified to learn of her death, as was her friend Amber, who found out about the murder during a telephone conversation with her foster mother. Just as Annie Mae's death had turned Stacey away from prostitution and inspired her to keep her promise to testify against her former pimps, Amber was similarly determined to stick to the straight and narrow. She had met Armstrong years before, on the crack stroll, and the two had become fast friends; Amber would not betray her memory by returning to the old life. Stacey, however, wasn't content to leave matters there, nor perhaps would Amber have been if she had been in Halifax to watch the story of Kathy Armstrong unfold—or, rather, to watch the story disappear from media reports almost as quickly as it made headlines when the murder occurred.

Stacey complained to anyone who would listen. Her frustration exploded into outrage a few months later, when the murder of a six-teen-year-old girl, unconnected to prostitution, remained a top news story for days and prompted the RCMP in Lower Sackville, where the body had been discovered behind a local school, to deploy a team of investigators around the clock in an effort to find her killer.

Where was the team investigating Kathy Armstrong's murder? Stacey called John Elliott to try to find out more; it turned out that the Halifax police were facing problems similar to their Montreal coun-terparts: the victim could have been killed by any number of sus-pects–drug dealers, pimps, bad dates—and the investigation was making little headway. A few days later, the Lower Sackville RCMP announced an arrest in the sixteen-year-old's murder, and John Elliott told his persistent former witness that the man in charge of the investigation was none other than Brad Sullivan, who had left the task force for a posting as a lead investigator.

Stacey called and left a message for the former task force officer. Brad Sullivan did not know what Stacey wanted when he received the message. He was very busy building a case and collecting evidence, but he took the time to find a phone and call Stacey. That response was a result of a habit most of the task force investigators had devel-oped. It did not matter that Sullivan and some of the other original task force members had been reassigned, they still felt a sense of responsibility toward the girls they had worked with in the battle against the pimps.

Sullivan knew Stacey could be volatile at times but he was shocked by the level of her anger and frustration. Stacey was in tears as she berated Sullivan for what she felt was his sudden change of heart. She wanted to know why he wasn't trying to solve the Halifax murder and would not accept the answer that it was not his jurisdiction. Stacey accused the former task force officer of abandoning the girls he had promised to help. She did not understand that by returning her call Sullivan had demonstrated a commitment to that promise. At the end of what turned out to be more of a lecture than a conversation, Stacey stated flatly that it was clear no one cared when a prostitute was murdered but if someone's daughter, a real person, was found dead the whole world had to stop until that case was solved. Not satisfied with the explanation given by Brad Sullivan, Stacey phoned Shane Kirk and went to meet with her former case worker. Kirk also tried to soothe Stacey and explain the differences presented by the two cases. In the end he realized Stacey was not looking for explanations, "the whole thing touched her a little too closely. It reminded her of how close she had come to being murdered that day in Toronto. Stacey thought that she would have been nothing more than a dead prostitute and it scared her, a lot." Stacey wanted comforting and Kirk provided it, letting her cry through her frustration.

The reprimand from Stacey was frustrating for Brad Sullivan who, despite being reassigned, still worked the Kimberly McAndrew file. Sullivan had changed his mind about McAndrew being abducted into the world of prostitution by an aggressive pimp. The years working on the task force taught him that this rarely, if ever, happened. While at first the police believed many of the girls had been abducted, they learned through investigation the girls were usually conned by conniving pimps. Kidnapping was not their style. Sullivan still felt McAndrew had been picked up by a pimp who tried to work her, but who panicked when he realized she was a police officer's daughter. Brad Sullivan believed Kimberly McAndrew had been murdered and he refused to let the case die with her. In fairness to Halifax police the case was not dead. The investigators in Halifax had a very different theory about what had happened to McAndrew, and they continued to investigate the possibility that she had been killed by someone she knew, not a stranger or a pimp.

On a balmy evening in August 1995, Darrell Gaudet and Mitch Ginn were out in their unmarked car, cruising around Halifax-Dartmouth—a typical night's work for the last of Operation Hectic's original investigators. They were looking for a pimp who was back on the street after being imprisoned more than two years before. The man had earned early release after serving a small portion of his sentence for living on the avails of prostitution. The officers were particularly concerned that he had returned to The Game. That was because the two officers were also looking for a fourteen-year-old girl who had been reported missing by a social services case worker. She was a runaway from a group home, a prime pimping target. They were hoping the two had not found each other; they were hoping the confidence—and budgetary restraint—that had all but dismantled the task force had not been misplaced.

A visit to Hollis Street on any given night would be all that politicians or police executives needed to justify drastic cutbacks to the anti-pimping unit, which now had four members—Ginn, Gaudet, and two newer officers—plus a supervisor. Originally there had been twelve on the team, but that was clearly not necessary now, the visitors would say, noting the slow action on the stroll, where, on average, there were less than half as many prostitutes working than in 1992—and where a juvenile was a very rare sight. Ginn and Gaudet, like the others who had participated in Operation Hectic, were justifiably gratified by the drastic reduction in prostitution activity.

Ginn and Gaudet were also worried. They had heard all the stories from the girls they had befriended about how the task force had forced pimps to stop mistreating prostitutes. Their concern was, how long would that last in the absence of visible deterrence? They also wanted a chance to target the clients. Almost nothing had been done to crack down on the men who bought the service, men as responsible for victimization of girls and young women as the pimps were. Gaudet also longed for the chance to go after the people he first began investigating when he developed an interest in prostitution in the days before the task force: the escort services whose operators could hide the presence of underage prostitutes—and any violent behavior towards them.

As their car descended the hill above the Nova Scotia Hospital, Gaudet glanced at an abandoned building on the grounds. Sullivan House, which once stood as a beacon for the terrorized and brutalized teenagers fleeing the kinds of horrors the officers feared would relapse if the preventive measures the task force provided were not restored. A smaller safe house had been set up in Halifax. The new house remained an integral part of the fight to protect young girls and keep them off the streets. The move was made because the larger facility was too expensive to run, and was not needed after the first year of Operation Hectic when the number of girls needing its services began to decline. The new smaller house in Halifax actually marked an increase in the role played by the community services counselors working with young prostitutes. Those workers had begun to take part in an active outreach program that targeted young girls at risk. To Gaudet though, the closure of Sullivan House just marked another step in the gradual dismantling of the police operation he believed was the most important work he had ever been involved in.

By the time the officers reached the Dartmouth stroll, in the city's north end, the orange glow was fading in the sky—the start of The Game's prime time, and another night of frustration for area residents. The stroll had been the subject of much media attention since spring, and a community group, intent on driving the street trade out of the neighborhood, was having its effect. Gaudet and Ginn saw no prostitutes on the stroll—not yet, anyway. The officers knew they would simply come out later, when most of the residents in the area had retired for the night. That way, there would be no angry calls from women who had been accosted by cruising clients. The players always adjusted when they saw the rules were changing, it was just a part of life on the street. At any rate, the officers agreed they wouldn't find their suspect here—or the girl he might be running. They'd been told he was renting an apartment in a nearby house, so they tried there. No luck, there was not even a car in the driveway. Mitch Ginn swore quietly as the officers returned to their car: seven teenagers were sitting on the doorstep of the house, four of them girls. "Another pied piper," he said; the kids, he was sure, were waiting for that pimp.

Maybe they'd have better luck across the bridge; Ginn and Gaudet crossed over Halifax Harbour and drove to Gottingen Street, the main thoroughfare that marks the city's north-end crack stroll, where prostitutes take their dates into abandoned lots on a lonely side street, or wait on poorly lit corners for a client to come by in a car.

The officers turned off Gottingen and onto one of the side streets. "There you go—it's never too early on the crack stroll," Ginn remarked, pointing to one of two prostitutes standing near a garage. "See her? She was still working at eight-thirty this morning, looking for one more high. Christ, look at her!" The emaciated woman had the unmistakable pallor of a crack addict; her hair was stringy and matted, her clothes soiled, her features a death-mask of sunken eyes, skeletal cheekbones, lips blue with cyanosis. As the car approached, she glanced eagerly inside, but when she recognized the men, she turned away and went on chatting with her companion. Ginn smiled and waved as he drove away.

"You know what really amazes me about this place?" Gaudet knew, but he also knew Ginn liked to talk, so he let him. "It's these stupid fucking dates," his partner continued. "These guys come down here because they know some of these girls will let them have sex without a condom. They flash a little money, and these girls will do almost anything to get to that next high. Stupid bastards think they're the only ones doing it. I mean, look at these girls. That's some serious danger, man—stupid bastards."

"Who's that?" Gaudet interrupted his partner as he noticed a new face working the next corner.

"Don't know, she looks young though." The girl did not have the crack addicted pallor that marked the other girls working the area. She still carried a healthy body weight. She did not fit the description they were given of the missing teen but she warranted a second look. There was something in the young girls' eyes that both investigators noticed as they slowly rolled past, fear.

"Could be a first timer, lets circle back and see if we can talk to her." Gaudet agreed and Ginn pulled the big car back up on Gottingen Street and drove up a block and headed back down to the stroll. There were a few people standing in front of the businesses on Gottingen, and they glanced at the car as it sped past and turned back down the side street. A few may have recognized the men for what they were, but most probably thought they were simply a couple of customers window shopping the stroll from their car.

"Hey look, she already broke." Ginn said as they returned to the stroll. In three years of interviewing prostitutes Gaudet and Ginn had picked up the language of the streets. The officers also never used the term "john" because prostitutes preferred to call the men they serviced clients or dates. Ginn and Gaudet had long ago stopped calling the sex trade prostitution. It was The Game and everyone involved was a player.

"Let's see where he takes her, Darrell." In the time it had taken the two men to circle the block a car had pulled up to the curb beside the young girl. As Gaudet and Ginn drove past a second time, she was getting inside. The car was an older model Chrysler in need of some body-work; the man behind the wheel looked to be sixty five or older. Ginn parked his car on a side street just beyond the stroll and the two officers turned to look back. Within seconds the big Chrysler rolled past.

"She's taking him to one of the lots." Ginn was certain he knew the destination. Prostitutes try to work in a specific area not far from their corner. They choose a parking lot or alley nearby and instruct all of their dates to take them there. There are several parking lots down near the waterfront. A few are used by the girls working the crack stroll. Ginn slowed the police car and let the Chrysler pull away. He didn't say anything but he already knew what he was going to do.

The Chrysler did not pull into one of the regular parking lots; it kept driving north along the harbor and beneath the newest of the two bridges that span Halifax Harbour. The officers had allowed the car to turn onto Barrington Street while they waited on a side street to give the man time to pull into the lot they believed the girl would select. They then pulled around the corner but when they looked into the gravel parking lot it was empty.

"Shit, she doesn't know where to take him." Ginn had lost too much ground and the big car was gone. His knuckles whitened on the steering wheel as he took the car up over one hundred kilometers per hour. He sped beneath the bridge and headed down toward the container pier.

"Slow down there he is." Gaudet could see the Chrysler headed back toward them. Ginn's anger began to build as he drove past the Chrysler. "Look at the silly old prick. He can't wait." The driver of the Chrysler was leaning across the seat with his left hand still holding the steering wheel. His head was positioned just below the rear view mirror as he alternately glanced at the road and into the lap of the young girl beside him. His right arm was stretched down in that direction. The man was wearing a ball cap and he must have bumped it on the mirror as he leaned across the front seat of the big car. The hat was now twisted sideways with the peak pointing back toward the driver side window. The man was grinning wildly as he slowly cruised along the road looking for a place to park. Mitch Ginn hoped the man was married. If he was, Mitch would have some fun. The officers turned their car around and headed back south along Barrington Street where they saw the Chrysler pull into a small park on the harbor side of the road. Mitch turned the car around and then slowed to a stop at the side of the road.

"Shit, why'd she take him here." Gaudet didn't like what he was seeing. Although it was already dark the park was not yet empty. A man and a young boy were walking up from the water's edge, headed back to their car. A young couple was also strolling in the park and a woman was walking with her dog.

"We better go in," Gaudet said. Mitch drove to the corner of the lot where the man had parked his Chrysler. The driver had backed it into the corner and he looked out as the dark green car pulled up at an angle blocking him in. He didn't appear to realize who had found him. The two police officers stepped out of their car. They left the doors open behind them and walked toward him. The young girl knew what was happening and she hung her head.

"You talk to her, he's mine." Mitch headed to the driver's side window. He pulled out his wallet and flipped it open to expose his badge. He pressed the shiny metal crest against the window and gestured with his free hand, instructing the driver to lower the glass. As Gaudet walked toward the passenger window he realized he had left his badge in the car. He reached into his shirt pocket and pulled out one of the task force business cards he carried. When he reached the car Gaudet gestured for the young girl to step out. He identified himself and asked if the girl knew about the task force. The young prostitute said she did, but Gaudet gave her the speech anyway because he had never dealt with her before. He told her the task force was designed to help young prostitutes, not prosecute them, but he could see the spiel would be useless. She wasn't even looking at him as she leaned against the car door, her arms crossed defensively. She did tell the officer she was nineteen years old, from Glace Bay, near Sydney, on Nova Scotia's Cape Breton Island, that she had just been released from prison after being convicted of breaking and entering, and that she was only working the streets to raise enough money for the trip home. After confirming her story, Gaudet let her go. Just in case, he handed her his task-force card, along with the best offer she'd probably ever had—although he doubted she would ever take him up on it: "If you ever need help, or you're being pressured by someone to keep working, call me."

Meanwhile, Ginn was taking an entirely different approach with the client, intensifying his usual street-smart tone as he asked the man just what he thought he was doing with the teenager—oh, he was looking for conversation, was he? And did he happen to be married. Really? "Okay, listen," the officer continued; "I'm really busy tonight, but I am going to have to talk to you about this. We're trying to get these kids off the streets, so tomorrow morning around ten, I'm going to come out to your place to ask you some questions about this incident, and I'd like to talk with your wife as well." He glanced at the man's anxious expression with some satisfaction. "Now I'll be back in a minute; you just stay here." The check on the client's license turned up nothing out of the ordinary—sixty-seven years old, no outstanding warrants, no criminal record. While he was waiting for the dispatcher's response, Ginn saw the man step out of his car and, using a cane, limp over to an outdoor toilet nearby; this, and the elderly client's utterly defeated look when the officer returned with his license, convinced Ginn that he should give the guy a break. He'd made his point, anyway. "Look, maybe I won't have to talk to you about this after all," he told the man, who looked as if he'd just been granted a reprieve from the firing squad. "You just go home, and don't let me catch you down here again." He didn't have to wonder whether the guy would follow his advice; Mitch Ginn's success rate for extracting confessions from cornered dates was unblemished.

Whenever he and Gaudet were feeling down, Ginn would play a cassette recording of his favorite exchange with a client. This was a man of twenty-seven with a wife and baby; he had picked up an underage prostitute on Hollis Street while Ginn was on patrol. When the officer caught up, he began by insisting that the girl had jumped into his car while it was slowing down to avoid another vehicle, but quickly changed his tune and admitted what he had done. As usual, Ginn gave his speech about talking to him—and his wife—at their home in the morning. The client's response was to follow Ginn to his car and kneel at the window, begging him just to settle the matter right then and there; almost in tears, he implored the officer not to charge him. Ginn had no intention of charging anyone; he couldn't. The man had not broken any laws. Driving around with a young girl is not an offense and getting a prostitute to testify that a man had "solicited" sex for money was impossible. The only real way to nail a client, and it was still done on occasion on the stroll in Dartmouth, was to send in an undercover female officer and charge the men who took the bait. The undercover officer had no qualms about testifying and new what phrases the client would have to use for the case to stand up in court. "How much for a blow job?" usually did it. That the date's Mitch hassled didn't know the law was their problem, and when he had one on the hook he enjoyed watching him squirm. Ginn considered the man a child abuser—the girl he was with was only fifteen years old—and it was only when he broke down entirely, repeating that he knew what he'd done was wrong and swearing never to return to the stroll, that Ginn relented. If the higher-ups wouldn't do anything about really going after the dates, Mitch Ginn would—one at a time. He had the recording to prove it, too; he'd switched off his tiny micro cassette recorder just after letting the man go.

After leaving the north end, Ginn and Gaudet headed downtown to Hollis Street; the girl they were seeking might be there, *if* the pimp had turned her out, *if* he had her in the first place. The officers thought the man might be back in The Game because a street source told them she thought she saw him with a girl fitting the description of the missing teen. It was slim evidence but neither officer had a great deal of faith in the rehabilitative capability of the federal prison system. When they got to the stroll, things weren't exactly hopping. It was with considerable pleasure that the officers observed that of the only seven prostitutes out that night, not one was under the age of eighteen. In 1992, when as many as thirty females could be seen working on Hollis any night, more than half of them were underage; a few were only twelve or thirteen years old. No such sight this evening—just a few of the regulars. There was Dawn, at twenty-seven a fixture on the stroll—hefty, self-confident, and in utter contempt of the police, the pimps, and any date stupid enough to give her a hard time. Ginn and Gaudet well remembered the time she'd ordered them to piss off when they tried to help her with a client who had tried to rip her off; at five-foot-six and one hundred and seventy pounds of muscle, she could smack the guy around herself if she wanted to. Then there was Pauline, who looked like a well-turned-out business-woman in her favorite get-up, a tailored skirt suit and smart handbag. "We all need to stand out somehow," as Gaudet put it. Yet another familiar face, a twentyish prostitute just walking back from a pay phone; she must have serviced a customer and called her pimp to report the transaction.

Maybe they'd come back later; it was still early, and there might be more activity on the stroll around midnight—perhaps even a lead on their runaway. Meanwhile, there was paperwork to do back in Dartmouth.

The task force office was empty, as it usually was nowadays. Once every cubicle was occupied by an investigator; dozens of teenagers were escorted through the large room by the officers assigned to their cases, and their young voices mingled with the sound of ringing phones behind the partitions that gave the cubicles their illusion of privacy. Darrell Gaudet went to his desk; there was space for three, but it was all his now, though he would have rather had the company. He glanced at the photographs on the walls around him—girls still listed as missing, believed to have been taken out of Halifax by pimps; girls like Kimberly McAndrew.

In a neighboring cubicle, Mitch Ginn thumbed through a three-ring binder filled with more than one hundred photographs—the teenagers who had been prostitutes, or still were, and who had had some kind of contact with the task force. Like Keri, some had only been photographed; maybe they'd spoken with an officer once or twice, then returned to The Game—only to be discovered months or years later, haggard from a crack addiction, beaten by a pimp or a bad date; dead. Here, too, were success stories of girls who left prostitution and never looked back. Amber Borowski, Lydia Chiasson, Teri

MacDonald, Taunya Terriault, Stacey Jackson. Mitch looked at the picture of Stacey and remembered the night Anne Mae Wilson was killed. Ginn had been in the office when John Elliott took the call, and watched as Elliott walked solemnly from the room to go to his car for the drive to Sullivan House. Breaking the news to Stacey must have been tough. Mitch Ginn would never have admitted to Elliott the extent of his sympathy; his style was to give the guy a rough time. He and Brad Sullivan, the "experts," or as Ginn had more frequently expressed it, "those two fucks." His crude humor wasn't intended as disrespect for his fellow officers; it was just his way of blowing off steam. He admired the two Mounties whose only real fault, according to Ginn, was that they were Mounties. Right now he wasn't in the mood for vulgarity or crude humor. He was overcome with sorrow, thinking of Kimberly McAndrew, of Keri Sherwood; he was struck by a painful memory, awakened by Stacey Jackson's photo, of the day her friend Annie Mae Wilson was killed. All the young faces, and the ones still out there, like that fourteen-year-old they would undoubtedly fail to locate tonight or tomorrow night, or the next.

At about midnight, after monitoring a suspect believed to be using juveniles in pornographic movies but who wouldn't be arrested for at least a few weeks, the officers made the rounds of the prostitution strolls again before giving up on the fourteen-year-old, and her alleged pimp. There was always tomorrow. Maybe they would find her tomorrow. "Hey, the lights are still on," Mitch Ginn remarked as they drove past Stacey Jackson's north-end apartment. "I hope she doesn't have any of the girls up there."

The officers cruised past Stacey's place almost every night, and Ginn's concern about the teenager inviting her street friends home was not so much a criticism of her choice of companions as a fear that the prostitutes could attract pimps, maybe even men connected with Michael Sears—or Smit, as he called himself. Ginn remembered with a sneer the often incomprehensible street names. As John Elliott had urged time and time again, Ginn and Gaudet felt Stacey would be much safer in the witness protection program, especially as the date for Smit's parole neared. They hoped she would eventually agree; the chances of a reprisal weren't worth gambling on.

Indeed, six months later, Stacey did decide to leave Halifax. It was bittersweet for Debbie Howard who wanted her daughter away from the city and the dangers it could present but who also knew she would miss the girl she had lost once before. Stacey left Nova Scotia behind and found a job and a new life in an undisclosed city.

As the spring of 1996 approached, Darrell Gaudet and Mitch Ginn had been reassigned to new postings with the recently created Halifax Regional Police Force. A nominal task force of four members remained in existence. The final two original members of Operation Hectic were sad to leave the unit but hoped the work they had done had been worth something. Craig Botterill whose six month posting to the special unit still had him prosecuting task force related cases almost four years later, preferred to put a positive spin on the reduced force. "It is smaller because there aren't as many juvenile working in Halifax. The task force was a success." He was also an optimist. "If the problem returns, we have the expertise and we will expand on the unit if we have to." The problem may well have left Halifax, but the East Coast connection to the sex trade had not been eliminated. Police in Toronto, where even Dave Perry had also been reassigned, were now reporting a new spin on the Scotian Game. In Perry's absence the JTF continued its work and the new members claimed pimps from the Halifax area were once again a predominant presence, now working Ontario or Quebec teenagers. Teenage girls were still being reported missing across Nova Scotia and in every other province, some of them seemingly disappearing without a trace, like that fourteen-year-old Ginn and Gaudet were seeking, like Kimberly McAndrew. Many more were simply presumed to have run away. Without a full-scale investigation of the wide range of hidden forms of prostitution, such as escort services, it was only possible to guess that some of these adolescents were vanishing behind brothel doors, before hitting the streets of the big city, as Taunya Terriault did at fourteen.

Without the consistent and strong presence on the street of task-force officers, as in the heyday of Operation Hectic, the street trade in children might easily resurface. Officers like Mitch Ginn and Darrell Gaudet were not convinced, as they accepted their new assignments, that the problem had vanished. Their view was that juvenile prostitution had been driven underground—into other provinces, if not Ontario and Quebec; or into escort services. They also believed that, with time, it would return to Halifax in the absence of the full twelve member task force. That was the opinion of the final two original investigators from Operation Hectic who shared the policemen's philosophy that only more investigators in the street can effectively reduce criminal activity. That opinion was not shared by the new front line workers who made up the true legacy of Operation Hectic.

Shane Kirk and the other members of The Association for the Development of Children's Residential Facilities are continuing to battle juvenile prostitution in the Halifax area. Like the officers assigned to Operation Hectic, Kirk had become an expert in the methods used by pimps and the personality traits exhibited by the girls who were most at risk. The police officers had developed the theory that sexually assaulting a young girl was the first step toward creating a juvenile prostitute but Kirk had another theory. "Many of them had suffered child abuse in some form, sexual or otherwise....but by far the biggest factor was a lack of self-worth. All of the girls shared that trait."

Kirk, who continues to work at the new smaller Sullivan House in Halifax, uses the resources of a large network of child care specialists dedicated to keeping young girls from becoming prostitutes. "We take a pro-active approach now; we work with social services counselors, teachers and parents who identify girls who are at risk and we work with those girls to try to keep them from making the mistakes the girls like Stacey made." While his background was in counseling, Kirk learned a lot from the police officers he befriended during the busy days of Operation Hectic and today he uses some of their techniques. With the pimps no longer maintaining a visible presence on the Hollis Street stroll Kirk does not hesitate to drive down there and park his car on a corner near the prostitutes in an attempt to bring them back to Sullivan House and away from The Game. "I do it if one of the girls we are working with runs and goes back to the street. I just sit there on the hood of my car and watch her.... She's only a few metres away and the cursing begins right away. My being there is very bad for business so the girls try to chase me off. I tell the girl I'm following I just want to talk with her. Sometimes it works, she gives up and comes back to the house."

Kirk also continues to take part in the school visits that were such an important factor in Stacey's return to square life. The outreach programs run by the Sullivan House counselors have been sighted as a model for other Canadian cities to follow. In 1992, when juvenile prostitution was a major problem in Halifax, the federal government commissioned a national consultation on prostitution. By the time the federal study was nearing completion, Nova Scotia's image had changed. In 1992, police in Vancouver and Toronto pointed to Halifax as the source of many of the under aged prostitutes working in those cities. The interim report released by the authors of the federal study pointed to Nova Scotia as an example of how to best handle the problem of juvenile prostitution. While Nova Scotia had modeled its safe house after the one used in Toronto, Sullivan House had a success rate that surpassed even the most optimistic projections in 1992.

The task force officers delivered close to one hundred young girls to the doors of Sullivan House, and while most of them decided they did not want to sign a statement against their pimps, those who did almost always remained off the street for good. By the late summer of 1996, thirty-seven girls had signed statements on one or more pimps; they followed through on the commitment and testified in court. Today twenty-seven girls remain free of The Game. Of the ten remaining girls, four may be free of prostitution; they have simply stopped communicating with Sullivan House counselors. Three girls have returned to The Game full-time; two work on an occasional basis and one has been jailed. Kirk and the other counselors working in Halifax maintain contact with the girls that have passed through the doors of Sullivan House, just as the task force officers continue to respond when a girl they were assigned to reaches out to them. That long term relationship demonstrates what Shane Kirk sees as the real problem faced by the girls: the serious lack of self-worth.

In August 1996, Stacey once again reached out to John Elliott and to Shane Kirk when, in her new home, she was again in contact with pimps. Stacey had continued to maintain her relationship with girls involved in The Game and one of those friends inadvertently led a pimp to her door. At first Stacey felt she was confident enough to resist his attempts to get her back on the street, but within weeks she began, once again, to remember the fun she had had with Annie Mae and to recognize that she still lacked education and could not expect to get a high paying job. A series of late night phone calls brought Stacey back into the fold. Once again she packed her belongings and headed to a new city, and another new start. Stacey's experience is not unique; even Taunya, who had been so strong on the witness stand and who had helped Teri and Gizelle when the aborted attempt to escape led them back to an angry Manning Greer, continues to suffer from self-doubt. Asked if she had any sense of accomplishment or pride at having turned her life around Taunya stated flatly, "No." Asked if she now had a higher self-esteem she responded, "No, not really," and lowered her eyes and walked away.

Criminologist John Lowman of Simon Fraser University believes that kind of response is evidence of what really is at the heart of a young girl's decision to follow a pimp. "The girl or woman can never recover any feeling of self-worth because she lost it long before she met the pimp. Signing on the pimp will not really help, because he is not the source of the problem in the first place." Shane Kirk agrees, comparing self-worth to an expensive Tiffany lamp. "It is very easy to shatter and very difficult to put back together, you have to do it one piece at a time." While self-worth may be easily destroyed, Kirk believes one positive adult role-model can make all the difference in a young girl's life. If a child does not receive the proper support at home he feels a teacher, who knows what to look for, or some other relative can help the child develop the self confidence needed to avoid the mental games played by the pimps. The serious players openly admit they seek out girls with low self-esteem because they are the easiest to manipulate and control.

As a criminologist, John Lowman has spent years studying prostitution in Canada and has published numerous papers on the topic. "The pimp's game is to take a girl with low self-worth and make her feel she's worth something. She's caught because she likes the feeling he gives her. Chances are, she has never felt this way before." Once a pimp has his target feeling good about herself, he then uses those feelings to his advantage. "The pimp convinces her that he is the only person who can make her feel like this. He then treats her like shit, so to speak, and withdraws his affection so she feels unworthy again. This way, he manipulates her into the position of continutally trying to please him so he will treat her the right way again."

By late August of 1996, the Canadian Government was acknowledging the serious social problem presented by juvenile prostitution. Canada was one of 130 countries to adopt the recommendations of the World Congress Against Commercial Sexual Exploitation of Children. The Congress, in Stockholm, called for tougher laws to govern the exploitation of children; laws that would make the commercial sexual exploitation of children a crime while recognizing the children as victims not criminals. The congress also called for a worldwide mobilization of resources aimed at eliminating the child sex trade. Canada has already taken steps in that direction by introducing a new tougher sentencing policy for pimps who lure young girls into the streets.

Tougher laws will not stop pimps from playing their favorite game. Pimps are survivors, and they will adapt to any rule changes that come with new laws in the same way they adapted to the reality of the task force in Halifax. Pimps intent on staying in The Game did not stop running girls; instead they stopped running juveniles on Hollis Street, preferring to move them to other provinces. Some also began to limit, but not eliminate, the use of violence. As long as grown men are willing to pay to have sex with these children of the night, the pimps will find a way to meet the demand. Pimps in Calgary long ago found a way to make money while keeping the young girls off the streets. They use what police call a "floating trick pad." Customers are contacted by the pimp and told to come to an apartment or a home at a specific time. During a single night a young girl will be forced to have sex with twenty or more men who have all paid in advance for the privilege. Police suspect these one-night encounters are the first exposure to prostitution for many of these girls. The location of the trick pad changes every time a new fresh girl is lured into The Game.

The law of supply and demand will continue to prevail in the sex trade. Perhaps the only way to prevent young girls from being used to supply the voracious appetite of The Game is to follow the advice of the experts and accept that self-esteem is the key. It is up to parents, teachers, and family friends to do everything possible to develop a sense of self-worth in young girls. If they do not, there are pimps who are more than willing to invest the time it takes to build and then destroy that self-worth. To them it is, after all, just an investment; one for which they expect a healthy return. To a pimp a juvenile prostitute is a profitable object and nothing more; she is certainly not somebody's daughter.